THE END OF ARCADIA

Gordon Browning

Courtesy Tennessee State Library and Archives

THE END OF ARCADIA

GORDON BROWNING AND TENNESSEE POLITICS

William R. Majors

MEMPHIS STATE UNIVERSITY PRESS

Manufactured in the United States of America

Library of Congress Cataloging in Publication Data

Majors, William R., 1929–
    The end of arcadia.

    Bibliography: p.
    Includes index.
    1. Browning, Gordon, 1889–   . 2. Tennessee—
Politics and government—1865–1950.   3. Tennessee—
Governors—Biography.   4. United States. Congress.
House—Biography.   5. Legislators—United States—
Biography.   I. Title.
F436.B86M34   976.8'05'0924 [B]   82-3412
ISBN 0-87870-098-6   AACR2

Contents

To Lynelle and Marcia

Preface

Tennessee has had many colorful and charismatic political leaders. Gordon Browning, governor of the state from 1937 to 1939 and from 1949 to 1953, was one. In a long and varied career in which he served in both World Wars, spent twelve years in the United States House of Representatives, and was elected to three terms as Tennessee's chief executive, he displayed an amazing resilience in politics. More than once he recovered from what appeared to be a disastrous defeat to regain stature and to be reelected to public office. Browning was one of the most controversial politicians in Tennessee history. He was usually a shrewd practitioner of the political arts, but when he made a mistake, it was one of enormous proportions. He could be eloquent and articulate when the occasion demanded and was at his best on the political stump. Browning was raised in a rural environment at the turn of the twentieth century and was greatly influenced by the small farmer radicalism that was prevalent in the countryside then. He was therefore a blend of Tennessee populism and southern states' rights conservatism. In the 1930s, Browning became the chief opponent of Memphis political boss Edward Hull Crump, the personification of urban progressivism in Tennessee, and he played an important role in breaking Crump's influence in the state. The power struggle between the two leaders was symbolic of the continuing clash between rural and urban interests in Tennessee. This narrative is largely concerned with the conflicts between Browning and Crump and because they fought for control of Tennessee, it is also the political history of the state from 1934 to 1954.

Space limitations make it impossible to acknowledge all those who made important contributions to this work, but several people deserve special notice: Joseph H. Parks for suggesting that Browning would be a good subject to research; Willard Gatewood who directed this work in its original form as a dissertation and whose incisive criticism contributed immeasurably to the final product; the late Governor Browning who graciously consented to three separate oral interviews; and Brenda Patton and Denise Tucker for suggesting improvements in style. Those who clarified many puzzling aspects of the Browning era and added color and drama to the narrative through oral interviews also deserve sincere thanks. Nor would this work have been possible without the generous assistance of many hardworking people associated with the Tennessee State Library and Archives, the Memphis-Shelby County Public Library and Information Center, the Memphis State University Library, and the University of Tennessee Library. Finally, I would like to express my gratitude to my wife, Lynelle and my daughter, Marcia. Without their patience and fortitude this manuscript may never have come to fruition.

William R. Majors
December 1978

THE END OF ARCADIA

Prologue

THE weather was crisp and clear in Nashville, Tennessee, on Friday, 15 January 1937. The day before an all-time high of seventy-two degrees had been set for that date at 4:00 P.M. It had been unseasonably warm for several days and forsythia and jonquils had actually begun to sprout. But shortly after 6:00 P.M. on Thursday a wind storm and hard rain struck the city as a cold wave crossed the state, sending temperatures tumbling, and by Friday morning the thermometer was at forty-two degrees and still falling. However, the cold wave could in no way chill the excitement prevailing in Tennessee's capital city, for on that day the thirty-seventh governor of the state was scheduled to be inaugurated. The governor-elect was forty-seven-year-old Gordon Browning of Huntingdon, a lawyer by profession, an artillery captain during World War I, and a former congressman from the seventh congressional district.

The inauguration of a new chief executive is traditionally a gala affair, and the schedule of luncheons, dinners, receptions, and balls sometimes spans several days. However, at the request of the governor-elect, the ceremonies were kept simple and brief. Tennessee's economy was seriously depressed, and Browning had charged in his campaign that the incumbent administration was wasteful and inefficient. So simplicity

would be more in keeping with his promise of efficiency in government
and austerity in administering the state's meager treasury. A parade was
scheduled to begin at 10:00 A.M., the oath of office was to be administered promptly at noon on a platform adjacent to the Capitol Building
and in front of the War Memorial Building, and a brief inaugural address
would conclude the events of the day. An informal reception at the
Andrew Jackson Hotel honoring the new governor and his wife was
planned for the evening.

Despite the simplicity, it was a colorful and exciting affair. The activities began as scheduled when Browning (in silk hat, morning coat, and
striped trousers), accompanied by Mrs. Browning (dressed in gray coat
and purple dress with a corsage of violets pinned to her shoulder) and
the outgoing Governor, Hill McAlister, boarded an automobile to lead
the procession to the platform and reviewing stand. In part because
Gordon Browning was the first veteran of World War I to become governor of Tennessee the parade that followed had a military flavor, as
units of the 117th Infantry Regiment and 114th Field Artillery Regiment
of the Thirtieth or "Old Hickory" Division of the National Guard
marched along with ROTC companies and school bands.[1] The American
Legion was prominent in the colorful parade, as veterans of the war
marched to honor the new chief executive. Browning had a special tie
with the 114th Field Artillery: he had served in France during the war
as captain of Battery A, a Guard unit based in Memphis. About sixty
veterans of his old unit were present at the inauguration, having traveled from Memphis to the state capital by motorcade. The trip had been
something of a lark; the men had shot fireworks along the way, and
stopped briefly in Huntingdon to give a seventeen-round salute from
an old French .75mm field piece in honor of their former captain before
proceeding on to Nashville for a torch light parade on the eve of the
inaugural. They stayed in the capital for about three days and, in the
words of one of the participants, had "a hell of a good time."[2]

The veterans of Battery A were honored guests on the platform and
one, Abe Waldauer, presented a battery flag to the new governor on
behalf of the men. "The men of this battery feel that this battery guidon
should be with the flag of the nation and of Tennessee in the governor's
office with you," he said. "We know that under its folds you will show
the same courage and ability as governor in peace as you did in war."
Browning acknowledged the presence of his comrades and declared:
"They are the identical men who stacked their lives up by mine in a
trying time of national peril and I have embalmed that service with them

among the holiest memories of the past. . . . Their loyalty will remain a perpetual inspiration, and if I am ever to experience a triumph I want them to share it with me."[3]

After the preliminaries, Grafton Green, Chief Justice of the Tennessee Supreme Court, administered the oath of office. When he proclaimed Browning the new governor, a great cheer went up from an estimated crowd of ten thousand along with a nineteen-round salute from a .75mm artillery piece. As the governor rose to address the throng assembled in front of the War Memorial Building, the American Legion band struck up the World War I favorite, "Over There."

Governor Browning's inaugural address was serious and in contrast to the excitement of the day. Indeed, his words were somewhat out of character for a political leader who was known for his wit and jovial manner. But his somber speech was fitting for the situation he faced. Tennessee, as other states, was still mired in the Great Depression. Moreover, the state government was in poor financial condition and a solution to the crisis would strain the competence of any man. Perhaps the gaiety of the day and Browning's words both were symbolic of a new beginning. Like Roosevelt on the national level, Browning had been elected by the widest popular margin in the state's history. Indeed, the critical situation confronting the new governor caused C. W. Bailey, a Clarksville banker and president of the Tennessee Taxpayers Association, to call Browning the Roosevelt of Tennessee and his program a "little New Deal."[4] The analogy was not altogether inappropriate, for the crisis at the state level faced by Browning was not unlike the one that President Franklin D. Roosevelt had faced four years earlier at the national level.

The new governor presided over a state that remained predominantly rural and composed of small farms; only about one-third of the population was classified as urban, and the cities were not heavily industrialized, remaining largely mercantile centers serving rural areas. Transportation was not adequate even by the standards of the 1930s. Although the massive highway building program launched a decade earlier was nearing completion, only the most populous centers were connected by hard-surfaced roads. There was a woeful lack of all-weather roads in rural areas, and often in seasons of heavy rains farm homes and even entire communities were isolated by high waters and muddy roads. But, of course, comparatively few Tennesseeans owned automobiles; the horse or mule-drawn wagon was still the principal mode of travel in the countryside. Browning would have agreed, at least privately, that his state was part of the region that President Roosevelt called the nation's number one problem. Although the per capita income in Tennessee compared favorably with other states in the Southeast, like them it remained far below the national average. There was still widespread illiteracy and poverty in rural Tennessee, especially among the large population of blacks. There were millions of acres of eroded, worn-out farmlands, caused in part by backward farming methods and in part by uncontrolled streams and rivers. Tenants and sharecroppers, living in unpainted shacks and suffering from malnutrition, were commonplace; endemic and epidemic diseases such as pellegra, typhoid fever, and ringworm had not been fully eradicated. Far too many Tennesseans had existed for years at the bare subsistence level in a life of monotony and drudgery.

Because of the nature of the state's rural–small farm economy and the small proportion of those owning stocks, the onset of the Great Depression in 1929 was barely noticeable to many Tennesseans. Most rural dwellers had experienced hard times for years, and their life-style did not change; only gradually did the economic decline become a problem in the state. Urban workers had been the first to feel the effects of the Depression; by 1933 at least one-third of the state's industries were closed. As unemployment increased, savings began to disappear, mortgaged homes were foreclosed, insurance policies lapsed, and more and more people began to live their lives on credit. Bank and business failures mounted. By 1933 declining farm prices, compounded by several years of drought, forced discouraged farmers to give up and move to the cities to join the already long lines of those looking for a job or for relief. But relief in the cities was at the bare minimum because most cities and the state were without funds. As the Depression deepened, revenue declined sharply and the legislature began the process of retrenchment, drastically slashing appropriations for all state departments in an effort to retain a balanced budget. Often state employees, particularly teachers, were issued warrants when no money was available to redeem them. Desperate to feed their families, these people were often forced to sell the warrants at discounts of as much as thirty percent. From the beginning of President Roosevelt's New Deal, Tennesseans, no less than the people of other states, had looked to the national government for assistance in relief. Although federal programs helped to alleviate suffering, they did not get at the root causes of the depressed economy. Even the Tennessee Valley Authority, the massive regional redevelopment program which would mean so much to the state's economy in the years ahead, had barely begun construction. Although conditions had improved because of relief measures by the federal government, most people in Tennessee still lived in or on the edge of poverty when Gordon Browning became governor in 1937.[5]

The most immediate problem confronting the new governor in 1937 was the state's debt. The debt had been a problem since Reconstruction days, but it became worse in the 1920s because of the growing need for new highways. A "pay as you go" plan to finance highways, inaugurated by Governor Austin Peay, proved inadequate; so in 1925, the General Assembly turned to borrowing to pay for roads and continued to do so until the Depression hit. From 1927 to 1933 the state budget was unbalanced, and after 1931, with the loss of funds in bank closures and decreased revenue, the state was forced to finance the deficits. A total of $21,950,000 in bonds was sold to finance deficits between 1929 and 1936, and the debt had risen from $96,702,000 to almost $129,000,000 when Browning became governor in 1937.[6]

No one was more conscious of the situation than the new chief executive, and his twenty-five–minute inaugural address demonstrated his concern for the financial crisis. He promised early relief from "this inelastic burden," but cautioned that the people would continue to be called on to make sacrifices because the state was obligated to improve its educational system and to care for the aged and needy. Much of his address was devoted to the need for honesty and integrity in public service. He noted that his election was the greatest popular victory in Tennessee history and stated his conviction that "the people of Tennessee in their great hearts want me to succeed."[7]

Gordon Browning's success in finding solutions to the state's economic problems would depend in large measure on his ability as a leader, for as governor he would possess a vast amount of administrative authority. By 1937, the chief executive of Tennessee had become the most powerful figure in the state even though the drafters of the state's constitution of 1870 had not intended that the governor exercise a great deal of power. Although that constitution appeared committed to the doctrine of separation of powers and "checks and balances" in government, those who had drafted the document intended the legislative branch to be more powerful than the executive. The constitution specifically delegated to the legislative assembly law-making authority and all responsibility for policy formulation; the chief executive was given responsibility for administering all laws and carrying out legislative policies. The constitution of 1870 limited the governor by setting a brief term (two years), with no more than three consecutive terms for six years' tenure. The chief executive's specified powers were few: the governor was delegated ordinary veto and pardoning power and he was commander-in-chief of the militia when that organization was not in federal service. The governor was expected to report to the legislative assembly from time to time and to make recommendations for legislative consideration. Otherwise, he had no control over regular meetings of the General Assembly or the business to be considered. However, the chief executive could call special, or "extraordinary" sessions, and no limit was placed on the number of these sessions that could be convened. Furthermore, only the governor could specify the business to be considered in extraordinary sessions. Finally, the constitution limited the governor's supervisory power in government by making four important administrative offices independent of the executive branch: the secretary of state, the state treasurer, and the comptroller were to be elected by the General Assembly, and the attorney general was established as the creature of the state's supreme court. The adjutant general, or head of the state militia, was the only constitutional officer the governor was authorized to appoint. [8]

But actual political practice was a far cry from the limitations set forth in the written constitution. If the drafters of that document had intended the executive to be weak and the legislative branch to be strong, the opposite was true by the time of Austin Peay's tenure as governor in the 1920s. A number of factors have contributed to increasing the power of the chief executive. First, the governor is selected by the entire electorate of the state, whereas members of the General Assembly are not. The govenor is also regarded as the first citizen, the chief spokesman for the state government, and as such is a public relations officer. He is almost constantly in the limelight, fulfilling innumerable ceremonial duties. Furthermore, the chief executive's office functions the year around, whereas, prior to 1968, the legislature was in session for only a few weeks between biennial elections. Moreover, the governor is in constant touch with the day-to-day routine of government and has at his immediate disposal detailed information necessary for policy making. Finally, the legislative branch itself has, from time to time, increased the chief executive's authority by statute. The General Assembly has also increased the number of departments in the administrative branch and delegated exclusive responsibility for appointment and removal of department heads to the governor. The prime example of delegation of authority by the General Assembly is the responsibility for making and administering the state's budget. As practiced in the 1930s, the governor's office drafted a budget, the legislature "rubber-stamped" it, and the chief executive administered it. Therefore, by 1937, despite constitutional limitations, a strong-willed individual could exercise enormous power as governor of Tenessee. Gordon Browning was such an individual.[9]

A governor of Tennessee also possesses a great deal of political power. With the Democratic party in the majority, both the governor and the General Assembly from Reconstruction days were invariably Democratic, and as leader of his party, the chief executive exercised a great deal of authority within its organization. He also had the tools to enforce discipline and insure factional regularity. Because nomination in the Democratic party's gubernatorial primary was tantamount to victory in the general election in Tennessee, the main contest for the governor's office was the primary and its winner generally carried supporters on his coattails into the General Assembly. Consequently, Tennessee governors seldom had difficulty having their programs enacted into law. Another factor enhancing the governor's strength was that local governments were literally creatures of the state, and therefore the General Assembly was obligated to act on a great deal of local legislation. Because the governor's organization controlled legislative machinery, it could use these local bills as bargaining points to insure loyalty to administration measures and to the statewide organization. Factional discipline and regularity were thus achieved.

Tennessee's chief executive had almost unlimited control of his party's machinery. The primary that nominated the Democratic candidate for governor also elected members of the party's State Executive Committee, and the chairman of that body was chosen by the candidate. The Executive Committee appointed county committees, and each county committee in turn controlled local election machinery. Of course effective control of election machinery enhanced the chances of the incumbent and his organization at the next primary. The administration-dominated General Assembly also elected members of the State Board of Elections which supervised general elections. But the most important single factor in political control of the state government was patronage. From time to time, the legislature increased the governor's appointive power, and appointments to state jobs were subject to political considerations. The result was a well-oiled machine, as each governor used patronage and other favors to entrench his organization. The machine then remained in power until it split over some controversial issue, the public tired of it, or some other circumstance disrupted the status quo. Since he was aware of the administrative and political powers he possessed, Gordon Browning was superbly confident that he could solve the critical economic problems facing Tennessee in 1937. How he exercised these powers would also have a bearing on the length of his career as a political leader in Tennessee.

NOTES

1. *Nashville Tennessean*, 16 January 1937.

2. Charles Gallena, interview with the author, Memphis, 23 August 1977; J. Chester Shields, interview with the author, Memphis, 22 August 1977.

3. *Tennessean*, 16 January 1937.

4. *Nashville Banner*, 11 November 1936.

5. Stanley J. Folmsbee, Robert E. Corlew, and Enoch L. Mitchell, *History of Tennessee* (New York: Lewis Historical Publishing Co., 1960), 2: 297–305, 321–328.

6. James E. Thorogood, *A Financial History of Tennessee Since 1870* (Sewanee: University of the South Press, 1949), pp. 121, 215–216, 229–231.

7. *Banner*, 15 January 1937.

8. Lee S. Greene, David H. Grubbs, Victor C. Hobday, *Government in Tennessee*, 3rd ed. (Knoxville: University of Tennessee Press, 1975), pp. 19–27.

9. Ibid., p. 91–116.

1

The Formative Years

CARROLL County is in nearly every respect typical of counties formed in the West Tennessee Uplands, a plateau of rolling hill country in the western section of Tennessee. The Tennessee River Ridge, which divides watersheds east to the Tennessee River and west to the Mississippi River, crosses Carroll County paralleling the Tennessee River. The land ranges from rolling hills to generally level terrain to river and creek bottomlands. The area was once a primeval forest with a great variety of hardwoods such as oak, gum, poplar, walnut, ash, and beech, with occasional stands of pine; it was inhabited by bear, deer, panther, wildcat, wolf, and numerous smaller animals. The forests have long since been cut, and the wild game has all but disappeared. The fertility of the soil ranges from rich river and creek bottomlands to sandy or clay hillside soil covered by thousands of years of leaf mold. Nature was not generous in endowing the area with mineral deposits; however there is some gravel, and deposits of clay are of adequate quality to use in pottery making.[1]

Created by the Tennessee General Assembly in 1821 as one of the second group of counties established after the Chickasaw cession of 1818, Carroll County was formally organized in 1822, and Huntingdon, near the center of the county, became the seat of government later that same year. The county was named for William Carroll who was then governor of Tennessee and one of the state's most popular chief executives. The area was quickly settled by migrants from Middle and East Tennessee as well as from North and South Carolina. Because the terrain was not conducive to a plantation type of economy based on slavery, the area was populated by small farmers producing staples such as corn, cotton, livestock, and fruits and vegetables. And like the rest of the West Tennessee Uplands, Carroll County remained throughout the nineteenth century a land of small farmers with an agrarian economy. But it did gain one advantage denied to most of the area. Transportation needs were more than adequately served by railroads. The trunk line linking Memphis and Louisville, Kentucky, crossed the northwestern corner of the county; the line connecting Memphis and Nashville by way of Jackson served the eastern part of Carroll County; and a branch connecting Hickman, Kentucky, on the Mississippi River and Union City, Tennessee, joined the Memphis to Nashville trunk at Hollow Rock. Politically, Carroll County was a Whig stronghold before the Civil War and voted against secession in 1861. After the war, the Republican Party became entrenched, and the county's most famous son prior to the twentieth century was a unionist and Republican, Alvin Hawkins, who served as governor of Tennessee from 1881 to 1883. The agrarian revolt in the last decade of the nineteenth century had an impact on Carroll County, and many, if not most, of the residents sympathized with the demands of the Populist Party, even if they were not active supporters.[2]

Few native sons of Carroll County and Huntingdon have gained distinction in public life in the state or nation. But the county can boast of one who made up for lack of numbers: Gordon Browning who became one of Tennessee's most popular, colorful, and controversial governors. Born in Carroll County, he spent the early years of his childhood there. He later set up law practice in Huntingdon in 1914, and in 1920 he launched a political career that spanned more than thirty years and had a significant impact on politics in the Volunteer State.

Gordon Browning was born on a small farm near Atwood in Carroll County on 22 November 1889, the son of James H. and Malissa Brooks Browning. Progenitors on both sides of the family were among the early settlers in the area. Little is known about the Brownings except that they were English in origin, that Gordon's great-great-grandfather was residing in South Carolina at the time of the first national census in 1790, and that his great-grandfather moved to Carroll County about 1830.[3] A good deal more is known about the maternal side of the family. Gordon's great-grandfather, Thomas Brooks, was a stone mason and helped construct Andrew Jackson's plantation mansion, the *Hermitage*. An often repeated legend about Brooks was his conquest of John Sevier in an all-day fist fight in the Jonesboro, Tennessee, town square.[4] There was a feeling in the Brooks family at the time of the marriage of James and Malissa, as well as among descendants, that the Brooks family was a cut above the Brownings. The Brownings were regarded as good, honest, hard working people, but none had achieved any great distinction. In contrast, there were "several ministers" and representatives of other professions in the Brooks family. Thomas B. Brooks, Malissa Browning's father, was a member of the Tennessee House of Representatives in the thirty-eighth and thirty-ninth General Assemblies (1873–1877) and his son, Malissa's brother, Thomas Joseph Brooks, was a state senator in the fifty-seventh General Assembly (1911–1913). Thomas Joseph later became a professor of rural economics at Mississippi Agricultural and Mechanical College at Starkville, where he wrote a number of books on a variety of subjects, including a widely used textbook.[5]

Gordon was the youngest of four surviving children born to James and Malissa Browning. The eldest was a son, Will; then came a daughter, Halford; the third was another son, Flavius; and finally, Gordon. The Brownings remained on the farm near Atwood until Gordon was about twelve. They lived only a short distance from Thomas Brooks, and in the manner common to extended families in rural America, farming was a joint enterprise. Life was difficult for the Brownings in those years, but it was typical of rural West Tennessee in the late nineteenth century. James Browning managed a grubby existence on marginally productive hillside land with long hours of drudgery. Cotton was the money crop, but because of low prices, there was very little cash income; hay and corn were raised for the livestock. The family also produced their own pork, poultry, milk and butter, and garden vegetables. Mere subsistence required that the entire family share in the work on the farm. Not only did Malissa Browning do housework and keep the vegetable garden, she also went into the fields with the rest of the family. Browning recalled "she would go to the fields and hoe cotton every day until we got over the crop. In the fall she would take a cotton sack and go to picking just like the rest of us did."[6] The children were taught to work and did indeed spend long hours in the fields and performed chores around the house and barn. "I was raised up pulling a cotton sack every fall, hoeing cotton every spring," Browning recalled. But the children were not required to perform beyond their physical ability; "we were not overworked," said Halford.[7]

James and Malissa Browning were strict disciplinarians, but they gave a good deal of parental affection. And each parent, with an individual character and personality, left an indelible stamp on the children. James Browning was a small man, weighing little more than one hundred and thirty pounds in his middle years; he was always cheerful, with a sense of humor, and was ever loquacious. Malissa Browning, a rather large woman, was strong willed and probably the dominant parent. The more serious of the two, she made the moral and religious training of the children her prime concern. An active member of the Women's Christian Temperance Union, she believed that drinking alcohol in any form was a sin, and even the use of tobacco was anathema to her. Of course young Gordon, along with the other children, took the temperance pledge at an early age. Both parents were God-fearing Christian fundamentalists who required that their children be regular in attendance at Sunday school and church; Gordon's profession of Christianity took place at the age of nine.[8] Browning declared that he was "raised under rather strict religious requirements of conduct, attendance at church, and so forth." But it "was typical of those fine parents wishing to control their children with a puritanic base, who were genuine in their hopes and dreams that their children would grow-up and be something worthwhile." He believed the results were gratifying, for the Browning children "developed into healthy specimens as far as our general makeup is concerned."[9]

Despite this austere life-style and Calvinistic moral environment, Gordon Browning had a happy childhood. Unaware that he lacked material advantages, he was a cheerful, exuberant boy, full of wit and brimming with optimism. As he worked hard, so he played hard, got into his share of mischief, and "had the common experiences of all country boys that rode calves and attended themselves anyway they wanted to during the days that they were not working." And like most boys raised on a farm, he enjoyed hunting and fishing when the requirements of work permitted. "I had a normal amount of that," he declared.[10] On rare occasions there were special treats such as fairs and traveling carnivals. Gordon was also a good athlete and especially liked to play baseball. "I was pretty good on first base at one time in my development and I played first base for the high school team that I was on," he recalled.[11] He also excelled in school, especially in classes that required speaking ability. His forensic talents caused his schoolmates to refer to him as "preacher," but the term was not always used in a derogatory sense; he was a well-liked leader among his peers. Malissa Browning, before anyone else, recognized that her youngest son was unusual, and perhaps because of his oratorical talent, she had hopes that he would "answer the call" and become a minister of the gospel. Committed as she was to the church, it would be her crowning glory for Gordon to enter the ministry. Because of his gifts and because he was the youngest child in the family, Gordon became the "pet" and was treated with a little more deference than the other children.

Gordon was especially close to Flavius, F. L. or Flavy as he was sometimes called, who was only twenty-two months his senior. The two boys were almost inseparable companions as children, working and playing together, and they never had a serious disagreement. But as with most brothers, Gordon and Flavius had their share of minor fraternal differences that culminated in combat. Browning declared "I used to fight F. L. He and I grew up just loosening up our hides on each other." However, the two would put aside their internal disputes to be allied against outside threats. The brothers were also in the same class in school. According to Gordon, Flavius was held out of school a year so that the two could attend together and save on the cost of buying books. "We went together and we sat at the same desk and had to use just one book. We didn't have but one because Dad couldn't afford another one. So we sat together through the whole thing. We didn't think it was tough because we had what we needed."[12] Sister Halford gave another reason for holding Flavius back: he was a frail child and was kept out for a year because of ill health. The contrast between the two was significant. Flavius was quiet, more serious and studious, while Gordon was aggressive, impetuous, and outgoing. Halford declared that Gordon always liked a good fight but did not know his limitations; F. L., more than anyone else, was able to restrain his brother. Flavius "held him down—only one who could." Browning conceded as much in later years.[13]

Largely through the influence of his family, Gordon Browning developed a consummate interest in the art of politics very early in life. The male members of the family were interested in public affairs, and Gordon heard many conversations and discussions concerning public issues. What he heard sounded exciting, and sometime in his boyhood he resolved to become a part of the fascinating game of politics. Halford believed that a high school civics teacher had some influence on his decision, but Gordon declared that his maternal grandfather, Thomas Brooks, was the source of his interest in public life; "I learned politics

16

at his knee," he said. [14] Brooks had served in the Tennessee General Assembly. Although on record as a Republican, by the 1890s he was a thorough agrarian radical, an opponent of the privileges of wealth, and an ardent advocate of free coinage of silver. Gordon spent many Sunday afternoons on his grandfather's front porch listening to him discourse on politics and the issues of the times. Brooks would "take his text on the idea that no man had honestly made a million dollars." The first intense political activity Browning remembered was William Jennings Bryan's presidential campaign of 1896. Bryan made free silver an issue in that race, and Thomas Brooks was keenly interested in the outcome and no doubt disappointed in the results. [15] Very likely James Browning had as great an influence on Gordon as his grandfather; he was active in local political affairs and once served as justice of the peace and member of the county court in Gibson County. Moreover, Gordon became a Democrat like his father. In setting politics as his career goal, he displeased and defied at least a portion of his family; his mother and sister opposed his ambition, believing that he was capable of better things. "We always hated that," Halford commented in regard to Gordon's choice of a career. And even after achieving success in politics, Halford believed that her brother "would have been better off" if he had gone into another profession. [16]

The rural environment in which Gordon Browning was born and reared played a vital role in his political conditioning. He was easily conditioned to rural values and the acceptance of what Richard Hofstadter calls "the agrarian myth." Without conscious effort, his family imbued him with the belief that country living was the nearly perfect way of life and farming was a unique calling; that farmers were the most valuable citizens and the most important producing class; and the yeoman farmer, with his special virtues, was the nearly perfect citizen. Yet Gordon perceived, perhaps only dimly understood in those formative years, that the farmer's way of life was threatened, and that his family and their neighbors were distressed. [17] Small farmers in Tennessee, like those all over the nation, were caught in a severe economic depression in the 1890s, a condition that had been slowly evolving over many years. The transition to commercial farming in America had produced surpluses in the staple crops; as a consequence, prices began to decline sharply. Cotton, for example, dropped from about fifteen cents a pound in 1870 to nearly five cents in the 1890s. At the same time, taxes and transportation costs remained high, the exactions of middlemen were unchanged, and money was in short supply, all of this caused tight credit and high interest rates. Especially depressing to southern and Tennessee farmers was the crop-lien practice whereby farmers were forced to pledge part or all of their cotton crops to merchants in order to secure credit for necessities. As cotton prices continued to decline, small proprietors sank deeper into debt, and many were eventually forced to give up their land and become tenants. The fact was that family farming was no longer a paying proposition. Realizing that they were no longer on a parity with other economic groups, small freeholders began to look for scapegoats.

Thus young Gordon Browning heard the standard grievances: he heard complaints about railroads and discriminatory freight rate differentials, unscrupulous middlemen and bankers, unfair tax burdens, and manufacturers who reaped great profits protected by the "mother of trusts," the tariff. And he also heard his parents and neighbors single out cities for special censure, for they were the centers of the forces that repressed the farmers: cities were controlled by corrupt political bosses, contained immigrants with foreign and blasphemous ideas, and the vices of gambling, prostitution, and alcohol flourished there. From his parents and neighbors, he heard the solution to the problems of the farmer: a government more responsive to the needs of rural and agrarian America. It was therefore easy for Gordon Browning to aspire to be a part of a positive government. Ironically, he, like many others raised in rural America, began early in life preparing to leave the paradise.

Browning's formal education was as good as the times and the area permitted. His first schooling was at House's School House, a one-room school located between Atwood and McLemoresville in Carroll County, and continued at Trezevant where he and his family moved in 1901. Two years later James Browning bought a farm, known as the old Cunningham place, in Gibson County near the town of Milan. The family seemed to prosper there, and the location of the new home also enabled Gordon and Flavius to attend high school. Both eventually finished the tenth-grade high school in Milan but not without some hardships; not only did they have to continue working on the farm, but they had to walk three miles into town each day to go to school. Active, energetic, and mentally alert, Gordon was a participant in most of the school's activities; he was especially drawn to those exercises that required talent in speaking, debate, and declamation. He read rather extensively, considering the limitations of library facilities in Milan, but did not finish at the head of his class; that honor went to Flavius who graduated valedictorian.

In an era when few Americans had the resources to obtain any kind of education beyond high school, it seemed out of the question for a poor farm boy to even consider going to college. But Gordon Browning was ambitious and persistent; he was determined to attain a college education. Since neither he nor his father had assets sufficient for such a venture, he had no choice but to work and save until he had enough money. Even though he was only a high school graduate, and merely ten grades at that, he was able to get a teaching position without much difficulty. He was also able to augment his teacher's salary when he and Flavius bought fifty acres of land to raise cotton. At the age of eighteen he began teaching. His first position was a one-room school in Ebenezer, a few miles south of Milan. Here he taught all grades, had approximately forty-two pupils, and earned about thirty-five dollars a month. How effective he was as a teacher cannot be known, but he probably did not experience many disciplinary problems. He was cheerful, outgoing, and a pleasure to be around, and few pupils would have been willing to challenge the husky five-foot, ten-inch schoolmaster. He continued farming and teaching for three years, and at the age of twenty, after he had saved seven hundred dollars, he was ready to commit himself to college. Gordon's choice was Valparaiso University in Indiana "because it was cheap," and he remarked with pride that "I bought all my own books, paid my own tuition, my own rent and board, all on less than $700." College brought about the first separation of the Browning brothers. Gordon tried to persuade Flavius to attend college with him, and his brother did go one summer, but he dropped out because he preferred to get married rather than go to school. Flavius did, however, become a teacher and was eventually a successful school administrator. Gordon Browning declared that he was always proud "of the fact that I took the attitude I did about going away to school." He admitted that he was intensely provincial and had a chip on his shoulder about where he was reared. At Valparaiso he was exposed to a quality education and to a more cosmopolitan environment. The chip apparently was knocked from his shoulder, and he lost his provincialism because "there wasn't any excuse for a man being provincial after he left there." Valparaiso was "a rugged institution and I put in twenty-four months to get what education I had over and above high school."[18]

After finishing at Valparaiso, Gordon returned to Milan in 1914 and immediately announced his desire to go to law school. A career in law did not hold any particular fascination for him; it was merely a means to an end. He was aware that the legal profession was traditionally the springboard for aspiring politicians because it provided a continuous source of income and allowed time for political activity. Law would therefore be the base from which he would launch his career in public life. Once again without resources, he asked his father to lend him the money to go to law school. As Gordon recalled, James Browning refused because " 'you wouldn't pay me back. I know you well enough to know you'd pay anybody else living their money back if you owed it to them. I'll sign your note.' " With that settled, Browning was off again, this time to Cumberland University in Lebanon, Tennessee, where he spent a year of intense study in law.[19] When he returned home and informed his family of his intention to set up practice in Huntingdon, his father expressed reservations about the location: "My father said, 'Son, you're making a terrible mistake setting up your office here. . . . Nobody in Carroll County has any money. You'll be taking your fees in jars of jam.' But I told him I didn't really intend to be a lawyer very long. 'I just came back to beat [Congressman] Thetus Sims out of his seat in Congress. Sims has had the seat too long and he isn't doing very much. I know I can take him.' "[20] It was no idle boast. Gordon Browning did not hesitate to set a high goal for himself; no lesser office would do.

In 1915 Gordon Browning joined George T. McCall's law firm in Huntingdon, and the handsome and personable young lawyer soon established himself in the community. He also quickly caught the attention of the legal profession and was made clerk of the chancery court. About six months after he began practice, Hillsman Taylor, district attorney general for Gibson, Carroll, Crockett, Henry, and Haywood counties, made Browning an assistant prosecutor for Carroll County. Taylor, the son of Tennessee Governor Robert Love Taylor of "War of the Roses" fame, had introduced Browning to the bar after the state examinations and had recognized his potential for politics.[21] Browning intended to make an early bid for Congress, but an event of major proportions forced him to modify if not delay his plans. In April 1917 the United States became an active partner of the Allies in World War I, and the Huntingdon lawyer quickly indicated his willingness to serve in the armed forces. Normally service in uniform during time of national conflict is an asset to an aspiring politician, but that was not Browning's only motive for going to war. He was raised in an era of intense nationalism, and his ultra-patriotic spirit enabled him easily to accept the leadership of America's crusading President Woodrow Wilson, who preached that the war was a war to end all wars and to make the world safe for democracy. Although Browning probably took the initiative and volunteered, he insisted later that Tennessee Governor Tom C. Rye called him in and offered him a commission in the Tennessee National Guard. His response was duly modest: "I said, 'Well, Governor, I don't know whether I'm capable of trying to command anybody until I get some training.' He said: 'Well, that's good. Everybody's in the same shape. Nobody else knows anything about it either so you go ahead and take it.' "[22] Browning was subsequently commissioned a second lieutenant in the First Tennessee Field Artillery. Governor Rye's appointment met with approval in Huntingdon; the *Carroll County Democrat* declared that the governor had made no mistake in conferring the commission, for the young lieutenant was a hard and faithful worker and would certainly do a creditable job.[23]

The Tennessee National Guard was a part of the Thirtieth or "Old Hickory" Division. In the weeks following the declaration of war, the division was involved in organizing, recruiting, and drilling locally. When the division was federalized on 25 July the artillery units became part of the 114th Field Artillery Regiment, and Lieutenant Browning was assigned to Battery D. The 114th Field Artillery was commanded by Colonel Luke Lea, former United States senator from Tennessee and publisher of the *Nashville Tennessean*. The regimental adjutant was Captain Leland S. McPhail who became famous in later years as an executive with professional baseball teams in Cincinnati, Brooklyn, and New York City. In September, West Tennessee units entrained for Camp Sevier, South Carolina, stopping in Nashville for a parade and at other locations on the route for meals provided by concerned women's groups. The days at Camp Sevier involved long hours of hard work; the enlisted men had to clear the primeval forest and build the camp before training could begin and the officers, with no prior military experience, had to study military procedures and tactics well into the night.[24]

In November 1917 Browning was promoted to first lieutenant, then to captain in May 1918, and before the division left Camp Sevier for Europe he was given command of Battery A. Battery A was a National Guard unit based in Memphis, and the greater portion of its personnel were recruited in that city, although a few came from the surrounding area of eastern Arkansas, northern Mississippi, and western Tennessee. The first lieutenants of the battery were Walter Chandler and Guy Joyner, both of whom would later become stalwarts in the Memphis political machine of Edward H. Crump. Chandler, who was soon appointed captain and placed in command of the 114th's supply company, would later serve as a congressman and mayor of Memphis, and Joyner

eventually became sheriff of Shelby County. Browning's company contained men of all kinds, including some rather tough characters, and it
gained a reputation as a "scrapping" outfit that the original commander,
Edward J. McCormick could not control. When he was removed, no
one wanted to take the battery except Browning who volunteered for
the job. He relished the challenge, and quickly demonstrated his leadership ability by developing a competent, disciplined outfit. According
to one of his men, Browning was a strict but fair disciplinarian who loved
his men. Because he put his men first, they loved him and "would fight
for him" even in political battles in later years. They continued to refer
to Browning affectionately as "Cap" after the war. [25]

After about seven months of training, often with simulated weapons,
the Thirtieth Division departed for France as part of the American Ex-
peditionary Force, arriving in Europe in June of 1918. In France, the
114th Field Artillery was detached from the "Old Hickory" Division and
was reassigned to a French unit. In the waning months of the war,
Captain Browning's battery participated in the battles of St. Mihiel,
Argonne, and Woevre. He described his combat as "rugged," for his
company was frequently under artillery fire, and he was knocked off his
feet twice by the concussion from exploding shells. Later he delighted
in describing amusing incidents such as the time when he, quite by
accident, captured a town single-handedly. Browning's wartime experiences were always related in such a manner as to give the impression
that the events were a mixture of heroism and high comedy. [26]

While serving in World War I, Browning made friends with Luke
Lea, the powerful Tennessee politician. It appeared at the time that
their relationship might eventually prove fruitful to the aspiring political
novice from Huntingdon. Browning was originally selected to participate in Lea's famous attempt in 1919 to kidnap Kaiser Wilhelm from his
exile in the Netherlands and present him to President Wilson at the
Paris peace conference. The Colonel planned to go into the Netherlands, use his credentials as a newspaperman to obtain an interview with
the Kaiser, and then take him as a hostage. Browning opposed that
method, advocating instead a simple direct assault to overwhelm the
exile's guards. However, he was removed from the expedition roster
because a superior informed Colonel Lea that there were too many cap-
tains on the list. Captain Browning was disappointed because "we were
kind of bored with time on our hands so we thought it would be a jolly
piece of business if we could do it." Lea's scheme failed because the
Kaiser would not cooperate by giving the interview. Moreover, army

authorities considered prosecuting the Colonel for attempting an adventure that would have violated the neutrality of the Netherlands with
repercussions for the United States. Charges finally were dropped, apparently because a court-martial would have been embarrassing to the
army, but Lea was given a reprimand by General John J. Pershing.
Nevertheless, Browning returned with a deep respect for Lea, who was
a fearless leader "well respected and very popular with his men because
he never did send them anywhere he wouldn't go."[27]

The Thirtieth Division and the 114th Field Artillery Regiment returned to Tennessee in April 1919 and Gordon Browning received a
hero's welcome when he arrived in Huntingdon. The politically ambitious young lawyer came home with his reputation enhanced. Already
possessing leadership ability and a dynamic personality, he now had a
commendable war record that would be helpful to anyone aspiring to
a career in politics. Moreover, he would have the support of a relatively
small but reliable and highly vocal pressure group—the veterans of the
war. Efforts to organize World War I veterans into what became the
American Legion had been initiated in France in the weeks after the
war, and the first national convention was held in May 1919 in St. Louis,
Missouri. The Tennessee spokesman at the St. Louis meeting was
Colonel Lea, and the following month he was one of the leaders at a
conference in Nashville to organize the Legion's Department of Tennessee. Also present at the Nashville meeting were Gordon Browning,
Walter Chandler, and Guy Joyner. The organizers of the American Legion were not unaware of its potential as a political pressure group, and
Browning, along with other political hopefuls, could count on the powerful veterans' organization to help get out the vote. Browning could
also count on the enthusiastic support of his former "buddies"from Battery A. That unit was unique; lasting friendships were made and held
together by regular reunions which began on 11 November 1919. Many
of Browning's comrades in Battery A became directly involved in politics
with him. The young veteran who returned to law practice in Huntingdon was sublimely confident that he could defeat anyone in political
battle. His ultimate goal at that time is not clear, but he probably hoped
eventually to reach the United States Senate. At any rate he began to
make plans to run for the eighth Tennessee congressional seat. The
Democratic primary in 1920 seemed to be the appropriate time.[28]

Tennessee's eighth congressional district in 1920 was composed of
twelve counties with a population of approximately 242,000. Made up
primarily of the West Tennessee counties of Benton, Carroll, Chester,

Decatur, Fayette, Hardin, Hardeman, Henderson, Henry, McNairy, and Madison, the district straddled the Tennessee River and included Perry County in the middle section of the state. The Democrats were the majority party, but Republicans had always been strong in Carroll, Hardin, Henderson, and McNairy counties. The congressman from the eighth district was Democrat Thetus Willrette Sims of Linden in Perry County. He had been in Congress since 1897 and was chairman of the House Committee on Interstate and Foreign Commerce until the Republicans won a majority in the House in the congressional elections of 1918. Sims had seniority, was entrenched in his home district, and would be hard to beat, but Browning apparently relished the role of giant killer because he had no reservations about taking on the incumbent nor did he consider the possibility of defeat. In April 1920 Browning formally announced his candidacy in the August Democratic primary for the nomination to the eighth district seat in Congress. A few weeks later he delivered his first speech of the campaign. He began by humbly asking for the honor of serving his people and denying the charge made by Sims that he was too young and inexperienced to hold a seat in Congress. Browning then attacked the incumbent's legislative record, which he characterized as insignificant, charged him with indifference shown by infrequent visits to the district, and declared that the overall record proved that Sims did not deserve to be reelected. The challenger concluded his opening address by venerating George Washington and the founding fathers for establishing a great democratic republic on America's virgin shores and applauding the recent efforts by the United States to destroy autocracy and to establish democracy in the world. Finally, he asked the people to support a measure to provide care and compensaton for the disabled veterans and the widows and orphans of those who made the ultimate sacrifice for victory over autocracy.[29]

Browning campaigned like a political veteran and displayed a bit of showmanship as well by carrying along a dog named Kaiser, a German shepherd that he allegedly "liberated" from the enemy. Whether the dog gained any votes for the challenger is impossible to ascertain, but surely it did no damage.[30] The ground swell of support which developed for Browning resulted in part from the help of veterans who organized to work for him in the district; a "Browning for Congress" Club was even organized in Memphis, which was outside the district, by former comrades from Battery A. One was a young attorney, Abe Waldauer, who had served as a private in the battery, and the Memphis *Commercial Appeal* reported that the Memphian's campaigning was a major factor in the Browning boom.[31] The challenger's bandwagon was rolling with such speed that one of Sims's supporters committed an error. On 23 July the *Lexington Progress* carried a brief article entitled "A New German Invasion." It read in part: "It appears from the newspapers that a band of political raiders from Memphis headed by one 'Von Abe Waldauer' is making a campaign drive through this congressional district . . . for Capt. Gordon Browning. . . . This is true political Prussianism. . . . This 'Von' Waldauer, with an unpronounceable, unamericanized name but with unexampled cheek and gall assumes that the Democrats of our district are too ignorant to know who to nominate for Congress."[32]

Because the article carried no by-line, quoted no one, and gave no indication that it was a paid political advertisement, it must be assumed that the editor was expressing himself in the form of a news item. Nevertheless, the article raised a storm among the veterans of the district, and a group of ex-servicemen from McNairy drafted a petition demanding that Congressman Sims explain and refute the statement.[33] He apparently gave no reply but even if he had, it would not have mattered, for the damage had been done. Sims had been in Congress for more than twenty years and had become complacent. His visits to the district were infrequent; he was overconfident at the beginning of the campaign and realized too late that he faced a formidable opponent in the attractive and aggressive Browning. On 5 August 1920 the voters repudiated Congressman Sims in the Democratic primary as Browning won by what some considered a surprising figure, approximately five thousand votes out of nearly thirty thousand cast.[34] The *Lexington Progress*, perhaps embarrassed by the storm it had raised, humbly reported that "Capt. Browning will have much to live up to in the fact that he has beaten one of the best men the 8th or any other Tennessee districts ever had in Congress—and he is capable of doing so."[35]

Politics was not the only matter of importance that occupied Gordon Browning in the months after his return from France, for he became involved in a courtship. One of the most eligible bachelors in Huntingdon, the young candidate had his eye on the most eligible girl, the petite and lovely Ida Leach, daughter of Edward and Madonna Baird Leach. Respected members of the community, Leach was a merchant and his wife operated the Industrial Training School, a secondary level boarding institution. Quiet and refined in manners, Miss Ida was an ideal prospect for the wife of a man in public life and Browning pressed his cause aggressively. She finally accepted his proposal and the couple planned to wed, or as Browning put it, "declare war" on each other on Armistice

Day, 11 November 1920. He fully expected to carry his bride off to Washington with him.[36]

Ordinarily victory in the Democratic primary in the eighth district was tantamount to victory in the general election, and the young Huntingdon lawyer, elated over his victory, was confident he would soon be in Washington as a member of the House of Representatives. But an ill wind was blowing for the Democrats in 1920, even in predominantly Democratic West Tennessee. The Republican party, perhaps sensing a possible upset, gave its nomination for the eighth district seat to the personable Lon Allen Scott of Savannah. Scott had served in the Tennessee General Assembly, enlisted as a private during the war, and was eventually promoted to lieutenant while serving overseas. Scott and Browning had been classmates at Cumberland Law School, were good friends and even canvassed together, participating in debates. Nevertheless, the campaign was a bitter one, focusing on issues that centered around the involvement of the United States in international affairs.[37] When the day of reckoning came on 3 November Browning was upset by the Republican candidate. The Democratic party in Tennessee was shaken by the Republican upsurge that swept the entire country that year when Republican Alf Taylor was elected to the governor's office in Tennessee. In the eighth district, Scott received 22,938 votes to Browning's 22,279; Browning even lost his home county by 1,398 votes.[38]

Several factors contributed to Browning's defeat in the general election. One was the failure of Congressman Sims's friends to give adequate support to the party's nominee. Browning was convinced that his support for the League of Nations also weighed against him; he declared, "That beat me."[39] No doubt many rural Tennesseans feared that the League would exercise too much influence over the government of the United States, but there were other factors which contributed to the Republican victories in the eighth district as well as across the state: discontent with President Wilson's policies, fear of Bolshevism, the economic recession of 1919–1920, an increase in the number of women voters, and a cleavage within the Democratic party in Tennessee.[40]

Although it was a bitter setback for the aspiring politician, in the long run it was merely a stumbling block to success. "Miss Ida married me anyway," he laughed, but there was no immediate journey to Washington.[41]

NOTES

1. Samuel Cole Williams, *Beginnings of West Tennessee In the Land of the Chicakasaws, 1541–1841* (Johnson City: The Wautauga Press, 1930). pp. 94–97.

2. Ibid., pp. 132–133, 271–279; Stanley J. Folmsbee, Robert E. Corlew, Enoch L. Mitchell, *Tennessee, A Short History* (Knoxville: University of Tennessee Press, 1969), pp. 248–266, 316–322.

3. Gordon Browning to Edgar Raymond Browning, 10 December 1951, Gordon Browning Papers, Tennessee State Library and Archives. Browning expressed little interest in his family's genealogy; he was fond of saying "ancestors are like potatoes—the best part is underground," Mrs. Bill Bowers, interview with the author, Milan, 24 June 1976.

4. Gordon Browning, "Gordon Browning: An Oral Memoir," ed. Joseph H. Riggs (Memphis Public Library, 1966), p. 16; George Barker, "Of War, Peace, and Politics," *Nashville Tennessean Magazine* (23 Sept. 1962), p. 11.

5. Mrs. Bill Bowers, interview; Dan Robison, *Biographical Directory, Tennessee General Assembly, 1796–1969: Carroll County* (Nashville: Tennessee State Library and Archives, 1969), p. 8.

6. Browning, "Oral Memoir," p. 12.

7. Ibid., p. 42; Mrs. W. S. Field, interview with the author, Milan, 24 June 1976.

8. Mrs. W. S. Field, interview.

9. Browning, "Oral Memoir," p. 3.

10. Ibid., pp. 4, 10; Mrs. W. S. Field, interview.

11. Browning, "Oral Memoir," p. 10.

12. Ibid., pp. 16–17.

13. Mrs. W. S. Field, interview; Browning, "Oral Memoir," pp. 16–17.

14. Mrs. W. S. Field, interview; Gordon Browning, interview with the author, Huntingdon, 28 December 1965.

15. Browning, "Oral Memoir," p. 42.

16. Mrs. W. S. Field, interview.

17. Richard Hofstadter, *The Age of Reform: From Bryan to F. D. R.* (New York: Vintage Books, 1955), pp. 23–59; see also Hofstadter, "The Myth of the Happy Yeoman," *American Heritage* 7 (April 1956): 43–53.

18. Browning, "Oral Memoir," pp. 4–5, 17–18.

19. Ibid., p. 5; repeated in Gordon Browning, interview, 28 December 1965.

20. Barker, "Of War, Peace, and Politics," p. 18; Browning, "Oral Memoir," p. 5–6.

21. Browning, "Oral Memoir," p. 20; Robert L. Taylor, interview with the author, Memphis, 10 August 1976.

22. Browning, "Oral Memoir," p. 22.

23. *Carroll County Democrat*, 22 June 1917.

24. J. Chester Shields, interview with the author, Memphis, 21 August 1977.

25. Ibid.; Charles Gallina, interview with the author, Memphis, 22 August 1977.

26. Barker, "Of War, Peace, and Politics," p. 18; Browning, "Oral Memoir," pp. 22–32. For the 114th Field Artillery's part in the war, see William J. Bacon, ed., *History of the Fifty-Fifth Artillery Brigade* (Memphis: William J. Bacon, 1919); Elmer A. Murphey and Robert S. Thomas, *The Thirtieth Division in the World War* (Lepanto: Old Hickory Publishing Co., 1936) pp. 14, 20, 183–184.

27. Browning, "Oral Memoir," pp. 29–30. For the story of the escapade, see T. H. Alexander, "They Tried to Kidnap the Kaiser," *The Saturday Evening Post* (25 October 1937), pp. 5–6, 84–89; Luke Lea, "The Attempt to Capture the Kaiser," ed. William T. Alderson, *Tennessee Historical Quarterly* 20 (September 1961): 222–261.

28. J. Chester Shields, interview; Charles Gallina, interview; Fred D. Estes, ed., *History of American Legion, Department of Tennessee, 1919–1953* (Nashville: American Legion, 1953), pp. 13–14; Cromwell Tidwell, "Luke Lea and the American Legion," *Tennessee Historical Quarterly* 18 (Spring 1969): 70–83.

29. *Lexington Progress*, 9 April 1920; Gordon Browning, "Announcement Speech of Gordon Browning, Candidate for Democractic Nomination For Congress," C. L. Majors papers, private collection.

30. "Sims is reported to have said later, 'Browning didn't beat me, the dog did,'" Barker, "Of War, Peace, and Politics," p. 18.

31. *Commercial Appeal*, 6 August 1920; William D. Miller [*Mr. Crump of Memphis* (Baton Rouge: Louisiana State University Press, 1964) p. 247] quoted Waldauer as saying "his [Browning's] campaign was planned in the dugouts of the Argonne Forest."

32. *Lexington Progress*, 23 July 1920.

33. Petition in C. L. Majors papers.

34. *Commercial Appeal*, 6 August 1920.

35. *Lexington Progress*, 6 August 1920.

36. Mary Leach, interview with the author, Huntingdon, 12 August 1976; Browning, "Oral Memoir," p. 25.

37. Gordon Browning, interview, 28 December 1965; Barker, "Of War, Peace, and Politics," p. 18.

38. *Tennessee Handbook and Official Directory 1921–1922* (Nashville, n.d.), p. 49.

39. Browning, interview, 28 December 1965.

40. Gary W. Reichard, "The Aberration of 1920: An Analysis of Harding's Victory in Tennessee," *The Journal of Southern History* 36 (February 1970): 33–49; Gary W. Reichard, "The Defeat of Governor Roberts," *Tennessee Historical Quarterly* 30 (Spring, 1971): 94–109.

41. Barker, "Of War, Peace, and Politics," p. 18.

2

The Congressman

ORDON Browning maintained that he was not discouraged after his defeat in 1920; rather, he was "more determined than ever" to win a seat in Congress.[1] There is no reason to doubt his sincerity, for if any trait stood out in Browning's personality, it was persistence. Even the most casual observer of Tennessee politics in the early 1920s realized that the Republican victory in the eighth congressional district in 1920 was probably a momentary circumstance, that the district remained predominantly Democratic, and that a strong Democrat could unseat Congressman Lon Scott in 1922. No one was more conscious of the situation than Browning; so without trepidation he entered the Democratic primary in 1922 and decisively defeated his only opponent, Arch Patterson. Now he was ready to challenge Congressman Scott in the general election in November. The campaign was almost a carbon copy of the one two years earlier, as once again they debated each other, often traveling together and sharing the same automobile. Browning declared that Scott again tried to make the League of Nations an issue, but he accepted the challenge "and very much to his surprise and everybody else's I fought it out the second time."[2] It was no contest, as the issues that plagued Browning and the Democrats in 1920 were no longer present or important to the voters in the eighth district. The predominately Republican counties of McNairy and Hardin went to Scott, but in the remainder of the district Browning won by the comfortable margin of 16,571 to 12,328. Considerable apathy was evident in the total vote since the two candidates together polled approximately 16,000 fewer votes than in the election two years earlier.[3] Browning interpreted his victory to mean that the League had ceased to be an issue: "I beat Scott in 1922 because people just quit Scott and the issue of the League of Nations just died out. But I was still for the League."[4]

In 1923 Congressman Browning began the long tenure that was typical of southern members of the United States House of Representatives. During his twelve years as representative from the eighth district, he had little political opposition in the Democratic primaries, and the Republicans offered no candidates in the general elections of 1924, 1926, and 1930. In 1928 Browning swamped Harvey E. Cantrell in the general electon by almost nine thousand votes. In 1932 he did even better by defeating two opponents, E. R. Dubois and Willoughby Stewart, by 20,000 to a mere 6,000 votes for both challengers combined.[5] Browning, however, did not achieve an outstanding record in Congress. Because the Republicans controlled both the legislative and executive branches of the national government after the Harding landslide in 1920, those were not propitious years for Democratic congressmen. Even the crumbs of patronage left to Democrats were more scarce for the representative from the eighth Tennessee district because the senior senator, Kenneth D. McKellar, had the honor of passing on all federal appointments in the state. McKellar was already exhibiting a tendency to look upon patronage as his responsibility. Congressman Browning did serve on a number of important committees in the House. In his first term, he was appointed to Elections Committee Number Two, Railways and Canals, Reform in Civil Service, and World War Veterans' Legislation Committees. In the Seventy-first Congress he was appointed to the Judiciary Committee and was a member when it investigated proposed repeal of the prohibition amendment and the short selling of securities on the stock market. However, he took no conspicuous part in the hearings nor did he have a significant influence on the committee's work.

Gordon Browning was a southerner with a populist background, and he viewed national issues in terms of that conditioning, modified somewhat by time and experience. His populism did not include the radical economic solutions proposed by his grandfather, Thomas Brooks, nor was he opposed to the acquisition of wealth. Browning simply believed that corporate interests had too great an influence on government policy. He maintained that government should exercise greater control over the economy and attempt to curb the power of great wealth. He was therefore out of sympathy with the policies of the Republican administrations of Warren G. Harding, Calvin Coolidge, and Herbert Hoover. Larger corporate and banking interests were favored in the twenties as those administrations sought to reduce regulations on business and to lower federal expenditures. Moreover, income taxes on those in the higher brackets were repeatedly reduced, placing a greater burden on those with lower incomes. The rationale was simple: the higher income groups would invest their tax savings in expansion which would eventually trickle down in the form of jobs or higher salaries and wages for the lower income groups. Congressman Browning was quick to join the opposition to the Republican tax policies, insisting instead, "The ability to pay ultimately must be the basis of our taxes."[6]

Browning was even more outspoken in his opposition to the Republican tariff policy of the 1920s, perhaps because he believed that it more directly affected his constituency of poor farmers than income taxes did. The Republicans, in deference to certain corporate interests, reversed the lower tariff policy of President Woodrow Wilson and reestablished very high rates in the Fordney-McCumber Act of 1922. The measure reduced foreign competition and trade and, by preventing Europeans from selling to the United States, also prevented them from paying the debts they incurred during the First World War. Against the protective tariff, Congressman Browning expressed a long-held southern grievance. He charged that the Fordney-McCumber Act destroyed the farmers' foreign market and at the same time forced upward the price of manufactured goods, thereby drastically reducing puchasing power. He believed that the tariff was damaging to the cotton farmers in his district because that staple was one of Tennessee's chief exports. "We didn't have any market abroad and the whole thing added up to the fact that the manufacturers had tremendous advantage and the farmers were limited," he declared. Browning also insisted that a majority of manufacturing actually suffered under a high protective tariff, and he urged Congress to enact a more moderate, or as he termed it, a "competitive" tariff.[7] Concerning the European war debt issue, he took a hard line and spoke in opposition to the proposed cancellation of those debts.

As a congressman representing small farmers, Browning was deeply concerned with national agricultural policy. The most important measure involving agrarian interests to go before Congress after his arrival in Washington was the McNairy-Haugen Bill. That measure would have authorized government purchase of farm surpluses at a high domestic price and in turn sold on the foreign market at whatever price could be obtained. Although in sympathy with any proposal to improve the lot of farmers, Browning proved to be a southerner first in this case. The congressman stated that he was opposed to the measure in its original form because "I used to pride myself on being an old-fashioned states' righter." He voted against the McNairy-Haugen Bill when it came up because it failed to make provision for the farmers to have a voice in the implementation of the law.[8] Browning's stands on taxes, the tariff, and other economic policies in the 1920s generally were in accordance with the wishes of his constituents. Secure in his seat, he was unlikely to violate the popular will and rarely went against the apparent will of the majority in his district.[9]

Like most Americans, Gordon Browning found the postwar years perplexing if not overwhelming. The decade of the twenties was an era of confusion, uncertainty, and insecurity. It was a time of accelerating technological and intellectual change, of fast-changing fads, fashions, and styles, all of which seemed to challenge the older values. It was also an era of intolerance for those of different color, religion, or ethnic background. Americans in the war years had been taught by specious propaganda to hate the enemy. Consequently this hatred spilled over into the postwar years and was expressed in many forms such as the move to restrict immigration and the rise of the Ku Klux Klan. Imbued as he was with rural values and religious fundamentalism, Browning joined the resistance to the unwelcome trends of this decade. And like most of those living or reared in rural or small-town America, he found it easy to blame the insecurity and anxiety of the period on the growth of the cities and industry, and the presence of Jews, Catholics, blacks, or those of foreign origin. Narrow provincialism and intolerance led to the National Origins Act of 1924, which sharply restricted immigration. Reflecting his rural background, Congressman Browning found it easy to endorse the move to restrict immigration. "I felt then, very strongly," he said, "that we had enough to engage our attention for a long time with trying to assimilate the ones that were already here. I've always been opposed to immigration for we have a virile and strong people and they'll stay strong by not being mixed with any other race."[10]

Browning was less open on another burning issue in the 1920s, the Ku Klux Klan. Born in the lingering prejudice of rural, small-town and white-protestant America, the Klan sought to unite whites in order to control or eliminate Jews, Catholics, and blacks by murder, kidnapping, flogging, cross-burning, arson, and other forms of terror. The Klan became a politically divisive issue, and although many Americans opposed the organization's use of violence, they supported its goal of maintaining white supremacy. The Klan was moderately strong in Tennessee with its greatest strength in the extreme eastern and extreme western portions of the state. It probably had peaked in 1923 but was still able to play an influential role in the Democratic gubernatorial primary in 1924.[11] Browning insisted that he opposed the Klan, because "I've always been against secret societies when they've tried to enter into the influence of government."[12] But he did not see fit to make an issue of the Klan in the 1920s. Like most of his constituents, he believed in the desirability of white supremacy and he was reasonably adroit in sidestepping controversial issues when faced with them directly. On the issue of prohibition, however, he could safely be outspoken. Prohibition, ratified as a constitutional amendment in 1919 and implemented by the Volstead Act, was perhaps the last-ditch victory of rural America against the rising tide of urbanism. Moralists in the countryside, particularly those of fundamentalistic sects, had long insisted that liquor was an instrument of the devil and the source of most of the nation's evils. But prohibition proved to be virtually unenforceable and urban "wets" began a drive to repeal the amendment. The congressman's opposition to repeal was an honest conviction, for throughout his public career he remained consistent in his opposition to legalizing the liquor traffic. His opposition was also a reflection of the views of his rural West Tennessee constituents.

Congressman Browning's chief legislative interest was World War veterans' affairs. During the 1920s one of the most vocal lobbies was the American Legion, and Browning demonstrated that he was one of the most vocal congressional spokesman for that pressure group. Indeed, he probably worked harder for veterans than anyone else in Congress. The measure calling for adjusted compensation for veterans of the First World War went before Congress during his first term. The "Bonus," as it was called, providing for a paid-up life insurance policy, had passed the previous session only to be vetoed by President Harding. Browning was one of the strongest supporters of the measure, but he fought to add a provision to allow the ex-serviceman the option of cash instead of insurance, a feature which the House Ways and Means Committee had considered but rejected. Browning then took the floor in an effort to either block the committee from reporting out the measure without the cash option provision or force a bill that could be amended. On 14 March 1924, in his maiden speech in the House of Representatives, he made an impassioned plea for a bonus bill with a cash option. Browning called the measure without a cash option an "absolute abortion under the guise of adjusted compensation." He had no quarrel, he said, with those who opposed adjusted compensation because it placed a price on patrotism. He conceded that no price could be placed on the patriotism of personal self-sacrifice, but he believed that a cash payment to the veterans would be a pittance compared to the profits others made during the war. He argued that a small cash payment was no "raid on the Treasury" as some called it; indeed, it would cost the government far less than the adjustments of uncompleted war contracts. He declared:

> When we came out of the war with 23,000 more millionaires than [when] we entered it we heard no loud denunciation of these shrewd individuals as being unpatriotic. On November 11, 1918, the War Department had uncompleted contracts outstanding of $6,700,000,000. It cost the Government approximately $3,400,000,000 to adjust these claims with contractors. Yet no one called them unpatriotic because they demanded and received this adjustment. . . . . Only the men who fought have been singled out and taken to task for even presuming they should recoup a part of their financial losses because of the war. They are being called mercenary, while all other elements without reflection are replete by adjustment.

Finally, he declared that the obligation to the veterans was just as moral an obligation as the obligation under any contract. The congressman conceded, however, that he would vote for the bonus measure without the cash option "if I can not get any better one."[13] The measure passed without the cash feature only to have President Calvin Coolidge veto it; but perhaps because 1924 was an election year, Congress overrode the veto, and the "bonus" became law.[14] Gordon Browning's work for the veterans' lobby did not end with adjusted compensation. Several measures concerning liberalization of the interpretation of service-connected disablity came before the Committee on Veterans Legislation and the congressman worked for the passage of those measures. One of his chief concerns was veterans' hospitals, and he participated in investigative junkets around the country looking into the operation of those institutions. The inadequacy of the facilities shocked him, and he frequently urged increased appropriations for operating and building new hospitals.[15]

In 1931, after the Depression had spread across the land, Congress again took up the subject of the veterans' bonus, and legislation was passed permitting ex-servicemen to borrow up to fifty percent of the face value of their life insurance certificates. But because of the severity of the Depression, the veterans' lobby demanded that Congress authorize immediate payment of the insurance certificates at face value; Congressman Browning was one of the advocates of the cause. President Hoover, however, announced that he would veto the proposed payment if it passed because it would produce a deficit in the federal budget. Browning rose on the floor of the House and angrily charged the president with ignoring thousands of sick and needy men. He maintained that the chief executive had no trouble getting funds for other projects, and that the secretary of the treasury, Andrew Mellon, had refunded millions of dollars to corporations from revenues collected under the excess profits tax. Browning also reacted in anger when the president announced his opposition to increasing benefits to disabled veterans and to widows and orphans of those killed in the service. Gordon Browning was undoubtedly sincere in his concern about the welfare of ex-servicemen, but a veteran himself, he was also aware that his efforts in their behalf would pay dividends at the polls. The congressman's comrades, along with the American Legion, provided him with a hard core of voting strength which reflected their appreciation of his efforts in their behalf. Browning also demonstrated special concern for individual veterans in trouble and made service in the First World War a prime consideration in his political appointments.[16]

The nation was stunned by the Wall Street Crash in 1929 and the advent of the Great Depressoin. The sudden onset of hard times was a shocking contrast to the apparent prosperity of the 1920s, and Congressman Browning, like most Democrats, found the cause of the disaster in the economic policies of the Republican party and its deference to big business. President Hoover, believing that government intervention in the economy would be pernicious at best, pursued a policy of "wait and see" despite evidence that the Depression was getting worse. Browning joined the growing chorus of those demanding positive governmental action in the crisis. It was almost inevitable that a Democrat would replace Hoover in the White House, and it came as no surprise when the governor of New York, Franklin D. Roosevelt, won the presidential election of 1932. The Democrats also won control of both Houses of Congress for the first time since the Wilson years. Browning, for the first time since he had arrived in Washington, found himself in the ma-

jority party. With his mandate in hand, President Roosevelt introduced
the New Deal, a complex of economic and political principles and policies designed to promote recovery from the Depression and to advance
the economic and social welfare of the American people. Tennessee, as
much as any state, benefited from the New Deal programs, but Congressman Browning did not play a significant role in their development
and implementation. For reasons not entirely clear, the congressman
and Roosevelt were not congenial; Browning described the President
as "two-faced," although he conceded that Roosevelt was "one of the
shrewdest of all the politicians that I've ever seen."[17] However, Browning's voting record on New Deal legislation was generally positive, and
he supported most of the measures the President presented to Congress
in the "hundred days" of 1933. But he refused to identify himself as a
New Dealer. He acknowledged, "most New Deal measures were proper
and good and I supported them because of party discipline. I believed
in party government. but I voted my convictions."[18] Browning's estimate of himself was reasonably accurate. His record in Congress revealed that he was a Democratic regular on most issues and a southern
states'-rights Democrat on particular issues. He opposed the Republican party because "I never did believe that they had any interest in
anybody except those that were worth a million or more." Browning was
a Democrat because the party was for the little man, but "I was not
raised as a rock-rib, hidebound partisan,"he declared.[19] Gordon Browning did indeed demonstrate occasional independence.

Of all the New Deal measures that most directly affected Tennessee,
the act creating the Tennessee Valley Authority in 1933 was by far the
most significant. Although Senator George W. Norris of Nebraska is
credited as being the father of TVA, the regional development agency
was the product of many minds concerned with problems such as flood
control, reclamation, navigation, and electric power. During the 1920s,
Senator Norris sought to expand the federal government's Muscle
Shoals Dam and nitrate plant on the Tennessee River in northern Alabama into a great regional development program for the entire valley.
The Norris plan provided for the completion of the Muscle Shoals facilities by the federal government for the manufacture of nitrate fertilizer and for the sale of surplus electric power. The measure also called
for the construction of a dam on Cove Creek, a tributary of the Tennessee River in East Tennessee. But the Republican administrations in
the decade sought to turn the dam and plant over to private enterprise,
and several individuals and concerns, including automobile manufac-

turer Henry Ford and the American Cyanamid Company, made bids for the facilities. Browning originally opposed the sale of the properties to private enterprise, for he feared that industry might absorb all the electric power generated by the dam and deprive his West Tennessee constituents of the potential use. He changed his mind, however, and supported the American Cyanamid bid when a study by the Corps of Engineers revealed that possibilities for water power sites existed in West Tennessee.[20] In 1928 Norris succeeded in getting his plan approved by Congress only to have President Calvin Coolidge pocket veto the bill. Although favoring the American Cyanamid bid, Browning was willing to accept the Norris plan in principle if it contained provision for orderly retirement of the cost of construction to the government. He subsequently voted against the bill because it failed to contain that provision. Browning fairly consistently opposed appropriations of the nature of Norris's project which did not provide sufficient revenue to pay for the cost of construction, financing, and retirement of the debt. It is interesting to note that Browning was not the only Tennessean voting against the measure. Several of his fellow Democrats—Congressmen Cordell Hull, Joe Byrns, Lamar Davis, and Edward Eslick—voted against it, while Sam McReynolds and Republicans B. Carroll Reece and J. Will Taylor voted in the affirmative.[21] When the Norris plan was brought before the House again in the following session in 1929, Browning changed his position again. In a radio address to the people of Tennessee, inserted in the *Congressional Record*, he praised the Muscle Shoals project for its contributions to the development of industry, agriculture, river navigation, and flood control. He declared that the government had to build the dams because the private power industry would never build them. However, he announced that he favored leasing the dams to private concerns and allowing them to produce fertilizer and power as a means to amortize the entire cost of construction.[22]

In 1931 the Norris bill once again passed Congress, but President Hoover vetoed it. When the bill was revived in 1933, the chances of its being enacted into law appeared to be excellent because President Roosevelt was sympathetic to the plan. During the hearings on Muscle Shoals before the House Committee on Military affairs, Congressman Browning appeared as a witness. In his opening remarks, he said, "I am not here to oppose any feature of the bill. . . . I am in hearty accord with the main purpose of this bill . . . and I would not do one thing to hamper its expeditious consideration." He pointed out, however, that in the present form the measure contained no provision for the construction of dams at places other than Cove Creek and Muscle Shoals proper. Other sites, he said, were recommended in the report of the Corps of Engineers and were part of the whole plan, and he saw no reason why the bill should not include provisions for the early development of those sites. Browning then went on to propose an amendment to the bill that would permit the government to lease power from the other dams to private enterprise. He said:

> I believe there would be no objection, and no conflict, to permit the board to construct these other dams now, or all of them where they can be leased under contract to private enterprise at the switchboard . . . and if a bid is offered by a private concern to lease this dam after completion for power purposes, providing for the amortization of the entire cost of construction of the dam and taking care of the interest on that part of it chargeable to power, I believe it would be a fine proposition for the Government, looking to its intention to develop the whole valley.

Browning contended that his amendment would meet some of the objections to government operation; it would "leave the government in control of the power at the switch, but at the same time, it would give private industry the privilege of using this power in its own way." He emphasized that the use of the electricity would be subject to regulation by the Federal Power Commission, which would insure that power would be sold at reasonable rates. He insisted that "the provision of the amendment would require the company leasing it to amortize the entire expense of the dam." In addition, Browning supported the provision that the states be paid five percent of the gross receipts received by the sale of power generated at the dams. It was reasonable and just, he said, for while the "government has a right to the navigation features of those rivers, and it has the obligation, possibly, to provide flood control," the states owned the power rights in those streams as well as the beds through which those streams flowed.[23] Browning apparently did not realize that his proposition might well have cut the heart out of the project, resulting in a higher rate for the power, and lessening the importance of TVA and its contribution to the welfare of the valley.

When the measure creating the Tennessee Valley Authority came before the House of Representatives without his amendment, Browning gave it his unqualified support. In speaking for the bill, he pointed out that it was a project in the public interest, that it was a wise and farsighted policy of reclamation, and that it would aid, rather than interfere with, private enterprise. He concluded, "this great national resource belongs to the people, and I am sympathetic with any enterprise, whether it is the manufacture of fertilizer or the production of power, that is about to be disturbed by progress; but I do not think progress should be disturbed because they are about to get in the way."[24]

Gordon Browning's stand on the river development program was motivated less by a rigid adherence to an economic philosophy than by the considerations of pragmatic politics. He supported the Tennessee Valley Authority because he saw the potential value to the people of Tennessee and the potentially valuable patronage to himself. He could scarcely oppose the appropriation of millions of dollars that would be utilized in Tennessee to develop the resources of the region. Why, then, did Browning propose the amendment to the TVA bill? In all probability he was seeking personal recognition. The measure would pass anyway and it would be of immeasurable political value to Browning if he could gain some credit for the formulation of TVA or have his name attached to the bill in some way. He apparently had no other motive in presenting his amendment; he also had a propensity to think up grandious schemes without considering details.

Browning's political enemies later charged that he was lukewarm on TVA and that he failed to vote for the measure when it came to a vote on the House floor. It is true that he did not vote for TVA, but his opponents did not set the record straight. The congressman was involved in other affairs on the day of the roll-call vote on TVA, for he was one of the House managers in impeachment proceedings then under way in the Senate. The session convened at ten in the morning of the day of the vote on TVA in the House and recessed at four in the afternoon with only one brief recess. Browning declared that it was a long and tiresome session and maintained that he asked the presiding officer for a recess which was not granted. Besides, he was paired with another congressman.[25]

The most controversial issue Congressman Browning was involved in during his tenure in Congress was President Roosevelt's economy measure in 1933. In an effort to promote economy and achieve a balanced budget during the crisis of the Depression, the President asked Congress shortly after his inauguration in March to give him the authority to cut the federal budget by half a billion dollars. That drastic slash called for the reduction of not only congressional and federal employees' salaries but a significant reduction of benefit payments to disabled veterans and to widows and orphans of those killed in action.[26] Members of Congress were astonished at the request; most were committed to the concept of economy, but the measure would make many constituents unhappy. Those who were obligated to the veterans' lobby were up in arms; Browning called the measure "inconsiderate," and a "slaughter" of the disabled serviceman. Because Congress was not yet organized at the time the measure was announced, the House of Representatives created a special committee for the sake of quick action and gave the committee's report privileged status. Angry Democrats, including Browning, Wright Patman of Texas, John Rankin of Mississippi, Fred Vinson of Kentucky, and John McCormack of Massachusetts, forced a party caucus in which Browning proposed amendments that would have emasculated the economy program. The caucus finally broke up in discord without endorsing the economy act. Administration leaders were fearful that the rebellious members would be able to defeat the measure on the House floor and threatened recalcitrants with retaliation if they succeeded. Browning maintained that President Roosevelt "tried to get me to give in" but the congressman would not be intimidated.[27] As one of the leaders of the rebellion, Browning gave administration spokesmen a great deal of concern. It was something of an anomaly that a firm believer in fiscal integrity should oppose the economy measure, but the congressman was concerned with the condition of disabled servicemen. Because the measure came from the special committee with privileged status, the only way for Browning to block the bill was to move to recommit to committee. However, Speaker of the House Henry R. Rainey refused to recognize him on the floor; this gag, plus the institution of a roll-call vote, enabled administration leaders to frustrate the rebels and the veterans' lobby.[28] Since few congressman wanted to go on record as opposing economy, the measure passed the House of Representatives and ultimately became law primarily because of concern about the federal deficit.

The reaction in Tennessee to Browning's stand indicated that opposition to the economy measure was politically dangerous. The state's press was indignant. The *Knoxville News-Sentinel* said that it took courage for President Roosevelt to propose economy and expressed regret that Congressman Browning did not show the courage of the other Tennessee representatives and support him. The *Chattanooa Times* suggested that Browning's actions demonstrated cowardice, while both the *Nashville Banner* and Memphis *Commercial Appeal* insisted that Tennessee was shamed by his actions.[29] To what extent those papers reflected the thinking of the people of the state, or of the eighth congressional district, is impossible to determine. A vote for the economy measure could have been politically dangerous. A powerful lobby, the American Legion, was aroused, and the protest from veterans and veterans' widows was loud. The angry letters flowed in such volume that a move to restore benefits began in short order. Browning insisted that many congressmen came to him later and "whined that they got their tails in a crack" for reducing pensions; "I was vindicated for my stand," he said.[30] Congress surrendered to the pressure, and a year later the economy program was liberalized and all veterans' benefits were restored. How large a volume of mail Browning received favorable to his stand cannot be estimated but it must have been considerable. Veterans in Tennessee were also outraged at what they regarded as vicious attacks on the congressman in the editorial columns of the state's press.[31] Apparently the outpouring of support was sufficient to encourage Browning to make a move in his political career.

Gordon Browning had never tried to hide his ambition to go to the United States Senate. Indeed, it is probable that the vast majority of members of the House of Representatives have aspired to move into what has been called the most exclusive club in the world. Browning was certainly no exception.[32] But a decison to enter a statewide race for the Senate was not to be taken hastily or lightly. As in any hierarchical structure, the higher the office, the stiffer the competition. Moreover, a senator's relatively long six-year term further restricted opportunities for challenges. Several important factors had to be considered: the nature and strength of the incumbent, the availability of other contenders, the ability to develop an organization and find sources of campaign funds, and finally, good issues. The decision also involved timing. Those who moved too quickly or impatiently flirted with disaster just as did the faint-hearted who hesitated. Many congressmen have spent entire careers waiting for an opportunity to materialize. The year 1934 seemed to Browning an appropriate time for him to make his move for he had an issue: his stand for veterans in opposition to President Roosevelt's economy act. For the first time, therefore, he became involved in the complexities of statewide politics in Tennessee.

NOTES

1. Gordon Browning, interview with the author, Huntingdon, 28 December 1965.

2. Gordon Browning, "Gordon Browning: An Oral Memoir," ed. Joseph H. Riggs (Memphis Public Library, 1966), pp. 33–34.

3. *Tennessee Handbook and Official Directory, 1923–1924* (Nashville: n.d.), p. 46.

4. Browning, interview, 28 December 1965.

5. *Tennessee Blue Book and Official Directory, 1929–1930* (Nashville: n.d.), p. 96; *Tennessee Blue Book and Official Directory, 1933–1934* (Nashville: n.d.), p. 97.

6. Browning, "Oral Memoir," p. 40.

7. Ibid., p. 39.

8. Ibid., p. 40.

9. For Browning's speeches and comments on economic issues, see *Congressional Record,* 68th Cong., 1st sess., 1923–1924, 65: 334–335, 1695; Ibid., 68th Cong., 2nd sess., 1924, 66: EE 2037; Ibid., 69th Cong., 1st sess., 1925–1926, 67: 5029–5031; Ibid., 71st Cong., 1st sess., 1929–1930, 70: 2753–2755; Ibid., 72nd Cong., 2nd sess., 1932, 74: 4516.

10. Browning, "Oral Memoir," 38.

11. David M. Chalmers, *Hooded Americanism: The First Century of the Ku Klux Klan 1865–1965* (Garden City: Doubleday, 1965), p. 153; Arnold S. Rice, *The Ku Klux Klan in American Politics* (Washington: Public Affairs Press, 1952), pp. 43–44.

12. Browning, "Oral Memoir," 39.

13. *Congressional Record,* 68th Cong., 1st sess., 1923–1924, 65: 4178–4180.

14. John D. Hicks, *Republican Ascendancy, 1921–1933* (New York: Harper, 1960), p. 52; Dixon Wecter, *When Johnny Comes Marching Home* (Cambridge: Houghton Mifflin, 1944), pp. 446–447; Willard Waller, *The Veteran Comes Back* (New York: The Dryden Press), 1944, pp. 220–221.

15. *Congressional Record,* 68th Cong., 1st sess., 1923–1924, 65: 10172; Ibid., 68th Cong., 2nd sess., 1924, 66: 1553–1554, 1559; Ibid., 69th Cong., 1st sess., 1925–1926, 67: 6987; Ibid., 69th Cong., 2nd sess., 1926, 68: 5398–5399; Ibid., 68th Cong., 2nd sess., 1924, 66: 1553–1554, 1559.

16. Ibid., 71st Cong., 2nd sess., 1930, 71: 11514; Ibid., 72nd Cong., 1st sess., 1931–1932, 75: 2968–2969; C. L. Majors papers, private collection. The proposal for immediate payment of the face value of the insurance was shelved but pressure from veterans, including the bonus marches of 1932 and 1933, persisted. Congress finally authorized payment in 1935.

17. Gordon Browning, interview with the author, Huntingdon, 28 December 1964; Browning, "Oral Memoir," p. 35.

18. Browning, interview, 28 December 1965. For Browning's voting record, see John Dean Minton, "The New Deal in Tennessee, 1932–1938" (unpublished Ph.D. dissertation, Vanderbilt Univerity, 1959), passim.

19. Browning, "Oral Memoir," pp. 40–42.

20. Preston J. Hubbard, *Origins of the TVA: The Muscle Shoals Controversy, 1920–1932* (Nashville: Vanderbilt University Press, 1961), pp. 251–252.

21. George W. Norris, *Fighting Liberal: The Autobiography of George W.*

Norris (New York: MacMillan, 1945), p. 250; *Congressional Record,* 70th Cong., 1st sess., 1927–1928, 69: 9956–9957.

22. *Congressional Record,* 71st Cong., 1st sess., 1929–1930, 71: 2978–2979.

23. House of Representatives, Committee on Military Affairs, *Hearings on Muscle Shoals, April 11 to April 15, 1933,* 73rd Cong., 1st sess., 1933, pp. 54–67.

24. *Congressional Record,* 73rd Cong., 1st sess., 1933, 77: 2201–2202.

25. Ibid., pp. 3502–3600; Browning, interiew with the author, Huntingdon, 23 June 1966.

26. E. Pendleton Herring, "First Session of the Seventy-Third Congress, March 9, 1933 to June 16, 1933," *The American Political Science Review* 28 (February 1934): 70–73; see also Arthur M. Schlesinger, Jr., *The Age of Roosevelt,* vol. 2, *The Coming of the New Deal* (Cambridge: Houghton Mifflin, 1959), pp. 10–11; William E. Leuchtenburg, *Franklin D. Roosevelt and the New Deal, 1932–1940* (New York: Harper and Row, 1963), p. 45.

27. Browning, interview, 28 December 1965; see also Minton, "The New Deal in Tennessee," 53–54.

28. Browning, "Oral Memoir," p. 38.

29. *Knoxville News-Sentinel,* 15 March 1933; *Chattanooga Times,* 13 March 1933; *Nashville Banner,* 15 March 1933; *Commercial Appeal,* 13 March 1933.

30. Browning, interview, 28 December 1965.

31. C. L. Majors papers.

32. Albert Gore once wrote that he knew of no member of the House, unless it was Speaker of the House, Sam Rayburn, who did not long to go on to the Senate, Albert Gore to Gordon Browning, 28 June 1950, copy, Box 9, No. 31, Edward J. Meeman Papers, Memphis State University.

3

State Politics

POLITICAL patterns in Tennessee are the result of geographical location and diversity, heritage, and the Civil War. Tennessee has long been regarded as a border or upper South state, but within its boundaries may be found characteristics of both upper and lower South. Less than one hundred and fifty miles wide from north to south, the state stretches more than four hundred miles from high in the Blue Ridge Mountains in the east to the banks of the Mississippi River in the west. In reality, Tennessee may be regarded as three states in one, and indeed, the state's constitution and laws acknowledge the existence of three "grand divisions": East Tennessee, Middle Tennessee, and West Tennessee. East Tennessee is an area of mountains, ridges, and long narrow valleys. Middle Tennessee is separated from the eastern division by the Cumberland Plateau and is characterized by the Central Basin of rolling hills and valleys surrounded by a plateau, the Highland Rim. West Tennessee is separated from Middle Tennessee by the Tennessee River and is an area of gently rolling hills that merge with the Mississippi River flood plain. Because of the terrain, East Tennessee did not develop a plantation economy in the years of settlement and consequently there were few slaves in the area. A Whig stronghold prior to the Civil War, the eastern division remained loyal to the Union during the war. The Republican party therefore came to dominate the section during the era of Reconstruction and remained entrenched there into the twentieth century. And because East Tennessee faced problems similar to those confronting the rest of the nation, it took on the characteristics of a border state. The race issue, for instance, was not a conspicuous feature of politics in the eastern section. In contrast, because much of West Tennessee is an alluvial plain, a plantation type of economy caught hold during the antebellum period, and this section was therefore more heavily populated with slaves than the rest of the state. Middle Tennessee, with its rolling hills and rich river valleys, developed an agricultural economy resembling that of West Tennessee. Both Middle and West Tennessee were Democratic before the Civil War, supported the secessionist movement in 1861, and resisted Radical Reconstruction after the war. The post-Reconstruction economy in West Tennessee was similar to that of the deep South where the one-crop agricultural economy was retained. Because blacks were more numerous in that section, the politics of West Tennessee, like that of the "black belt" in the deep South, remained the politics of race. Appropriately, Middle Tennessee stood somewhere in between the other sections in its social and economic problems. In both West and Middle Tennessee the Democratic party remained dominant after the Civil War and, because of its numerical superiority, it controlled the state. East Tennessee Republicans could win statewide political races only when the Democrats were badly divided.

At the same time, however, Democrats in post-Reconstruction Tennessee did not establish a cohesive, unitary party; on the contrary, the party was continually rent by factionalism. Scholars have long attempted to identify and interpret those factions. Dan Robison, for example, found three clearly defined factions with individual leaders and historical continuity: states'-rights planters, Whig industrialists, and small farmers.[1] Roger Hart, in challenging the Robison thesis, insisted that there were no disciplined factions in the Democratic party. "Any attempt to trace continuing factions in the careers of individual politicians ends in a labyrinth of inconsistencies, reversals, and contradictions. . . . A characteristic of Tennessee politics which emerged repeatedly throughout the late nineteenth century was a preference for local associations over broader ones. . . . Statewide political structures were loose and weak.[2]

If absence of order was the rule in political structures, there was, as George Brown Tindall has postulated, a "persistent tradition" of community in Tennessee politics. As was the case throughout the South, a conservative oligarchy' ruled and was usually referred to, perhaps for want of a better label, as Bourbon. As a coalition of states'-rights planters and Whig industrialists, often differing on issues such as debt retirement, the Bourbons, as Tindall observed, "kept alive the vision of an organic traditional community with its personal relationships, its class distinctions, its habits of deference to the squirearchy,"The ruling class also accepted the creed of the New South, thus achieving "the reconciliation of tradition with innovations."[3] Bourbon hegemony was eventually challenged late in the nineteenth century by pressures exerted by small farmers in what became known as the Populist Revolt. Long plagued by falling prices and high interest rates and transportation costs, the farmers blamed corporate and banking interests allied with a pliant government for their troubles. Small farmers became well organized, set as goals a long list of reforms that required more active governmental participation in the economy, and came close to overthrowing conservative control in Tennessee.[4] Although forced to make concessions, the conservatives were able to crush populism by division, intimidation, and racial demagoguery. Nevertheless, populism left a legacy of a more active government, and populistic complaints and doctrine in only slightly revised forms remained the creed of rural Tennessee for more than half a century.

The progressive reform movement followed hard on the heels of the small farmer revolt and had as pervasive an influence in Tennessee as elsewhere. While historians are not in agreement as to the meaning, scope, and place of progressivism in American history, they agree generally that populism had some influence on it and that progressives adopted and put into effect some of the reforms demanded by the small farmers. But whereas populism drew its support from one class, progressivism was a more broadly based movement that included the ranks of labor as well as the urban middle class. Historian J. Joseph Huthmacher argues convincingly that the major portion of reforms during the progressive era was actually instituted by urban political bosses and their lower class constitutents.[5] Tennessee's experience in reform seems to verify this interpretation. At any rate, the progressives, like the populists, generally agreed that the chief problem in America was the excessive influence of monopolies allied with corrupt city governments. Their solution was to restore popular democracy; to institute more active, honest, and efficient government; and to implement a variety of reforms which would remedy social injustices. But, as Tindall observes, although the progressives accomplished much in the South, the old conservative oligarchy was able to temper progressivism by adopting some of the demands while beating back others.[6]

More important in the long-range view than specific problems and proposed solutions, or even the meaning of both populism and progressivism, was the changing face of the nation. During the very years of populism and progressivism, the United States was making the painful transition from being a predominantly rural and agrarian nation to one largely urban and industrial; thus, William E. Leuchtenburg notes, "small-town America was being challenged by the rise of the city to the dominant position in American life."[7] Similarly, as Robert H. Wiebe suggests, rural values were also being challenged: the years between 1877 and 1920 saw the transformation of American values from those of the small town to those of a bureaucratic, and largely urban, middle class.[8] Rural Americans, thoroughly imbued with the agrarian myth, came to believe that their way of life and political preeminence were being threatened. The reality of incredible drudgery and boredom coupled with the chronic low income of the small farmer was in conflict with his presumed status. Facing an identity crisis, rural peoples found convenient scapegoats for their declining status in the influence of corporate interests and urban areas on political authority. Cities became special targets because urban mores and folkways seemed so contrary to rural values. To Americans in the countryside, cities were the centers of the economic forces that repressed the farmers. Moreover, they believed that cities were controlled by cynically corrupt political bosses and contained immigrants with foreign and blasphemous ideas. It is therefore not surprising that rural Americans looked upon urban America as symbolic of all the evils in the nation and responsible for their declining status.[9]

Rural Tennesseans exhibited the same status anxiety that troubled rural Americans all across the nation. Indeed, in the first half of the twentieth century the crucial underlying conflict in the state was between the forces of agricultural and small-town Tennessee and the ever increasing power of urban areas. The issues dividing the two forces were not articulated at times, nor for that matter were they always clearly understood by the people as a whole. Neither were the lines delineating the two always clear; and there were frequent crossovers, as political leaders and factions sought the rewards of power and spoils. The lines held firm, though, when the interests of the two were clear-cut, as on issues of apportionment, taxation, and services. Initially, the countryside had the upper hand. In the first place, Tennessee cities were relatively insignificant at the beginning of the century, and although they grew rapidly, especially after World War I, they were populated by migrants from the country. Imbued with rural values, this new city population was slow to support urban interests. More important, state government was completely under the control of the countryside. The legislature had been reapportioned only once since ratification of the state constitution in 1870, despite a provision requiring reapportionment every ten years. General Assemblies were therefore dominated by rural representatives while cities were underrepresented. Tennessee governors also tended to be rural in outlook. Moreover, Tennessee cities were literally creatures of the state; local autonomy or home rule was virtually nonexistent, except in routine day-to-day matters. Urban areas were therefore at the mercy of the General Assembly, which had to ratify any changes in local governmental structure or taxation. As a result, a great volume of local legislation came before the assembly each session. It was inevitable that the growing cities would eventually rebel against those restrictions. The struggle between rural and urban Tennessee grew with intensity over the years, and, in spite of holding certain trump cards, the countryside could not halt the onrushing urbanization and industrialization. Eventually the cities would become preeminent in Tennessee.

The continuing conflict between the cities and the countryside did not, however, result in any cohesive or relatively permanent political factions in Tennessee. Contrary to V. O. Key's accepted interpretation of political factionalism to the middle of the twentieth century, factions in the Volunteer state remained weak and did not always correspond to the rural-urban cleavage. Key examined political patterns in Tennessee and found a relatively consistent bifactional pattern in both parties. In the Republican party, one faction was conservative and business-oriented while the other was made up of mountain agrarians. The former group, the "presidential Republicans," was composed of many who registered Democratic and voted in Democratic primaries in order to have a voice in local and state affairs, but who voted the Republican ticket in presidential elections. The mountain agrarians voted the straight Republican ticket. Key also found two major factions within the Democratic party and characterized each as a holding company or a coalition of various interests and individual organizations. According to Key those factions had historical continuity and relatively consistent geographical bases. One coalition, based in Memphis and Shelby County, dominated

West Tennessee; the other, based in Nashville, controlled much of Middle Tennessee. Despite assertions by scholars, the bifactional pattern does not hold up under close examination. Key admitted as much when he refered to the factions as "shifting alliances," or "fluctuations" resulting from "frequent alterations" in the alliance system, and went on to say, "the line of political descent has of course, been blurred by movements both ways across factional lines."[10] This suggests that Roger Hart's interpretation concerning Democratic factionalism in post-Reconstruction Tennessee may also be applicable in the twentieth century. In short, "inconsistencies, reversals, and contradictions" remained the rule.

Demonstrating this lack of political unity in Tennessee, the Democratic party was wracked by bitter internal conflict during the progressive years. Added to the usual personal rivalries and factional struggles that had long been common to the party was the controversial and emotional issue of prohibition. From time to time small victories characterized the long campaign to end the liquor traffic in Tennessee, so that by 1908 the legal sale of alcholic beverages was generally limited to the state's largest cities. The pressure for absolute prohibition continued and left Democrats badly divided. The highlight of the struggle was the shooting of former United States senator and prohibitionist editor Edward Ward Carmack and the hasty pardon of one of his accused slayers by antiprohibitionist Governor Malcolm Patterson. The incident stirred prohibitionists to even greater zeal and the General Assembly was forced to make Tennessee a dry state in January 1909. The issue was not completely resolved, however, and for the next several years the struggle revolved around the problem of enforcement of prohibition. The rift among the Democrats enabled the Republicans to elect Ben W. Hooper governor in 1910 and to reelect him two years later. A measure of unity restored, the Democrats elected governors in 1914, 1916, and 1918 but personal rivalries once again disrupted the party in 1920 and Republican Alf Taylor, brother of Robert L. "Our Bob" Taylor and participant in Tennessee's famous "War of the Roses" in 1886, was elected governor.[11] But with the controversial disputes that had divided the party largely resolved, Democrats elected a governor in 1922 and the party entered a long period of ascendancy. This did not mean that the party had achieved cohesiveness in the 1920s; rather, as David Lee has suggested, "The Tennessee Democracy was a party deeply riven by constant strife among amorphous, impermanent coalitions."[12]

The Democratic governor elected in 1922 was a Clarksville attorney,

Austin Peay. A strong leader and an astute politician, Peay was dignified in appearance, looked the part of governor, and became one of the state's most popular chief executives—he was the first governor since the Civil War to be elected to three consecutive terms. The achievements of his administration were notable: reorganization of state government, a massive highway construction program, and increased expenditure for public education. Elected as a progressive, Peay initially garnered widespread urban and business support. His reorganization of state government was clearly in the mold of business progressivism: a hodgepodge of sixty-four agencies was consolidated into eight departments, eliminating duplication of services, and achieving greater efficiency at less cost to the taxpayers. As a consequence, however, Peay, through newly delegated appointive authority, increased the power of the chief executive at the expense of the legislature. As time passed, the governor demonstrated an agrarian bias by catering more and more to the interests of rural and small-town Tennessee and by developing a strong following in the countryside. Some of his measures and policies clearly reflected sympathy for rural Tennessee. In education, for example, poor rural counties benefited from the equalization fund instituted in 1925, because the tax burden to pay for equalization and other services favoring rural areas was proportionally greater for the cities. As the social transformation caused by increasing urbanization and industrialization intensified in Tennessee in the 1920s, Governor Peay's policies and practices contributed to the polarization of politics in the Volunteer State.[13]

One of Austin Peay's most valuable allies was Colonel Luke Lea. A protege of Tennessee's editor-politician and prohibitionist Senator Edward Carmack, Lea came into his own after the shooting of Carmack in 1908. He had a good political personality, and with the aid of his newspaper built up a strong following in Nashville and Middle Tennessee. In 1911 Lea was sent to the United States Senate by the Tennessee General Assembly, but in the Democratic primary of 1916 he was defeated by Kenneth D. McKellar of Memphis, who went on to become the state's first popularly elected senator in the November general election. In 1917, with the entry of the United States into the First World War, Lea was commissioned a colonel by Governor Tom C. Rye and helped organize the Tennessee 114th Field Artillery Regiment. The publisher served with distinction until his attempt to kidnap the German Kaiser shortly after the Armistice. However, the escapade gained him much publicity and he returned home a hero. Continuing his struggle for political power in Nashville, he was opposed by a faction led by

Mayor Hilary E. Howse, attorney K. T. McConnico, and E. B. Stahlman, publisher of the *Nashville Banner*. The rivalry between the two
groups was so bitter that in 1920 Lea refused to endorse the Democratic
nominee for governor, A. H. Roberts, enabling Republican Alf Taylor
to become Tennessee's chief executive. Lea gained a powerful ally in
Rogers Caldwell, the wealthy founder of Caldwell and Company, a business concern organized to deal in municipal bonds. Founded in 1917
by the twenty-seven-year-old Caldwell, the firm rapidly expanded into
other areas: real estate mortgage bonds, industrial securities, insurance
companies, banking, and even an investment trust. In thirteen years
Caldwell and Company became the largest investment banking house
in the South. Although Luke Lea owned no part of Caldwell and Company, and the firm had no interest in the *Tennessean*, the publisher and
Caldwell were jointly involved in a number of banking and real estate
ventures. In 1927 Caldwell financed Lea's purchase of the Memphis
Commercial Appeal and the *Knoxville Journal*, which gave Lea additional organs for his political organization. The interests of the two men
were so closely related that the political organization soon came to be
called the Lea-Caldwell machine.[14]

Luke Lea supported Austin Peay in all three of his successful races
for governor, but clearly the governor was the dominant figure in the
alliance. In October 1927 Peay died suddenly, and Henry H. Horton,
speaker of the state senate, and a Lea man, succeeded to the governor's
office. The event was fortuitous for Lea and Caldwell because Horton
was politically inexperienced, perhaps a little naive, and pliant. The
following year he was elected governor with the all-out support of the
Lea-Caldwell machine and Luke Lea had reached the crest of his power
in Tennessee. He not only had the backing of a financial empire but he
also had a man he could control in the governor's mansion.[15]

Meanwhile, in the state's largest city, Memphis, a powerful urban political machine headed by Edward Hull Crump had emerged to challenge Lea's dominance in the state. Born near Holly Springs, Mississippi,
in 1874 of Bourbon ancestry, Ed Crump migrated to Memphis in 1894
where he got his start in business with a buggy and harness company.
He eventually became successful in insurance, real estate, and investment banking, but politics soon attracted his attention and it became
his passionate interest in life. He was a natural politician. Handsome,
shrewd, and dynamic, he early demonstrated a capacity for leadership.
In 1905 he became a member of the Memphis Board of Public Works;

two years later he was made Fire and Police Commissioner; and in 1909 Crump was elected mayor, a post he held until 1916. The rise of Ed Crump and the progressive reform movement were synonymous; indeed, he was the personification of business progressivism. His career demonstrated the validity of George Brown Tindall's thesis that there was a persistent tradition of community in New South politics: Crump was the Bourbon-progressive reconciling tradition with innovation. Mayor Crump was instrumental in reforming the charter of Memphis, he achieved more efficient administration in the city, and, although taxes were reduced, he increased services. Like many progressives, the mayor's chief concern was utilities. According to Crump, the greatest evil was private utility corporations because they milked the public and unduly influenced affairs of government. His fight with the utilities in Memphis became a personal struggle and he waged many epic battles with the utility concerns as he sought public control and even public ownership, of power, gas, and street railway services. Crump's dream of public ownership was consummated with the advent of the Tennessee Valley Authority in the 1930s. [16]

In 1916 Ed Crump suffered a rare setback and it left a lasting imprint on him. Despite statewide prohibition, enforcement proved difficult and the urban centers, including Memphis, were especially lax in complying with the law. Therefore, the rurally dominated and prohibitionist legislature, probably with Mayor Crump in mind, established a procedure for the removal of public officials who failed to enforce the liquor laws. Shortly thereafter charges were brought against the Memphis mayor for failure to enforce prohibition and he was subsequently ousted from office. Crump's pride was hurt and, believing that the utility interests were behind the ouster, he neither forgot nor forgave. He was more determined than ever to exercise control over Memphis. If indeed the utilities were responsible, they were in error if they thought they had seen the last of Ed Crump. His removal as mayor of Memphis did not result in a loss of prestige, for he remained a popular and strong leader and the following year he was elected trustee of Shelby County, a post he held for several years. At the same time he was perfecting his organization, which became one of the most cohesive and efficient urban political machines in the nation; by 1928 all opposition was silenced and Crump was in almost absolute control of Memphis and Shelby County. In building his organization, the Memphis boss effectively united the business and professional class, the Irish and Italian ethnics, rural migrants, and the blacks. The black vote was especially important as a source of strength. Memphis blacks were nominally Republican but, by providing a measure of service, Crump was able to obtain their support. The Memphis boss had the Bourbon's paternal attitude toward the Negro and perhaps a sincere regard for his welfare but the fact remains that the black vote was vital and well worth the schools, parks, and health services it cost. Crump's machine was the target of charges of corruption and tampering with the vote count, charges that were often more hopeful than accurate. But no hint of scandal ever touched the machine. The Memphis boss himself was scrupulously honest and lieutenants such as Watkins Overton and Walter Chandler were men of the highest integrity. It is possible that petty graft was practiced by those in the lower ranks of the organization, but evidence of widespread manipulation of vote counts has never surfaced. There was indeed intimidation of those whose loyalty to the organization was questioned. Once the machine was established, it was impossible for Crump to restrain the emotions and activities of the more enthusiastic members in the lower ranks. The secret of the machine's strength was simple: efficient organization. Workers knew their supporters, made sure they paid the poll tax, and got them to the polling places on election day.[17]

Ed Crump's most valuable ally was Senator Kenneth Douglas McKellar. For nearly forty years the two maintained a friendship and an alliance unequaled in the annals of Tennessee politics. They were alike in many respects. They came from similar backgrounds, and both were dynamic leaders, had similar personalities, shared similar interests, and had like political and economic philosophies. McKellar was born in 1869 during the Reconstruction era in Dallas County, Alabama, into a prominent but financially distressed family. After completing his formal education which included a degree in law, he migrated to Memphis in 1892 and quickly established a prosperous practice. Law led eventually to politics, and, like Crump, he was caught up in the progressive movement. Although the two were not originally associated in politics, their similar economic and political philosophies eventually led them into an easy alliance. McKellar became involved in local affairs as a reformer, was elected to Congress in 1911, and in 1917 he became a United States senator. In the years that followed he put together an effective but unstructured statewide organization that was held together by a coterie of lieutenants who were astute and hard-headed practitioners of the art of politics. And McKellar, more than any other Democrat, established rapport with East Tennessee Republicans. The senator liked his job, worked hard at it, answered his mail, and followed through on every complaint or request for service, large or small. Like Crump, McKellar was honest, shrewd, partisan, temperamental, spiteful, and ruthless; he was intolerant of those who disagreed with him and was given to harassing those who questioned his wisdom. Contrary to contemporary opinion, the senator was not Crump's errand boy nor, for that matter, was he a lieutenant. Instead, he created a statewide organization while Crump's machine was limited to Memphis and Shelby County.[18]

Once secure in his control of Memphis, Ed Crump began to try to exercise greater influence at the state level. It has long been assumed that the Memphis boss was simply power-hungry, but that does not explain why Crump sought more control in state-wide politics. Certainly a man of his intelligence must have understood it clearly: continued control of Memphis and Shelby County required the exercise of considerable influence in state politics. In short, the boss of the "Bluff City" needed allies, if not friends, in the governor's office and in other positions of power. There were three areas where Crump required assistance: patronage, conducting elections, and effective home rule. And in all three of these areas, Tennessee's governors exercised significant power.

In the 1920s Tennessee governors had an increasing number of clerical, technical, and supervisory positions to fill across the state, and the number in an urban area such as Memphis was significant. A voice in making appointments was important to a local leader such as Crump; a governor dispensing patronage through enemies of the local machine could effectively weaken the organization. Even more important to Crump and other local political organizations was control of election machinery. But the governor was in virtual control of election machinery across the state. The primary that nominated Democratic gubernatorial candidates also elected members of the party's State Executive Committee which supervised primaries, and supporters of the nominee usually won positions on the committee by riding on his coattails. The Executive Committee in turn appointed county committees which appointed elections officials, selected polling places, and controlled registration books. In effect the Executive Committee controlled the franchise. County committees therefore had weapons to intimidate opponents and otherwise manipulate local elections without practicing graft. Crump was conscious that an enemy in the governor's office could significantly weaken his organization by the Executive Committee's control over local primaries.

Even more vital to the Memphis boss than patronage and primary machinery was effective control over municipal affairs. Prior to 1953, home rule for municipalities was absent; cities were creatures of the state and at the mercy of the legislature. Crump himself, by painful experience, was aware of how a rural-dominated General Assembly could impose policy on urban areas. The legislature could also impose its will upon municipalities by its power to tax and allocate services. Cities frequently had to go to the General Assembly for enabling legislation, or local bills as they were called, on important matters ranging from governmental organization to taxation. A governor who controlled the legislature or powerful legislative leaders could expedite or hamper local bills by veto or by holding them up in committee, depending on whether the local leader was a friend or an enemy. It was therefore vital to Crump to have sufficient influence in the governor's office and in the General Assembly either to block legislation that might penalize Memphis or to obtain passage of local bills. Without the influence to obtain passage of local bills, especially, Crump's power at home would have been significantly curtailed. Lee Greene and Jack Holmes are correct in observing, "there is considerable reason for believing that Crump's interest in state affairs would have been different if home rule for cities had been in the constitution before 1953."[19]

In any event, the power of the Memphis boss had increased in the 1920s to the extent that he could deliver nearly twenty-five thousand votes out of about two hundred thousand cast statewide in a Democratic primary. In a three-way race for governor in 1928 involving Henry Horton, Hill McAlister, and Lewis Pope, the Crump-endorsed McAlister came within about five thousand votes of defeating the Lea-Caldwell-backed Horton.

After 1928 it appeared that the Lea-Caldwell-Horton régime was in complete control of the Democratic party and state government. Profits from Caldwell and Company's connection with the state were large indeed. The business gained in a number of ways. In 1926, for example, Caldwell and Company established the Kentucky Rock and Asphalt Company, or Kyrock as it was called by its trade name, to quarry and sell crushed rock for road building purposes. After Horton became governor, the Tennessee State Road Department specified Kyrock for several roads without competitive bidding. By far the greatest advantage was state deposits in the Bank of Tennessee, and in other Lea-Caldwell banks. State deposits in the Bank of Tennessee were "in effect, unsecured advances to the company by the State at 3 per cent interest."[20]

However, the régime was on the road to self-destruction, for Caldwell's financial empire was tottering. The company was a paper conglomerate and after years of poor management, relaxed standards, and the underwriting of poor securities, it began crumbling in 1929 in the manner of many of its contemporaries around the nation. The state quickly came to Caldwell's aid with additional deposits in the Bank of Tennessee, but they were not sufficient to save that institution. The collapse came in November 1930, when the bank closed its doors with more than seven million dollars of state money on deposit.[21]

The aftermath of the fall of Caldwell and Company shook Tennessee from one end to the other. Luke Lea's opponents demanded an investigation and prosecution of those involved with the company. Across the state, people came to believe that Lea, Caldwell, and Horton were thoroughly crooked. Criminal indictments and civil actions were brought against Lea, Caldwell, and others associated with the empire for conspiracy to defraud, not only in Tennessee, but also in Arkansas and North Carolina. A federal grand jury in Knoxville indicted Lea for conspiracy to violate the national banking laws. But of all the indictments and charges, only the North Carolina indictment resulted in conviction and imprisonment, and Lea received a six-to-ten-year sentence. John Berry McFerrin, the historian of Caldwell and Company, considered the failure to convict Lea and Caldwell on more indictments "little short of a travesty of justice."[22]

The fall of Caldwell and Company had political repercussions: Lea, Caldwell, and Horton were discredited and Crump moved to fill the vacuum. When the General Assembly met in January 1931, Crump insisted upon a thorough investigation of the scandal, and articles of impeachment against Governor Horton were brought up in the House of Representatives, charging him with failure to protect state funds and having given special benefits to Lea-Caldwell interests. The House voted down the articles, in part because the administration used all the resources at its command to defeat them. David Lee has suggested that the Horton forces successfully made the Memphis boss the issue and the vote in the House divided on rural-urban lines.[23] Yet despite the failure to impeach Horton, Lea, Caldwell, and the governor were tagged with the onus of corruption and the Crump-McKellar alliance emerged as the dominant political force in the state. The events surrounding the fall of the régime left the Democratic party in disarray and the confusion carried over into the gubernatorial primary in 1932. Three candidates entered the race: State Treasurer and Nashville attorney Hill

McAlister; former governor and leader of the antiprohibitionist forces earlier in the century, Malcolm Patterson; and Commissioner of Institutions under Austin Peay, Lewis Pope. A candidate twice before, McAlister had Crump's support and much of Senator McKellar's organization worked for him, although the senator himself did not make a public endorsement.[24] Patterson was the administration's candidate and had Lea's support. Lewis Pope, who had also been a candidate for governor in 1928, was an independent without organization support. The 1932 campaign was one of the bitterest of modern times. Violence at several polling places across the state marred the primary, and charges of vote fraud were common. McAlister won with a plurality but Pope, starting from far behind, came in second, only 9,000 votes short of McAlister's 117,454. Indicative of the disarray of the old Lea coalition, Patterson came in a poor third, with only 60,522 votes. Clearly, the 31,441 votes delivered to McAlister from Shelby County made the difference between victory and defeat. Even so, the rural-urban cleavage was more pronounced in 1932 than in earlier races. McAlister polled forty-one percent of the vote, most of which was obtained in Tennessee's cities; the remaining fifty-nine percent, divided between Pope and Patterson, was largely rural. The divided vote in the countryside, therefore, enabled the Crump-backed McAlister to become the Democratic nominee. A bitter Pope, charging that the election was stolen from him, ran in the general election campaign as an independent but was unable to generate much enthusiasm. Rank and file Democrats coalesced behind the nominee and McAlister defeated Pope and Republican John McCall easily.[25]

With McAlister's victory in 1932 the balance of power in the Tennessee Democracy shifted from the coalition put together by Luke Lea to the Crump-McKellar axis. The Memphis boss was in a commanding position at the state level for the first time. He had been instrumental in electing a governor, and a Tennessee chief executive was indebted to him. Crump now had friendly election commissioners, a voice in state patronage in Memphis, and freedom from threats from hostile attorney generals, grand juries, and judges. Crump could hardly be called boss of Tennessee but he was in a position of immense power; he controlled ten percent of the vote in any Democratic primary and any candidate had to act in accordance with that fact. The triumph of the Crump-McKellar coalition did not mean that urban Tennessee had triumphed over rural Tennessee; the countryside still held a numerical majority and Crump would not muddy the waters by trying to force the interests of cities on the rural areas. But operating from a position of power he could trade for legislative and other favors with rural leaders and factions. The rural-urban cleavage remained, but the lines of difference blurred as shifting alliances crossed over for power and spoils, holding firm only when the interests of city versus country were clearly delineated.

Senator McKellar also benefited from the election of McAlister because he also had a voice in naming election commissioners across the state. But more important to the senior senator, 1932 was a Democratic year across the nation. Both houses of Congress went Democratic and Franklin D. Roosevelt became president, ushering in the New Deal; for the first time in many years McKellar had federal patronage in Tennessee entirely in his hands. He had been one of the first to endorse Roosevelt's candidacy and approved in principle of New Deal policies; he, therefore, more than any Tennessean, had the ear of the President. McKellar had the tenacious ability to get the things he set out to obtain, an ability enhanced by his being chairman of the Senate's Post Office Committee and senior member under the chairman of the Committee on Appropriations. He was thus able to milk the New Deal for all it was worth, obtaining for Tennessee perhaps more than its rightful share of projects. The increasing number of positions in federal agencies enabled the senator to dispense jobs to his friends and he never apologized for his partisanship because he understood the value of patronage. It strengthened his organization in the state, and as he gained more power in Tennessee, he gained more strength in Washington, which in turn enhanced his prestige in the state. The Crump-McKellar axis was an alliance of equals between two dynamic and aggressive men who shared similar interests and similar political and economic philosophies. The combination became one of the most powerful forces in the history of politics in the Volunteer State.[26]

In 1934 Congressman Gordon Browning became embroiled in state-wide politics in Tennessee for the first time. His great ambition was to become a United States senator from Tennessee, and after waiting in the wings of the House of Representatives for twelve years, he believed that the election year of 1934 was an appropriate time to attempt the move. Both of Tennessee's United States Senate seats would be before the electorate, a regular term and a short term. The contest for the regular term was for the seat occupied by McKellar who obviously had no intention of retiring. The other contest was for two years to fill out the term of Senator Cordell Hull, appointed secretary of state by President

Roosevelt. Governor McAlister had appointed Nathan Bachman, a Chattanooga jurist and one-time associate justice of the state Supreme Court, to fill the vacancy until the next election. The appointee soon found that he liked the job and therefore became a candidate for the short term. But because both seats were available did not mean that Browning had two choices; on the contrary, tradition limited his choice to the long term. There was an unwritten code in Tennessee that no one of the three "Grand Divisions" was to monopolize the senate seats. Since both Browning and McKellar were from West Tennessee, the congressman would violate the code by running against Bachman; his choice was thus effectively limited to challenging McKellar. Considering the senior senator's strength, that was not an attractive proposition.

No doubt impatience was a factor that impelled Browning to commit himself to the Senate race in 1934. He was aggressive with a tendency to be impulsive and he was becoming frustrated while waiting for an appropriate opportunity to make his move. But there were two factors that encouraged him. He had gained considerable publicity for his stand against reduction of payments to disabled veterans and widows and orphans in Roosevelt's economy measure in 1933. Indeed, Browning later admitted that he was influenced to make the move because of the popularity of his opposition to the reduction of pensions.[27] Undoubtedly his friends in the American Legion encouraged him to try for the senate. A second factor was the rumor that the friendship between McKellar and Crump had cooled almost to the breaking point. There was some substance to the talk. And it was an irony that during the very years when their alliance was winning control of the machinery of the Democratic party, friction developed between the two leaders. In 1930, for example, McKellar was dismayed when Crump joined his old antagonist, Luke Lea, in endorsing Horton for governor. The senator also resented Crump's treatment of his old friend, Congressman Hubert Fisher. In 1930, the Memphis boss unceremoniously dumped Fisher and ran and won the first of the two terms he served in the House of Representatives.[28] McKellar had friends in the eastern and middle sections of the state who had long mistrusted Crump and they no doubt took this opportunity to warn the senator about the motives of the Memphis boss in going to Congress. Once, in a petulent mood, Crump wrote to McKellar, "You no doubt permitted many, including false friends, to thoroughly sell you on the idea I would be a candidate against you for the United States Senate."[29] The Memphis boss may have also had friends who questioned McKellar's loyalty. More important, he had rea-

son to be jealous of the senator, for in Washington Crump soon realized
he was a little fish in a big pond; the responsibilities there were nothing
compared to the authority he exercised in Memphis. McKellar, on the
other hand, had power and prestige. Crump also took offense at some
of the senator's actions. During the legislative session in 1931, for example, McKellar made a hurried trip to Nashville on legal matters and
left without calling on the Memphis boss. Whereupon a displeased
Crump wrote: "Our Memphis crowd . . . felt that your getting out of
Nashville so elusively and mysteriously would have formed a splendid
subject for one of Sir Conan Doyle's spiritualistic thrillers."[30] Crump
also felt that McKellar did not provide enough assistance in the attempt
to impeach Governor Horton. Finally, one dispute erupted in public:
when the senator approved the appointment of his brother, Clint, as
postmaster of Memphis, Crump condemned it as unethical.[31] The friction between Senator McKellar and Boss Crump was grist for the rumor
mills and was magnified as stories circulated in Washington and across
Tennessee. In reality, the two were not near the breaking point. Both
were acutely sensitive and their feelings could easily be hurt by the most
unintentional slight. But their friendship ran too deep for them to split
over petty matters and, besides, both were pragmatists: a break would
destroy the balance of power they had achieved in Tennessee. Nevertheless, the stories gave Browning cause for hope, for a break would be
a decided advantage to him. As one long-time observer of Tennessee politics noted, every candidate for statewide office had to be concerned
with Memphis.[32]

It was well known in the early months of 1934 that Browning was
seriously considering a race against McKellar. Properly conscious of the
unwritten code prohibiting two senators from the same section, he
wrote, "We realize that only one Senator should come from West Tennessee. I have no idea of opposing Senator Bachman."[33] Even so, a race
against the senatorial appointee was not ruled out entirely and he made
discreet inquiry among his closest friends about the possibilities of challenging Bachman. McKellar, for his part, had long considered the congressman a potential threat, and was anticipating the challenge. Always
protective of his position, the senior senator kept a watchful eye for
possible rivals, often looking years ahead. Browning returned to Tennessee in the early spring of 1934 to tour the state and assess the situation and he found no shortage of advice. Some within the American
Legion were loud and vocal in urging him to be a candidate. Positive response even came from within the Crump organization: Abe

Waldauer was openly soliciting support for his former captain. Undoubtedly Browning received some pressure to run from the forces of Lewis Pope, who was once again challenging McAlister for the gubernatorial nomination. Although coalition campaigns were not common within Tennessee's Democratic party, an effective challenger to McKellar would aid Pope in his efforts to break Crump's power in the state. On the other hand, some urged Browning to avoid getting involved in the Senate race. Although they could hardly be considered objective observers, some of his friends who were also committed to the senior senator tried to keep him out of the race. R. A. Greene, editor of the *Tennessee Republican*, a Huntingdon paper, warned Browning that "unscrupulous individuals" were trying to get him into the race against McKellar.[34]

Some of Browning's friends advised him to avoid getting involved in either race. Captain Tom Henderson of Franklin, for example, went to great length to dissuade him. A World War I comrade and an old friend, Henderson counseled Browning that he would likely be linked with the discredited Lea-Caldwell-Horton machine. Moreover, because Governor McAlister was running for renomination and would have the backing of the Crump organization, his effective control of party machinery would be to the advantage of both McKellar and Bachman. Henderson advised that it would be difficult to keep the contest for governor and the Senate separate, and therefore Browning would be associated on the ticket with the gubernatorial candidate generally regarded as a Lea man, Lewis Pope. McKellar, he declared, would have the endorsement of most newspapers and grass roots support because of his control of federal patronage. Finally, he stressed that Bachman would have only two years to serve and undoubtedly would not run for reelection in 1936 because he did not like Washington. Henderson concluded his missive by advising Browning to wait until 1936 to run for the Senate.[35] Priestly Miller, Nashville minister and close friend, recalled that he urged Browning not to run but that friends who were not sincerely interested in his career maneuvered Browning into the Senate race.[36] McKellar's allies across the state kept the senator abreast of the situation. One supporter reported to McKellar that it looked like a conspiracy by Luke Lea and others to get Browning to run against him, and that Browning mistakenly took the clamor of support by members of the American Legion as a good sign. He added that the Congressman's real friends were trying to keep him from getting involved.[37] Quite possibly Browning attempted to sound out Crump directly or indirectly during his tour of the state in March, for the Memphis boss was the most important key to the race. The tour could not have been encouraging as Browning gained a sense of McKellar's strength across the state. He also found that he could not count on significant campaign contributions nor could he expect important press support. He admitted years later that no important political leader in Tennessee would make a commitment to him.[38]

When McKellar made the official announcement of his bid for renomination and Crump added his subsequent endorsement, Browning realized that challenging the senior senator was a hopeless proposition. Others came to the same conclusion and on 4 May Joe Hatcher, political writer for the *Tennessean,* predicted that the congressman would not make the race against McKellar; instead, he would run for reelection to his old congressional seat.[39] But then came the biggest surprise of the campaign. On the same day Hatcher's prediction appeared in print, Browning announced that "after a close personal survey of the state," he had decided to enter the race for the short term against Nathan Bachman.[40] Browning thus demonstrated his propensity for doing the unexpected and a willingness to accept a difficult challenge. A subdued Hatcher reported that "not even the wildest of political prognosticators" had expected Browning to announce for Bachman's seat.[41]

The lines for the Democratic primary of 1934 were thus drawn: Congressman Browning was in the race against Senator Bachman for the short term; Senator McKellar had only token opposition in John R. Neal, a financially independent, absent-minded, and eccentric law school professor at the University of Tennessee who was a perennial candidate for state office; and Lewis Pope was aligned against Governor McAlister. The efforts of McKellar, Bachman, and McAlister very nearly became a coalition campaign. The governor of course controlled party machinery and had at his command an army of state employees; but the senior senator was the directing force in the campaign. Although Crump had lost his enthusiasm for McAlister, McKellar persuaded the Memphis boss to endorse the governor for renomination; the balance of power achieved by the Crump-McKellar axis would have otherwise been destroyed. The senior senator very clearly wanted Bachman to remain in Washington because he was pliant, unobtrusive, and cooperative; Browning, on the other hand, was aggressive and would challenge McKellar's hegemony. McKellar's office was therefore the source of strategy and campaign material for the junior senator.

Browning, for his part, without significant press support or the endorsement of any important local or regional leader or contributor, did not have a well-organized campaign. Unable to find a prominent Tennessean to manage his efforts, he chose a young, unknown, and politically inexperienced school administrator from Carthage, Albert Gore.[42] It was not, however, a poor choice; Gore proved to be intelligent, aggressive, and willing to learn. Browning remained clear of the efforts of Lewis Pope, who directed his fire at Crump with charges of bossism, corruption, and vote frauds. Browning launched a vigorous campaign against the lackluster Bachman, which stressed his support for legislation to aid disabled veterans, aid to farmers, support for TVA, and his opposition to cancelling the European war debts. For good measure, he praised President Roosevelt's efforts to achieve economic recovery, but emphasized that reform of the economy was necessary to prevent depression from recurring. One of Bachman's most repeated charges against Browning, used at the insistence of McKellar, was that the congressman was not sincere in his support for the Tennessee Valley Authority. Browning countered by charging that Bachman was a tool of private power interests. Neither charge, of course, had any substance. The incumbent's most potent theme was that a Browning victory would mean preferential treatment for the western "Grand Division." That charge was given substance when a letter conceding the wisdom of the code barring two senators from the same section, written by the congressman in March, was made public. Browning could only respond, somewhat lamely, that the unwritten code was no longer valid because "modern transportation has moved us so close together that this fiction has no use except as a political bogey."[43] Nevertheless, the *Chattanooga Times* probably expressed the sentiments of many in East Tennessee when it declared that two senators from the western section would be inequitable. Even the West Tennessee newspaper, the Memphis *Commercial Appeal*, suggested that it would be only fair to have one of the senators from the eastern part of the state.[44] The issue of two senators from the same section was to Browning's disadvantage but he had an even greater liability: the political powers of the state—McKellar, McAlister, and Crump—were working for Bachman. Neither the incumbent nor the challenger generated much enthusiasm; no important issue erupted during the senatorial campaign and the voters had little to choose between the two because they were not far apart on the important questions of the day.

Consequently on 2 August, Senator Bachman won the senatorial nomination in the Democratic primary by a little more than 45,000 votes out of just over 287,000 cast. As expected, Bachman ran strong in the first, second, and third congressional districts in East Tennessee where McKellar had considerable influence; Browning made up some of the deficit in Middle Tennessee but not enough to overcome the senator's lead. Bachman won Memphis and Shelby County by an overwhelming 42,000 votes out of 48,000 cast. Outside of Shelby County in West Tennessee, the senator carried only four counties by slight majorities while Browning won the remaining thirteen by comfortable margins and a total majority of 16,000. But Browning lost West Tennessee, including Shelby County, by a few more than 21,000 votes. The challenger's greatest strength, as expected, was in West Tennessee outside of Shelby County. Statewide, he demonstrated strength in the rural counties and Bachman was clearly the favorite in the urban centers. The election results appeared to indicate that the tradition prohibiting two senators from one section may have played a part in the decision of many East and Middle Tennesseans. Browning did poorly in East Tennessee and only moderately well in Middle Tennessee against a colorless opponent.

In the other races, McKellar, who had not been forced to active campaigning against token opposition, won by an overwhelming vote. In the gubernatorial contest, McAlister defeated Pope by about 54,000 votes but the results reveal more than simple victory for one and defeat for another.[45] McAlister's margin of victory came from the urban counties; outside of the cities, the contest between the governor and Pope was almost dead even. The cities had therefore elected a governor, but only because the rural vote was split. This remained the pattern for the next generation. Urban areas in Tennessee could not alone elect a governor, but they held the balance by endorsing the most desirable, or the least objectionable, as the case may have been, among the candidates. The election returns, especially from East Tennessee, also suggest that Senator McKellar's support for both Bachman and McAlister was an important factor in their victories. And just as clearly, the continued dominance in the Tennessee Democratic party of the Crump-McKellar axis required the senator's continued influence in East Tennessee and the splitting of the rural vote across the state.

Gordon Browning lost his bid for the Senate in 1934 but, although his defeat was not a pleasant experience, in retrospect he gained more than he lost. While the race seemed to most observers an obvious exercise in futility, there was a measure of calculation in Browning's decision to challenge Senator Bachman; and as two of his contemporaries insisted, he was well advised to run.[46] According to an old adage, an aspirant to high office in Tennessee was required to make an initial and futile statewide race in order to establish name recognition and to make contacts for a future organization. Although Browning always entered a political contest to win and always put forth his best efforts, he was aware that, even if he lost, he could become a viable challenger for the governor's office in 1936. If he became governor, had a good record, and won reelection in 1938, with a sound organization based on his control of patronage and election machinery, he would be in a good position to challenge McKellar in 1940. A more timid soul might have been repelled at such a long-range prospect, but Gordon Browning was superbly confident that he could succeed.

The results in 1934 were gratifying. The voters all over the state were treated for the first time to what Joe Hatcher called a "rare type." Captain Gordon, or "Cap," as he was known to his friends and comrades, had a certain charisma that attracted the voters of the state.[47] On the platform in a formal setting, he could be articulate with a flair for classical oratory. On the stump platform he could hold audiences with his earthy humor and was adept at castigating his opponents with scathing caricatures, reducing them to humiliation. "Campaigning in the late summer heat, he would stand before the people in his shirt sleeves, his loud necktie resting against a bulging beltline, and he would pitch scalpel-sharp humor at his political enemies," one observer recalled.[48] He enjoyed mingling with people, and few voters could forget the warm handclasp and hearty hello in a chance meeting with Gordon Browning on the street or at some crossroads store. Moreover, he had carefully avoided antagonizing any important leader or faction. He kept a discreet distance from Pope's gubernatorial campaign and had not indulged in violent attacks on Crump. And by running against Bachman, he had not offended those friends he had in common with McKellar. Neither did he endorse Pope's Republican-independent "fusionist" coalition against McAlister in the general election campaign in 1934. Gordon Browning emerged from the senatorial primary in 1934 as the most available challenger for the governor's office in 1936.

NOTES

1. Dan Robison, *Bob Taylor and the Agrarian Revolt in Tennessee* (Chapel Hill: University of North Carolina Press, 1935), pp. 14–22, 217.

2. Roger L. Hart, *Redeemers, Bourbons, and Populists: Tennessee, 1870–1896* (Baton Rouge: Louisiana State University Press, 1975), pp. 225, 234.

3. George Brown Tindall, *The Persistent Tradition in New South Politics* (Baton Rouge: Louisiana State University Press, 1975), pp. xii, 22.

4. Robison, *Bob Taylor,* passim; see also J. A. Sharp, "The Farmers' Alliance and the People's Party in Tennessee," *East Tennessee Historical Society's Publications* 10 (1939), pp. 91–113.

5. J. Joseph Huthmacher, "Urban Liberalism and the Age of Reform," *Mississippi Valley Historical Review* 49 (September 1962): 231–241; see also John D. Buenker, "The Urban Political Machine and the Seventeenth Amendment," *Journal of American History* 56 (September 1969): 305–322.

6. Tindall, *The Persistent Tradition,* p. xii.

7. William E. Leuchtenburg, *The Perils of Prosperity, 1914–1932* (Chicago: University of Chicago Press, 1958), p. 7.

8. Robert H. Wiebe, *The Search for Order, 1877–1920,* in David Donald, ed. *The Making of America* (New York: Hill and Wang, 1967), passim.

9. Leuchtenburg, *Perils of Prosperity,* pp. 7–8; Richard Hofstadter, *The Age of Reform: From Bryan to F. D. R.* (New York: Vintage Books, 1955), pp. 23–36.

10. V. O. Key, Jr., *Southern Politics in State and Nation* (New York: Alfred A. Knopf, 1949) pp. 58–75, 277–281; William Goodman [*Inherited Domain: Political Parties in Tennessee* (Knoxville: Bureau of Public Information, University of Tennessee, 1954) pp. 30–32, 39–44] did not find such clearly delineated factions in the Republican party.

11. For the story of the prohibition struggle, see Paul E. Isaac, *Prohibition and Politics: Turbulent Decades in Tennessee 1885–1920* (Knoxville: University of Tennessee Press, 1965); see also Ben W. Hooper, *The Unwanted Boy: The Autobiography of Governor Ben W. Hooper,* ed. Everett Robert Boyce (Knoxville: University of Tennessee Press, 1963).

12. David Dale Lee, "Tennessee in Turmoil: Politics in the Volunteer State, 1920–1932" (unpublished Ph. D. dissertation, The Ohio State University, 1975), p. 24.

13. Ibid., pp. 1–113; see also Joseph T. MacPherson, "Democratic Progressivism in Tennessee: The Administrations of Governor Austin Peay, 1923–1927," *East Tennessee Historical Society's Publications* 40 (1963): 50–61.

14. John Berry McFerrin, *Caldwell and Company: A Southern Financial Empire* (Nashville: Vanderbilt University Press, 1969), pp. 1–115; Gary W. Reichard, "The Aberration of 1920: An Analysis of Harding's Victory in Tennessee," *The Journal of Southern History* 36 (February 1970): 33–49; Gary W. Reichard, "The Defeat of Governor Roberts," *Tennessee Historical Quarterly* 20 (Spring 1971): 94–109; MacPherson, "Democratic Progressivism," pp. 50–61.

15. McFerrin, *Caldwell and Company,* pp. 102–107.

16. William D. Miller, *Mr. Crump of Memphis* (Baton Rouge: Louisiana State University Press, 1964), pp. 3–184; see also William D. Miller, *Memphis During*

the Progressive Era, 1900–1917 (Memphis: Memphis State University Press, 1957), pp. 178–179.

17. Miller, *Mr. Crump,* pp. 117–143; Key, *Southern Politics,* pp. 62–63; Goodman, *Inherited Domain,* pp. 35–36.

18. "Memoirs and Tennessee Senators," Box 6, Kenneth Douglas McKellar Papers, Memphis-Shelby County Public Library and Information Center; Robert Dean Pope, "Senatorial Baron: The Long Political Career of Kenneth D. McKellar"(unpublished Ph. D. dissertation, Yale University, 1976), passim.

19. Lee S. Greene and Jack E. Holmes, "Tennessee: A Politics of Peaceful Change," *The Changing Politics of the South,* ed. William C. Havard (Baton Rouge: Louisiana State University Press, 1972), pp. 189–190; see also Key, *Southern Politics,* p. 68; Alexander Heard, "Comments of Tenn. Politics," Box 10, Southern Politics Collection, Vanderbilt University Library.

20. McFerrin, *Caldwell and Company,* p. 113.

21. Ibid., pp. 176–188.

22. Ibid., p. 221.

23. David D. Lee, "The Attempt to Impeach Governor Horton," *Tennessee Historical Quarterly* 24 (Summer 1975): 188–201; see also McFerrin, *Caldwell and Company,* pp. 199–202.

24. Memorandum, 19 July 1932, Crump-McKellar Correspondence, Box 2, McKellar Papers.

25. David D. Lee, "The Triumph of Boss Crump: The Tennessee Gubernatorial Election of 1932," *Tennessee Historical Quarterly* 25 (Winter 1976): 393–413.

26. Pope, "Senatorial Baron,"pp. 212–287.

27. George Barker, "Of War, Peace, and Politics,"*Nashville Tennessean Magazine* (23 September 1962), p. 18; Gordon Browning, interview with the author, Huntington, 28 December 1965.

28. Pope, "Senatorial Baron,"pp. 214–217; Miller, *Mr. Crump,* p. 154.

29. Crump to McKellar, 20 January 1932, Crump-McKellar Correspondence, Box 2, McKellar Papers.

30. Crump to McKellar, 17 January 1931, Ibid.

31. Pope, "Senatorial Baron,"pp. 217, 229–230; Miller, *Mr. Crump,* p. 180.

32. Frick Stewart, interview with the author, Winchester, 25 May 1977.

33. Browning to Alvin Zigler, 29 March 1934, copy, Political Correspondence, Box 26, McKellar Papers; *Nashville Banner,* 21 June 1934.

34. R. A. Greene to Sen. McKellar, 10 April 1934, McKellar Papers.

35. Tom Henderson to Browning, 13 April 1934, Tom Henderson Papers, Tennessee State Library and Archives. Henderson failed to explain why Bachman, if he did not like Washington, was a candidate for the short term in 1934.

36. Priestly Miller, interview with the author, Nashville, 23 June 1966.

37. Neill Wright to McKellar, 7 April 1934, McKellar Papers.

38. Gordon Browning, "Gordon Browning: An Oral Memoir," ed. Joseph H. Riggs (Memphis Public Library, 1966), p. 62.

39. Joe Hatcher, "Politics," *Nashville Tennessean*, 4 May 1934.

40. *Commercial Appeal*, 5 May 1934.

41. Hatcher, "Politics," 6 May 1934.

42. Albert Gore, interview with the author, 15 May 1977; Albert Gore, *The Eye of The Storm: A People's Politics For the Seventies* (New York: Herder and Herder, 1970), pp. 200–201.

43. *Banner*, 5, 17 May, 20, 21, 30 June 1934; *Commercial Appeal*, 5 May 1934; *Tennessean*, 28 July 1934; Barker, "Of War, Peace, and Politics," p. 19.

44. *Chattanooga Times*, 28 July 1934; *Commercial Appeal*, 2 August 1934.

45. *Tennessee Blue Book and Official Directory* (Nashville, 1936), pp. 121–123, 126–128.

46. William C. Bateman, interview with the author, Memphis, 28 June 1966; W. R. Jarrell, interview with the author, Springfield, 21 June 1966.

47. Hatcher, "Politics," 4 May 1934.

48. Barker, "Of War, Peace, and Politics," p. 11.

4

The Governorship I

GORDON Browning had no great desire to become governor of Tennessee because his interests were national rather than parochial. Years later he declared that he had wanted to run again for the United States Senate in 1936 but allowed his "friends" to persuade him to make the gubernatorial race instead.[1] He might have added that his friends had persuaded him that he was the most available candidate for that office, that he could win, and that the best route to the Senate was through the governorship. As he assessed political conditions in Tennessee in the eighteen months following the primary in 1934, Browning learned that a great many leaders would climb aboard his bandwagon should he commit himself to the governor's race in 1936. It also became clear that he would have no great difficulty in obtaining pledges of contributions or in building an organization. Although rumors that he was seriously considering the governor's race were prevalent throughout 1935, he withheld a final decision until early 1936. In February, he made his formal announcement of candidacy. In his statement, Browning briefly described his position on various issues, emphasizing his dry record and opposition to local liquor option, and pledging to reform Tennessee's budgetary system. Cementing his ties with the old organization of Governor Austin Peay, he named A. B. Broadbent of

Clarksville as his campaign manager. Broadbent's credentials were more than adequate: he had masterminded Peay's three successful campaigns.

The position Memphis political boss Ed Crump would take in the gubernatorial contest was the biggest question on the minds of Tennesseans in early 1936. Only one thing was certain: the honeymoon between Crump and Governor Hill McAlister was over. The marriage had been a rocky one from the beginning and the boss had supported McAlister's bid for reelection in 1934 with something less than enthusiasm. McAlister had sought to reverse the administrative reform instituted by Governor Peay and had succeeded in obtaining passage of a measure by the General Assembly requiring senate approval of appointments to cabinet posts and the removal of the functions of budgeting and accounting from the hands of the chief executive. That weakened the power of a governor by decentralizing the administration and may have been offensive to the old efficiency-minded business-progressive, Ed Crump. The Memphis boss also found McAlister indecisive in administering the state's affairs and the governor's commitment to continued prohibition was contrary to Crump's wishes. The final break came during the meeting of the General Assembly in 1935 when the governor tried, against the wishes of Crump, to push a retail sales tax through the legislature. With the help of the boss of Shelby County, the opposition organized and prevented the passage of the tax. An upset Crump described McAlister as "our sorriest governor, who had tried in a sneaking way to put the sales tax on us—kept it hidden in his stony heart—before the election."[2] Having no chance of Crump's support in 1936, McAlister declined to run.

The attitude of the Memphis boss toward Browning was not clear. Although the Crump organization had opposed Browning in his race for the Senate in 1934, no personal antagonism existed between the two. They apparently got along reasonably well when they served in Congress together, and Browning had said and done nothing in his campaign for the Senate that offended the Memphis boss. A few days after the general election in 1934, during festivities attendant on a visit to Nashville by President Franklin D. Roosevelt, Crump was observed greeting Browning warmly and inviting him to ride in his automobile in the parade. Columnist Joe Hatcher shortly reported a rumor that the Memphis organization was ready to groom Browning as a candidate for the governor's race in 1936.[3] Crump probably had no intention of trying to bring Browning along as a candidate, for he seldom put up his own man for any major office; instead he usually looked over the candidates and endorsed the one that appealed to him. The Memphis boss probably had reservations about the former congressman; they differed on prohibition for example, and Crump may well have been suspicious, as he declared later, of Browning's sincerity in his support for TVA. Still he would not arbitrarily reject a potential gubernatorial candidate on principle alone, especially one whose availability was so readily apparent. Nevertheless, he made no commitment, and in January 1936 Crump said that he was "indifferent" to the governor's race and might withhold support from all candidates and certainly would not ask anyone to run.[4] Tennesseans found it difficult to believe that Crump could remain indifferent in a governor's race.

Senator Kenneth McKellar viewed Gordon Browning's ascendancy with a great deal of alarm. The senator had come to regard Browning with hostility and dislike, largely because of his inability to separate abstract from personal differences. Already more than sixty years old and showing no indication of retiring, McKellar had come to think of his senate seat as a private possession and anyone who was a potential challenger was a personal enemy.[5] Having long regarded Browning as a probable opponent, the senator was aware that his defeat in the senatorial contest in 1934 had not removed him as a threat. Undoubtedly it came as no surprise when, in October 1934, a friend warned that Browning's goal was to win the governor's office in 1936, earn a second term on precedent, and then run for the Senate in 1940.[6] Preventing Browning's election as governor therefore became an obsession with McKellar.

More closely allied with the McAlister administration than Crump, McKellar might well have endorsed the incumbent for a third term; but McAlister's withdrawal required the forces in alliance with the administration to search for a viable candidate to run for governor. The senator may not have hand-picked the eventual candidate, but he most certainly played an important role in making the selection.[7] Of course the candidate had to be satisfactory to all leaders and factions in the administration's alliance system, but anyone chosen in this manner was not necessarily the strongest choice. At any rate, Burgin Dossett, prominent educator and McAlister's state campaign manager in 1934, became the administration candidate. His campaign manager was McKellar's personal friend, District Attorney General Tom Stewart of Winchester.

In the early months of 1936, before the gubernatorial campaign had begun to take shape, political alignments were still in flux. A number of trial balloons were floating across the state. A frequently mentioned potential candidate was George L. Berry of Pressman's Home, Tennessee, president of both the International Pressmen and Assistants Union of North America and the Non-Partisan League. Rural Tennessee, however, demonstrated a decided lack of enthusiasm for a leader of organized labor, so Berry declined to run and eventually endorsed Browning. Often mentioned as a possible candidate for both the governor's race and the Senate seat occupied by Bachman was former senator and then Secretary of State in President Roosevelt's cabinet, Cordell Hull. It is not clear whether he seriously contemplated running for governor, but he was popular, would have been a strong candidate, and hard to beat. In January he announced that he would remain at his post in the State Department.[8] One officially announced candidate was a Nashville attorney and state senator, George Cate. It was common in Tennessee for lesser lights to enter a race for governor, gather some strength, and then bargain with the stronger candidates for a significant reward. In April Cate announced his withdrawal, endorsed Browning, and was appropriately rewarded later. Thus by late spring, the Democratic gubernatorial primary had been reduced to two serious contenders, Gordon Browning and Burgin Dossett. And for the first time since 1918, no third candidate strong enough to prevent a majority victor was in the race. Senator Bachman had only token opposition in the senatorial primary.

True to his character, Gordon Browning launched a vigorous stump campaign. On 10 June, he formally opened his drive at Murfreesboro with a hard-hitting attack on the incumbent administration and its candidate, Burgin Dossett. Browning pledged to clean up state government, which he characterized as completely corrupt, promised to reform state finances to keep the state from bankruptcy, and, for good measure, endorsed Roosevelt's New Deal. During the following two months, Browning outlined a broad program of reform. He charged the McAlister-Dossett "machine" with corruption and dishonesty in elections, declaring that he would take graft and stealing out of state government and see that elections were honest. Further, he pledged a merit system in civil service to promote greater efficiency in government and to end the evils of political payoffs in the awarding of jobs. He said that he would provide better roads for the state and would establish an adequate welfare program that would include pensions for the aged. He promised to reorganize the administration of government for greater efficiency. His most important pledge, however, was the promise to reorganize the state debt to provide for its orderly retirement.

Although he did not endorse Dossett publicly until late in the campaign, Senator McKellar was deeply involved. He quietly contacted his friends across the state to urge them to support Dossett's election, and his office continually bombarded the candidate with advice on how to run his campaign. Dossett never failed to be appropriately "grateful for the suggestions recently made."[9] One of Dossett's often repeated charges, undoubtedly at the suggestion of the senior senator, was that Browning was not a sincere friend of the Tennessee Valley Authority. Indeed, he declared that Browning was a foe of TVA when the bill was pending in Congress and had tried to destroy it by amendment during the hearings before the House Military Affairs Committee. Dossett also pointed out that Browning had not voted for TVA when it came to a roll-call vote in the House of Representatives. Dossett's charge probably did not influence the electorate greatly; nevertheless, it worried campaign workers and necessitated a reply. One county campaign manager was sufficiently concerned that he wrote state headquarters requesting information to counter the attack.[10] State manager A. B. Broadbent then forwarded pamphlets exaggeratedly entitled "Browning Supported and Assisted in Drafting T. V. A. Measure" for distribution. The most important plank in Dossett's platform was a pledge to press for local liquor option, a measure that would effectively repeal the state's "bone dry" prohibition law. He claimed that repeal would allow the state to collect taxes from the sale of whiskey and bring badly needed revenue into the state's almost "bone dry" treasury. Dossett's stand on repeal, however, clearly worked to Browning's advantage. For a politician to advocate repeal of prohibition in Tennessee was almost tantamount to heresy, although the logic of the argument probably appealed to many thoughtful Tennesseans.

Handicapped by his alignment with the incumbent administration, Burgin Dossett was unable to generate popular enthusiasm in his campaign. Most of the large daily newspapers were for Browning or remained neutral. The *Nashville Banner* recommended to the voters that they simply vote their conscience. The *Chattanooga Times* refused to endorse either candidate because they had similar platforms and gave the electorate little choice. The Memphis *Commercial Appeal* probably reflected the general sentiment by saying that the main difference was that Dossett proposed to legalize whiskey for increased revenues and Browning promised to keep the state dry. The paper agreed that the state lost tax monies by its prohibition law, but thought Browning offered the greater promise of cleaning up the "mess in Nashville." The *Commercial* declared that Dossett was supported by the political ring in the state's capital and represented the continuation of the bungling, inept, spendthrift, McAlister administration.[11]

Browning had widespread support. Veterans of World War I, especially members of the American Legion, were among his most enthusiastic supporters, and he had a devoted following of those who had served in Battery A, the company he had commanded during the war. On the final night of the campaign, Browning led a torchlight parade of his war buddies in the streets of downtown Nashville. The scene was one of great excitement and emotion as former comrades-in-arms paid tribute to one of their own. Dossett was also a veteran of the war, a member of the American Legion and a past state commander, but he did not have the advantage of having been a leading spokesman for that lobby in Congress. A few groups did find reasons for opposing Browning, however. *The Labor Advocate*, for example, a Nashville paper which reflected the thinking of conservative labor forces in Tennessee, charged that Browning was unsympathetic toward organized labor and had voted unfavorably in Congress on most of the measures advocated by labor. The *Advocate* also thought his record on TVA was suspect.[12]

Crump remained the enigma of the campaign because of his continued silence. It was unusual for the Memphis boss to remain quiet, but the absence of commitment suggests that he was conforming to his cherished maxims: "observe, remember, compare" and "read, listen, ask." His reticence had the effect of splitting his own machine; top aide Frank Rice was in Dossett's camp while stalwarts Walter Chandler and Abe Waldauer were active for Browning. Of course both sides tried to influence Crump. It was generally assumed across Tennessee that the candidate receiving his endorsement would win the primary and guessing his inclination became a popular exercise in a state rife with speculation. One widely circulated story was that the price of Crump's support for Dossett was the dropping of several members of the McAlister administration from the candidate's inner circle of advisors, including Dancey Fort, commissioner of the Department of Finance and Taxation, and Secretary of State Ernest N. Haston. The Memphis boss had developed a consummate dislike for Haston, former attorney for the Southern Bell Telephone Company, because he was convinced that the secretary of state, as a member of the board that assessed property taxes on utilities, had accepted money from private power interests. However, those the Memphis boss wanted removed were the backbone of Dossett's organization and he could hardly dismiss them in the middle of the campaign without some disorder in the machinery. Crump also wanted Haston removed as secretary of state.[13] Although Dossett desired Crump's support, he could not afford to take a stand on Haston's position, because the post was a constitutional office responsible to the legislature, and involvement in the matter might impair his efforts to get that body to enact his program.[14] On the other hand, Browning was under no compulsion to keep any of the McAlister administration if elected and had in fact promised to drive them out of government. Also, he declared that if he became governor, he would use his influence with the General Assembly to block the reelection of Haston as secretary of state. As long as Crump remained silent, Browning walked softly. In 1936 he was the front-runner, and his campaign oratory reflected that knowledge. Except for frequent attacks on members of the incumbent administration, he was cautious in his comments about personalities and placed greater emphasis on issues; absent were the caustic attacks on urban bossism that would be characteristic of later campaigns. He shrewdly avoided saying anything that might antagonize the leader of Shelby County. Regardless of what had happened in the senatorial race of 1934, he would wait until Crump made his move. If he really believed that the senatorial nomination was stolen from him in 1934 by the Shelby machine, as he later claimed, he was not going to damage his chances now by a rash attack on Crump.

No one tried harder to influence Crump than Senator McKellar. He early began a campaign to win the Memphis boss over to Dossett, using all the persuasiveness at his command. When Crump wavered, the senator pleaded with him to remain uncommitted until they had had a chance to discuss the matter.[15] McKellar apparently believed that he had finally convinced Crump to endorse Dossett, and the senator's friends across the state, especially in East Tennessee, were almost certain that Crump would line up with them. Even the press expected Crump's endorsement of the administration's candidate, perhaps because it was inconceivable that the Memphis boss and McKellar would split their support.[16] At any rate, Dossett's forces exuded optimism based in part, perhaps, on an unwillingness to admit that their candidate was doing poorly and in part on the hope that Crump would come out for their man.

However, in mid-July McKellar received word that Crump was about to publicly endorse Browning and the senator made a last-ditch effort to save the situation. He summed up by letter the reasons why he thought Dossett's election would be to the best interests of Shelby County. He declared that Dossett was "an up-standing, honest and intelligent" self-made man. The senator then pointed out that nearly all of his friends were for Dossett and "all of my friends outside of Shelby County, as well as in Shelby, are as a rule your friends, and in my judgment Mr. Dossett being friendly towards us it would be better for all of us to support Mr. Dossett." Moreover, McKellar continued, the administration candidate "stands four square on the platform which you outlined some time ago,"and would "consult you and other friends" concerning appointments. He then urged Crump to consider the fact that some of their old opponents such as Lewis Pope and Luke Lea were probably in Browning's camp. Finally, he made clear his own reason for wanting to see Browning defeated: "I think Captain Browning made it plain to you by inference . . . that he wanted the senatorial nomination in 1940. His course in the past makes it perfectly plain that he will be a candidate for the Senate then. I have no desire to further his ambition in that behalf." McKellar concluded with a prediction that Dossett would win East Tennessee by a good majority and break even in Middle Tennessee; Browning would win West Tennessee outside of Shelby. But "if you support Mr. Dossett, Mr. Dossett will carry the eighth. With your support Mr. Dossett will be overwhelmingly nominated."[17] But the senator's appeal came too late.

On 18 July, Ed Crump ended the suspense and the months of silence when he announced that Gordon Browning was his choice for governor. Crump gave his reasons for endorsing Browning. He declared "I served in Congress with Gordon Browning for four years. He was a fine, high minded upstanding man—active, wide awake, and had the respect of every Democratic and Republican member." Moreover, Crump had checked Browning's congressional record and found that Dossett had erred in charging his opponent with being unsympathetic to the TVA program. He pointed out that Browning did not vote for TVA because he was in the Senate prosecuting a federal judge at the time of the roll-call vote in the House of Representatives. "I would not," he said, "vote for any man for governor who would not . . . protect everything for TVA." Finally, he continued, Browning "will throw the unworthy out of office."[18] As Crump's biographer suggests, he may have had misgivings about Browning and might have preferred Dossett, but the "unworthy Ernest Haston," whom Crump thoroughly disliked, was a member of the Dossett camp. A more important consideration was that Browning's political popularity indicated victory. Crump had surveyed the state, sounded out sentiment, and arrived at the conclusion that Dossett's cause was lost.[19] Others had reached the similar conclusion that if Crump came out for Dossett the race might be close, but if Crump gave support to Browning the administration's candidate would be defeated by a large vote. One contemporary observer suggested that Browning would win regardless of Crump's support.[20] At any rate, the Memphis organization immediately went to work, and Walter Chandler, a comrade from World War I and a Crump lieutenant, led the drive for Browning in Shelby County.

Browning was outwardly calm but happy with Crump's endorsement. He declared, "I welcome the support of Memphis. That makes it unanimous."[21] The Dossett camp was stunned. Frank Rice exclaimed: "I can't understand it! I just don't understand it!"[22] According to one report, "Dossett's headquarters took on the hush of a funeral parlor, and some of his county campaign offices closed up. He could not raise a dime for campaign expenses. A reporter remarked to him that Crump's announcement sort of left him out on a limb. 'Limb, hell!' was the reply, 'Out on a twig.' "[23] The Dossett people were so surprised they could scarcely find words for public expression except a few weak charges about bossism being rampant in Tennessee. McKellar, who had issued a statement publicly endorsing Dossett for the first time a few hours prior to Crump's announcement, received letters criticizing the Memphis boss and urging him to take an active role in the race; he was in turn chastized when he did not.[24] Perhaps the senator realized the futility of any effort on his part.

Tennessee, along with the rest of the nation, was experiencing a drought and heat wave; the temperature hovered around one hundred degrees fahrenheit daily, and the national death toll from the heat wave was rising with no relief in sight. As the campaign neared its close, tempers flared and rose with the thermometer each day. In desperation, the Dossett people attacked Crump and made bossism in Tennessee a campaign theme. At the end, Browning directed some parting shots at the Dossett forces for attacking Crump. He said Dossett was trying to array the people against an outstanding citizen of the state and insisted that the Memphis leader wanted the mess in Nashville cleaned up like every "red-blooded Tennessean." The bossism in the state, Browning insisted, was in reality the machine led by Hill McAlister and Burgin Dossett. He added, "neither Ed Crump or Hilary House have extracted a promise from me."[25]

The Democratic primary of August 1936 was over the day Crump came out in support of Gordon Browning. The returns made that abundantly clear. In the final tally, Dossett had an edge of about 13,000 in the first three congressional districts in East Tennessee. The tally changed in Middle Tennessee as Nashville and Davidson County gave Browning a majority of 16,000 and the fourth and fifth congressional districts gave him a lead of 34,000. Thus Browning crossed the Tennessee River into West Tennessee in front by 37,000 votes. Outside Shelby County, he carried every county in the western section by a margin of 33,000. Shelby County gave Browning just under 60,000 votes to only 825 for Dossett. Browning won even without Shelby's overwhelming total; the vote in the Crump-controlled community was frosting on the cake. The final official count was 243,463 for the victor to 109,170 for Dossett, one of the largest margins ever received and one of the highest vote totals ever cast for an individual candidate in Tennessee.[26]

Many contemporaries of the political scene in Tennessee in the 1930s, as well as later scholars, have assumed that Ed Crump determined the winner of the Democratic gubernatorial primary in 1936, that if he had endorsed Dossett some fifty-nine thousand votes would have automatically shifted and Dossett would have won, that Crump was motivated to endorse Browning in order to reduce McKellar to the position of number-two man in the alliance. In short, Crump's endorsement made Gordon Browning governor.[27] Clearly the Memphis machine, the largest single voting block in the state, was able to determine the outcome of any statewide election if it was sufficiently close. But the assumption that Crump made Browning governor in 1936 is wide of the mark. Browning had generated considerable enthusiasm at the grass roots by presenting to the electorate a personable and aggressive campaigner with a positive program. Moreover, he had a hard core of vociferous supporters in Memphis that would have delivered at least ten thousand votes to him regardless of Crump's endorsement. In contrast, Dossett did not have the personality to match—as one observer put it, he was brusque and "crusty."[28] Finally, Dossett was tied to an administration that had an image of ineptness and had alienated some rural voters with his proposal to replace "bone dry" prohibition with local option.

In truth, Ed Crump was perceptive and possessed an uncanny ability to sense trends almost before they developed. He realized that Dossett would win East Tennessee by only a small majority, that Browning would win the middle section by a clear margin, and that West Tennessee outside of Memphis would go to Browning by a large vote. Just before the primary in 1936, political writer Joe Hatcher explained why Crump endorsed Browning: the Memphis boss had surveyed the state and found that the former congressman could not be beaten. As Crump's biographer notes, "With or without Crump, Browning would have been governor."[29] The Memphis leader may have gained some satisfaction in embarrassing Senator McKellar, and he may have liked the thought of being kingmaker. But E. H. Crump was a practical man. He was motivated to endorse Browning by a simple expedient: he wanted to be on the side of a winner. Throughout his career, Crump invariably chose winners and as often as not he chose those for whom he had little enthusiasm. While Mr. Crump was a man of principle, he often allied his organization with those with whom he differed. In the end, power was more important than principle. The election of Browning was not a repudiation of McKellar by the electorate or an indication that his strength had waned. It did, however, demonstrate that the senator could not always transfer his personal popularity into votes for any candidate he supported. In his almost neurotic efforts to prevent Browning's election, McKellar had backed the wrong candidate.

Dossett actually carried East Tennessee in part because of the senator's influence, and then lost the middle section where McKellar was never especially strong. In West Tennessee, Browning and McKellar were both popular and had "friends" in common; those friends could vote for Browning in 1936 without repudiating the senator. Finally, if any political foes of Crump and McKellar thought that serious division had developed within the alliance, they were mistaken. The two remained friends and Crump's biographer found no indication of bitterness on Crump's part; the Memphis boss considered it merely a difference of opinion. McKellar viewed the split in the same light. He wrote that he and Crump were on good terms, that Crump had supported him many times, and that he could not criticize a man who had given him such strong support in the past.[30] Crump and McKellar remained useful to each other and their alliance would eventually prove vital in maintaining political control in Tennessee.

Although victory in the Democratic primary was tantamount to victory in the November general election, the gubernatorial candidate, now titular head of the party in Tennessee, had the task of restoring harmony in the Democratic party. That was especially important for 1936 was a presidential election year and the leaders were anxious to demonstrate loyalty to the party by an overwhelming vote for the nominee, Franklin D. Roosevelt. Browning went about his task with vigor and confidence and was generally successful in uniting the factions of the party behind the ticket; any dissension within the ranks evaporated after his overwhelming victory in the primary. But Browning had a propensity for making rash statements and for expressing thoughts and emotions in haste without considering ramifications. In his zeal to inspire greater effort for the ticket, he expressed a sentiment that would one day return to haunt him. In September, he wired Memphis Mayor Watkins Overton urging greater efforts to get out the vote for the Democratic presidential nominee. He stated that Roosevelt depended upon fine organizations such as the one in Shelby County and that the efforts there would "be an inspiration to [the] rest of Tennessee." He concluded by saying that it was "a privilege to fight by your side [stop] More than sixty thousand reasons why I love Shelby County."[31]

In the general election of November 1936 the Democratic gubernatorial nominee faced only token opposition from Republican P. H. Thach and Socialist Mrs. Kate Stockton. Thach received a total of 78,000 votes and Stockton less than 4,000, while Browning polled more than 332,000. Much of the large turnout for Browning may have been attributable to the large vote for the Democratic presidential nominee, Franklin D. Roosevelt. On the other hand, Browning ran 5,000 votes stronger than Roosevelt; his victory was therefore impressive in any interpretation.[32] Flushed with his triumphs, governor-elect Gordon Browning believed that he had a mandate to keep his pledge of a reform administration. Pessimists said that he would have trouble carrying out his promises since the state was facing a deficit, and that he could not pay state employees and teachers their salaries, much less increase them and pay old-age pensions and welfare benefits. Claiming that he would make enemies in trying to outlaw the spoils system, the pessimists argued he had pledged too much and would be a one-term governor.[33] Although he realized that he would have a difficult time, Browning was confident as always that he was equal to the task. Moreover, for the moment, harmony existed between the newly elected governor and the Shelby organization. Shortly after the November election, Browning visited Memphis and had a conference with Crump and Senator McKellar. As the meeting broke up, Crump commented to representatives of the press: "Yes, everything is fine and dandy. Everybody is happy. A fine victory. We are all smiling." The press promptly dubbed the meeting a love feast.[34] But, as with all feasts, this one was of short duration.

Although a semblance of unity had been achieved in the Democratic party, Governor-elect Gordon Browning faced the prospect of one of the most serious crises in the state's history as he prepared to take the oath of office as Tennessee's chief executive in January 1937. Revenue was not sufficient to meet the ordinary expenses of government and the enormous interest on the state debt. To solve this problem would require the best in any man. But three positive factors were in Browning's favor: first, the electorate saw the need for creative action and gave him an overwhelming mandate for reform; second, he had his own fearless confidence and optimism; and third, he could wield the power vested in the office of governor.

Almost immediately after the general election in November 1936, Browning began to map out a program to conform to his campaign pledges and to reorganize the executive department. One of his first moves was to call in A. E. Buck of the Institute of Public Administration in New York to help formulate a plan to reorganize the administrative branch of government. Buck, an internationally famous specialist in public administration, was the author of several books on state and local government, had aided reorganizations in Virginia, Maine, and New Jersey, and had helped Governor Austin Peay in a reorganization program in Tennessee in 1923. He began his study in late November. A second major step was to employ Norman S. Taber of Norman S. Taber and Company, consultant on municipal finance, to act as financial adviser to the state, to survey existing conditions, and to make recommendations for a debt reorganization measure. The governor-elect also began to carry out the promise of civil service reform in November when he set up a preliminary personnel office in Nashville to screen applicants for state jobs. A. B. Broadbent was placed in charge of the office and announced that job seekers would have to demonstrate merit in order to receive appointments. Applicants would have to fill out personnel forms setting forth experience and qualifications, he said, and "those who are incompetent and unworthy should not apply."[35] No doubt loyalty to Browning was also a criterion for selecting new employees. Broadbent, a Clarksville attorney, president of Tennessee's Board of Law Examiners, and former speaker of the state senate, had earlier announced for the post of secretary of state. He was one of the most politically sagacious of the governor-elect's inner circle. Demonstrating continuing harmony between the governor-elect and the Shelby organization, Ed Crump quickly endorsed Broadbent. The factions also agreed on the legislative leadership for the upcoming session of the General Assembly: Walter "Pete" Haynes, representative from Franklin County, to be Speaker of the House, and Byron Pope, senator from Sequatchie County, to be Speaker of the Senate.

Late in November, Browning announced that his legislative program was complete except for the actual drafting of bills. The program included civil service reform through a merit system, the reorganization of the administrative branch of government with the creation of a new department of administration, a welfare division to replace the Department of Institutions, the probability of establishing a department of conservation, the enactment of a statewide driver's license law, the enactment of the Tennessee Education Association's eight-point school program, and finally, the reorganization of the state debt. Browning earlier had suggested that the state needed more money to meet its obligations in welfare, Social Security, and education. He believed that some funds could be saved by lower interest rates and reduced payments on the indebtedness under a refinancing plan. Moreover, he thought that up to one million dollars could be saved by eliminating waste in the operation of state government. Thus Tennessee could take care of its obligations without a significant tax increase.

In the meantime, Tennessee was confronted with the prospect of losing its share of Social Security taxes collected in 1936 unless the legislature passed enabling legislation to allow the state to participate in the program before 31 December 1936. The outgoing governor, Hill McAlister, hesitant to take affirmative action, had failed to call the General Assembly into session to act on implementing legislation. As of 1 December 1936, no action had been taken, although the governor was under pressure from all sides to call the assembly into extraordinary session. McAlister had been uncertain whether to call the old Sixty-ninth Assembly or the newly elected Seventieth in advance of its regular meeting. Finally, after consulting with Social Security officials, the attorney general, and Governor-elect Browning, McAlister called the new legislature into special session. The measure that came from the assembly was in large part Browning's work because his administration would have the task of developing a Social Security program of a more permanent nature.[36]

When the Seventieth General Assembly met in regular session early in January 1937, it immediately elected A. B. Broadbent secretary of state; Grover Keaton, a lawyer from Milan, was named treasurer; and John W. Britton, an accountant from Lenoir City, a veteran of World War I, and a member of the American Legion, was elected comptroller. Britton and Keaton, like Broadbent, were important members of Browning's inner circle and had his endorsement. One of the earliest measures considered by the assembly was a bill to empower the governor to appoint and discharge at will his cabinet members. That had been a long-standing practice but reversed at the insistence of Governor

McAlister in 1933. The delegation from Shelby County sponsored the new act and it received final approval on inauguration day as the first bill presented to Governor Browning for his signature. Meanwhile, Browning made known his administrative appointments. His brother, F. L. Browning, would serve as his private secretary until the assembly adjourned. Loyalists were rewarded with cabinet appointments and the official family was heavily flavored with Legionaires: John M. Goodman, a farmer from Adams in Robertson County, and a veteran, was made commissioner of the Department of Agriculture; another veteran, Walter Stokes, a Nashville businessman, was named commissioner of finance and taxation; and George Cate, a Nashville attorney, state senator and a veteran of World War I, was selected as commissioner of the to-be-created Department of Welfare and Institutions. Nonveterans who received appointments included: Albert Gore, Smith County superintendent of schools and Browning's campaign manager in his bid for the Senate in 1934 who was named commissioner of the Department of Labor; W. A. Bass, executive secretary of the Tennessee Education Association, who was named commissioner of the Department of Education; Dr. W. C. Williams of Franklin who was made commissioner of the State Health Department; M. O. Allen, a Newport engineer and waterworks executive, who was named commissioner of the Department of Highways and Public Works; and James McCormack, a Memphis insurance executive, who was made commissioner of the Department of Insurance and Banking. McCormack's position was apparently the only cabinet appointment in which the Memphis political machine had any voice, for the Nashville Banner reported that McCormack's appointment was announced shortly after a meeting between Browning and Frank Rice, the "coordinator" for Shelby County's delegation to the General Assembly.[37] For two weeks after convening the assembly marked time acting on local bills and awaiting the inaugural of the new governor. Finally, on 15 January 1937, Gordon Browning became the state's chief executive in colorful ceremonies in Memorial Square in front of the Capitol Building. Even then the General Assembly did not get down to serious business until 25 January, because the new governor took time out to attend the second inaugural of President Roosevelt in Washington. Upon his return to Nashville, Browning promptly presented to the legislature two major pieces of "must" legislation: the reorganization of administration, and a measure that would complete the implementation of the federal Social Security Act.

When Browning became governor he faced a situation similar to the one that had confronted Austin Peay in 1923. State government in Tennessee had been a jumble of bureaus, boards, and departments with overlapping and conflicting responsibilities which often resulted in confusion. Under Governor Austin Peay, some 68 agencies had been organized to achieve greater efficiency. In 1932, however, Hill McAlister campaigned on a pledge to reverse the trend toward greater centralization in the governorship, and once in office he proceeded to dismantle the administrative structure created under Peay.[38] Browning had promised during the campaign to restore efficiency in the executive branch and, as noted, employed the services of an administrative expert, A. E. Buck, to survey the situation. By the end of December 1936 Buck completed his study and submitted plans for reorganization to the governor-elect. His proposals, as outlined by Governor Browning in a special message to the General Assembly, followed generally the same form as the reorganization act of 1923. First, Browning asked for the creation of a department of administration, which would include a division of the budget to be responsible for preparing a budget and eliminating duplicate functions in various agencies; a divison of accounts which would approve contracts and certify expenditures; the Division of Purchasing would be transferred from the Department of Finance and Taxation, authorized to purchase and store materials used by the state, and establish uniform standards of purchasing; and finally, a division of personnel to put into effect a merit system in civil service. Browning's request had the effect of redefining the duties of the comptroller, who was keeping both accounts and auditing. In this way, the budgetary and accounting phases were to be separated. The new department would shoulder all financial responsibilities and would leave to the old Department of Finance and Taxation the job of collecting taxes. The head of the new department would in effect be an executive assistant second only to the governor in authority and responsibility. Browning also proposed the creation of a department of conservation, which was not only to have charge of forestry, state parks, geological surveys, and fish and game management, but also to have authority to establish a state advertising and tourist information agency. The proposed conservation department was one of the least controversial and most heartily approved measures in the governor's program.

The General Assembly quickly took up the governor's administrative package and passed it in a short time with few changes. But the final act went further by adding a fifth and sixth division to the Department of Administration. The Division of Highway Patrol was transferred from

the Department of Finance and Taxation to the new Department of
Administration, and a division of local finance was established with authority to set up procedures for accounting, budgeting, and reporting
of financial affairs for local governing bodies. Some voiced opposition
to the latter division with the argument that cities would then come
under even greater scrutiny and "move all county governments to Nashville." In addition, the comprehensive act specified a greater integration
of welfare functions of the state by bringing the Tennessee Welfare Commission and Department of Institutions together as the Department of
Institutions and Public Welfare. The larger department was authorized
to supervise state correctional institutions, charitable agencies, and similar local institutions receiving state aid. The assembly also specified
that the new Department of Institutions and Public Welfare would administer all functions of the federal Social Security Act and other welfare
activities, although unemployment compensation and workman's compensation would remain under the Department of Labor. The administrative reorganization act was signed by the governor on 1 February
1937 and he immediately announced the appointment of Wallace
Edwards, a Paris businessman, as commissioner of the Department of
Administration. Edwards was a veteran of World War I, having served
in the headquarters company of the 114th Field Artillery, and had been
private secretary to Governor Henry Horton.[39]

Tennessee, perhaps as much as any state, benefited from President
Roosevelt's New Deal, and Tennesseans supported the president with
enthusiasm. Indeed, the New Deal wrought a revolution in the state
by means of more jobs, increased wages, government spending, and the
creation of the Tennessee Valley authority. As a congressman, however,
Browning had not played a significant role in the development of the
President's legislation, and, after he became governor, he occasionally
obstructed Roosevelt's goals. One of the issues that developed in 1936
was a proposed constitutional amendment Congress had submitted to
the states to prohibit child labor. In January the governor-elect announced that he would not recommend the ratification of the amendment to the General Assembly, despite a letter of appeal from the
president. He believed that control of child labor was a state function,
and that Tennessee, having had no great problem with it in the past,
could take care of it if child labor became a problem at any time in the
future.[40] Browning's real reason was that the proposed amendment was
not popular with his rural constituents: children were still a vital source
of labor on the farm in Tennessee. In the realm of Social Security and

welfare, however, Browning took his place in the unfolding of the New Deal in Tennessee. Late in January he sent to the assembly a package of bills that called for public assistance for the aged, aid to dependent and crippled children, and the provision for Tennessee's participation in Social Security. The packaged passed with little change and without a dissenting vote. It specified the powers and responsibilities for putting the welfare program into effect and placed them in the hands of the enlarged Department of Institutions and Welfare.[41] Thus within two weeks after his inaugural, Governor Browning claimed two important pieces of legislation: administrative reorganization and a state Social Security and welfare program.

Not content with resting on his success, Browning submitted additional bills in rapid succession. He sent to the assembly his civil service merit system, which passed on 10 February. The act placed implementation of the system under the Division of Personnel in the Department of Administration. The director of the new division was given power to prescribe rules and regulations for employment in civil service which would become effective when approved by the commissioner of the Department of Administration and by Governor Browning. The goal of the act was to remove as many government workers from politics as possible and comparatively few posts were exempted. The regulations were to include tests for prospective employees, a classification system, and a compensation plan. The act, to be commended as a step forward, was weak in several respects. The politicians could still appoint favorites from those qualifying for various jobs; more important, those discharged from service did not have the recourse of appeal, nor was there any safeguard against arbitrary firing. A. E. Buck, the specialist in administration, also suggested that, to be really effective, a civil service merit system required a constitutional amendment. Browning believed that the merit system was one of the most important accomplishments of his administration but his opponents made it ineffective as soon as he left office.[42]

Candidates trying to unseat an incumbent chief executive frequently charge that a "mess" exists in the administration and then promise to clean it up if elected. There was a measure of justification for Browning's charges of corruption in government during the McAlister administration, for several firms had successfully evaded paying taxes on oil sold in Tennessee. The revelation of such activities had resulted, by February 1937, in two persons being convicted, and others being under indictment on the charge of conspiracy to defraud the state of revenue.

Since Browning had promised to eliminate corruption, he was compelled to make a perfunctory house cleaning, if for no other reason than to comply with his campaign pledge. Therefore, the governor sponsored a measure to create a commission for the "investigation of the oil tax situation for the purpose of recovering for the State all taxes that should have been paid to it." The proposed investigation passed in March after a stiff fight in the senate and Browning named Lewis Pope, Nashville attorney and three times gubernatorial candidate, to head the "Probe." The final act went further than the original request. It authorized a complete and exhaustive probe of all state departments and institutions to expose all corruption if and where it existed and to settle allegations where it did not. The commission, which was given broad authority that included subpoena power, was directed specifically to determine if back taxes were due from any source, and if so, to bring suit to collect them.[43] The "Probe" went to work immediately in a flurry of activity; a small amount of corruption was exposed, particularly in purchasing for the various state institutions, and several minor officials were dismissed for incompetence and misuse of state funds. By midsummer Pope had filed suits to obtain back taxes totaling several million dollars. The commission continued its work through the summer and fall of 1937, but the "Probe's" most significant political activity was to come in 1938.

One of the most pressing problems facing the administration was public education. The schools of Tennessee desperately needed funds, and teachers, when they were paid, scarcely received a living wage. In 1936 the Tennessee Education Association adopted the "Eight Point Program," aimed at raising the state's minimum educational standards and teacher's pay. The program obviously required increased appropriations from the General Assembly. Browning, in his campaign, endorsed the "Eight Point Program" and made it an administration bill after the election. With his enthusiastic support, the General Education Bill passed the assembly on 4 March. The act increased grants to both high schools and elementary schools, and established a minimum term of eight months for elementary schools and nine months for secondary schools. The act did not raise teachers' salaries across the board, but it required the State Board of Education to establish a higher minimum salary schedule for all teachers and principals based upon education and experience, thus, in effect, raising the income of most teachers. Browning wrote a year later that no accomplishment of his administration gave greater pleasure than the enactment of the "Eight Point Program."[44]

Most of the governor's bills sailed through the assembly with little difficulty. The legislature enacted a comprehensive statewide driver's license registration law, a strict hunting and fishing code, and a law setting sixteen as the minimum age for receiving a marriage license.[45] The measure that encountered the greatest opposition during the first two months of the session was the governor's general revenue bill. Browning had promised a balanced budget and established the policy that no money would be spent unless revenue covered expenditures. Yet his legislature had already appropriated larger sums for education and welfare benefits. The appropriations were made with the understanding that certain fixed expenses would be met first and the remainder used for educational and welfare purposes. The problem was that the remainder was not always available in sufficient quantity. If Browning's ambitious program was to succeed, he had to find additional revenue. So the general revenue bill, the first of its kind since 1931, proposed several new levies and increased others. The new levies were primarily privilege taxes and designated over one hundred enterprises on which taxes were to be collected. They included, among other things, a tax on merchants, some public utilities, manufacturers of patent medicines, vending machines, restaurants, cold storage plants, warehouses, insurance companies, and theaters. Other provisions increased taxes on beer sales, the corporation excise, and inheritance. No large increases appeared in the measure. Philosophically, Browning was opposed to high taxes in general, advocating instead a broad network of low rates. After more heated debate than on any other bill, the General Revenue Act passed on 5 March. The result was a substantial increase in revenue, and funds were available for most expenditures. An authority on economic history in Tennessee suggested that the Revenue Act of 1937 demonstrated how completely the state had turned away from *ad valorem* taxes to privilege taxes. Except for a retail sales tax, other sources of revenue were limited because of constitutional prohibitions.[46] Governor Browning was unalterably opposed to a sales tax because he considered it the most inequitable form of taxation. On the other hand, he favored a graduated income tax and proposed that the legislature issue a call for a constitutional convention to consider it, as well as a provision for the classification of property for tax purposes. He added that he would stump the state in support of those sources of revenue. In March 1937 the governor hinted that he might call an extraordinary session of the General Assembly to consider a call for a constitutional convention. However, there was a decided lack of enthusiasm in the assembly for his proposition and he did not pursue the matter.[47]

An exhausted assembly, with two major pieces of legislation pending—the governor's debt reorganization plan and the General Appropriation Bill—recessed for two months on 5 March. A pleased governor commented:

> I am entirely satisfied with the cooperation the Legislature has given me. . . . It is the best Legislature I have known to assemble. It is fortunate that the platforms of legislators conformed to mine. That enabled us to get together quickly on the entire program. And, I think they have done more work than any similar group, for the length of time they have been in session.[48]

Although he agreed that government had a responsibility to provide services, Governor Browning was generally orthodox in his economic philosophy. He opposed deficit spending to provide those services, even at the cost of increased taxes, unless absolutely necessary. Most people agreed that Tennessee's debt had gone far beyond the bounds of reason and that the problem demanded solution. Shortly after the general election in November 1936 Browning employed Norman S. Taber to study Tennessee's financial situation. Taber made his first report to the governor in January, but most of what he said merely confirmed what was already known. The total indebtedness as of 1 January 1937 was $128,900,000, of which a little more than $97 million was in bonds with an average interest of 4.78 percent. Over $73 million of the debt was the result of refunding or deficit funding, so that the taxpayers were paying large sums in interest "for which they are receiving no evident benefit." Moreover, in the previous twenty years, only about $3,500,000 had been retired without funding or refunding. Taber pointed out that the state could have saved millions of dollars had a proper debt plan been in effect to provide for retirement, and he concluded that the state faced continued waste unless a complete reorganization of the debt was undertaken.[49]

When the General Assembly recessed on 5 March, the governor, Wallace Edwards, Walter Stokes, Grover Keaton, Walter Haynes, and Byron Pope left for New York City to confer with financial leaders and work out the details of debt reorganization. A plan was completed in less than a week, and the governor returned to the state to present it to the legislature. The *Nashville Tennessean* reported that the refunding proposal had elicited wide acclaim in financial circles and that the bondholders were in agreement with it.[50] The wide approval in financial circles was not echoed by all the members of the General Assembly as it reconvened on 5 May to consider the proposal. The Shelby County delegation in particular opposed the Debt Reorganization Bill. The county's three senators signed and sent to the governor a statement giving the reasons why they would vote against the measure. They contended first that it violated the contractual relationship between the state and bondholders; second, that the program had never been tried in any other state before; third, that the fees of Taber and Company were exhorbitant; fourth, that it was a bondholders' bill in entirety; and fifth, that the state would save nothing.[51]

The opponents of debt refinancing attempted to block passage of the measure by raising other issues. For example, the Shelby delegation proposed a measure that would end "bone dry" prohibition and replace it with local option. Indeed, for a time the administration's refinancing bill was ignored, and the Shelby group threatened a filibuster after Browning announced he would veto local option if it passed. The liquor bill died, but in the last-minute rush before adjournment, the assembly set up a referendum, to be held in September 1937, to determine the wishes of the people on prohibition. The act required that two alternatives be placed on the ballot—for repeal of prohibition and against repeal. The act was a meaningless gesture because the referendum was not binding on the legislature.[52]

After much bitter debate, the refinancing measure received the approval of the General Assembly on 13 May 1937. The Debt-Reorganization Act embodied a comprehensive plan that consolidated the existing debt by funding and refunding and setting up a retirement program. In brief, it brought all the various debts of the state into a single integrated plan for orderly retirement. The State Funding Board was authorized to issue consolidated bonds with maturity dates which could be met from revenue. The new issue consolidated twenty-nine categories of interest-bearing bonds which ranged from 3.25 to 6 percent interest. The act pledged five cents of each seven cents of the gasoline tax, all the gasoline and kerosene inspection fees, fifty percent of the automobile registration fees, the receipts from the corporation franchise tax, and the first $307,500 from the tobacco tax for retiring the debt. The act further specified that no other obligation could take money from those revenues unless they provided more than enough to meet the amortization of the debt. The state also pledged not to reduce those revenues until provisions of the act had been caried out.[53] With sufficient revenue pledged to retiring the debt and an adequate budgetary plan, Tennessee's credit went to an all-time high. The program received applause from the financial world, and one leader commented that it should go down in state financial history as a constructive program.[54] How well it worked was demonstrated by the fact that neither of the two subsequent governors attempted to change the structure of the program, and the debt was reduced by more than forty percent in ten years; between 1937 and 1948, the debt was reduced by more than $54 million.[55] Gordon Browning stated, without hesitation, that refinancing the state debt was the greatest accomplishment in all his years in public life. "I wanted to pay off the debt and avoid paying all that interest that was leaving the state," he said. "I never cease to wonder how I ever got it through."[56]

When the General Assembly adjourned in May 1937 it ended one of the most productive and effective sessions in the state's history. Indeed, the assembly set a record by passing 1,216 bills. When it closed, virtually all of the governor's pledges had been enacted into law. In four months, the assembly passed all of his priority bills, reorganized state government, established a merit system, materially improved public education, balanced the budget, provided for a comprehensive welfare program, and refinanced the debt. Perhaps the only discordant note was sounded by the forces of organized labor which charged Browning with breaking his promise to appoint a union member to lead the Department of Labor and being responsible for the defeat of the resolution to ratify the amendment to the federal constitution to ban child labor.[57] Complaints from labor, however, carried little weight in predominantly rural and agrarian Tennessee and had little impact on Browning's popularity. The *Nashville Banner* concluded that "no Governor in the history of the State ever held more complete control over a General Assembly. And the oldest observers on Capital Hill cannot recall another session so peaceful and composed."[58] Gordon Browning left a legacy that few succeeding governors and legislators could wisely repudiate.

NOTES

1. Gordon Browning, interview with the author, Huntingdon, 28 December 1965.
2. William D. Miller, *Mr. Crump of Memphis* (Baton Rouge: Louisiana State University Press, 1964), pp. 176–178, 226–227, 231–232.
3. Joe Hatcher, "Politics," *Nashville Tennessean*, 19 November 1934.
4. *Tennessean*, 8 January 1936.

5. McKellar to H. D. Derrick, 29 May 1936, Political Correspondence, Box 33, The Kenneth Douglas McKellar Papers, Memphis-Shelby County Public Library and Information Center.

6. J. R. Rison, Jr., to McKellar, 25 October 1934, Political Correspondence, Box 30, Ibid.

7. McKellar to K. T. McConnico, 29 January 1936, Political Correspondence, Box 34, Ibid.

8. Hatcher, "Politics," 17 January 1936; *Tennessean*, 19 January 1936.

9. Dossett to McKellar, 10 June 1936, Political Correspondence, Box 33, McKellar Papers.

10. Tom Henderson to A. B. Broadbent, 9 July 1936, Tom Henderson Papers, Tennessee State Library and Archives.

11. *Nashville Banner*, 28 July 1936; *Chattanooga Times*, 6 August 1936, *Commercial Appeal*, 20, 22 July 1936.

12. *The Labor Advocate*, 30 July 1936.

13. Hatcher, "Politics," 8 April 1936; *Banner*, 11 July 1936.

14. Burgin Dossett, interview with Frank B. Williams, Jr., Johnson City, 17 September 1976.

15. McKellar to Crump, 29 May 1936, Crump-McKellar Correspondence, Box 3, McKellar Papers.

16. Robert Dean Pope, "Senatorial Baron: The Long Political Career of Kenneth D. McKellar"(unpublished Ph. D. dissertation, Yale University, 1976), pp. 254–255.

17. McKellar to Crump, 13 July 1936, Crump-McKellar Correspondence, Box 3, McKellar Papers.

18. Quoted in *Tennessean*, 21 July 1936.

19. Miller, *Mr. Crump*, pp. 232–233; William D. Miller, "The Browning-Crump Battle: The Crump Side,"*East Tennessee Historical Society Publications* 37 (1965): 77–88.

20. Hatcher, "Politics," 19, 21, 23 July 1936.

21. Quoted in *Banner*, 19 July 1936.

22. Dossett, interview with Frank Williams.

23. V. O. Key, Jr., *Southern Politics in State and Nation* (New York: Alfred Knopf, 1949), p. 63.

24. Pope, "Senatorial Baron,"pp. 255–256.

25. Quoted in *Commercial Appeal*, 30 July 1936.

26. *Tennessee Blue Book, 1937–1938* (Nashville, 1938), pp. 172–173. Senator Bachman won a full term, Ibid., pp. 174–175.

27. Key, *Southern Politics*, pp. 62–63; Pope, "Senatorial Baron,"pp. 253–259.

28. Brainard Cheney, interview with the author, Smyrna, 19 November 1977.

29. Hatcher, "Politics," 23 July 1936; Miller, *Mr. Crump*, p. 233: Clark Porteous, in an interview with the author (Memphis, 22 June 1977), also believed that Crump supported Browning because he was destined to win.

30. Miller, *Mr. Crump*, pp. 232–233; Pope, "Senatorial Baron,"pp. 255–256.

31. Browning telegram to Watkins Overton, 29 September 1936, Box 1, Watkins Overton Papers, Memphis State University Library.

32. *Tennessee Blue Book, 1937–1938*, pp. 167–168, 176–178.

33. *Commercial Appeal*, 7 November 1936.

34. Quoted in *Banner*, 5 November 1936.

35. Quoted in Ibid., 8 November 1936.

36. *Public Acts of the State of Tennessee, Passed By the Seventieth General Assembly, Extra Session, 1936 and Regular Session, 1937* (Nashville, 1937), pp. 19–65.

37. *Banner*, 10 December 1936, 3, 12 January 1937; Miller, *Mr. Crump*, p. 211.

38. Lee S. Greene, David H. Grubbs, and Victor C. Hobday, *Government in Tennessee*, 3rd ed. (Knoxville: University of Tennessee Press, 1975), pp. 109–110, 127.

39. *House Journal of the First Extraordinary and Regular Session of the Seventieth General Assembly of the State of Tennessee* (Jackson, 1937), pp. 318–321; *Banner*, 28 January 1937; *Public Acts 70th GA*, pp. 89–131; see also James E. Thorogood, *A Financial History of Tennessee Since 1870* (Sewanee: University of the South Press, 1949), pp. 139–142; William H. Combs and William E. Cole, *Tennessee: A Political Study* (Knoxville: University of Tennessee Press, 1940), pp. 127–132.

40. Browning to Roosevelt, 11 January 1937, Gordon Browning Papers, Tennessee State Library and Archives.

41. *Public Acts 70th GA*, pp. 151–204. The Social Security Act required that some agency carry out the program and the legislation passed in the extraordinary session in December 1936 had not provided for this.

42. Ibid., pp. 208–221; Greene, Grubbs, and Hobday, *Government in Tennessee*, p. 146; *Banner*, 23 November 1936; Gordon Browning, interview, 28 December 1965.

43. *Banner*, 8 February 1937; *Public Acts 70th GA*, pp. 500–510.

44. *Public Acts 70th GA*, pp. 532–549; see also John U. Whitaker, Jr., "Influence of the Governors on Education in Tennessee, 1937–1955" (unpublished M. A. thesis, University of Tennessee, 1958), pp. 11–20; Edell M. Hearn, "Public Educational Changes Through Legislation in Tennessee, 1935–1959" (unpublished Ed. D. dissertation, University of Tennessee, 1959), pp. 112–263; Browning to A. D. Holt, 2 May 1938, Browning Papers.

45. *Public Acts 70th GA*, pp. 347–360, 271–318, 262–265.

46. Ibid., pp. 403–495; Thorogood, *A Financial History*, pp. 144–156.

47. *Banner*, 18 February, 31 March 1937.

48. Quoted in ibid., 4 March 1937.

49. N. S. Taber and Co., "Debt Reorganization Plan, Purpose of the Bill," n. d., Browning Papers.

50. *Tennessean*, 21 March 1937.

51. Senators [Blan] Maxwell, [Gerald B.] Stratton, and [Wesley] Harvell, statement, n. d., Browning Papers.

52. *Tennessean*, 11, 12 May 1937; *Public Acts 70th GA*, pp. 926–931.

53. *Public Acts 70th GA*, pp. 643–673; see also Thorogood, *A Financial History*, pp. 142–143, 232–233.

54. Frederick L. Bird, Director of Municipal Research, Dun and Bradstreet, to Browning, 20 May 1937, Browning Papers.

55. Thorogood, *A Financial History*, p. 233.

56. Browning, interview, 28 December 1965.

57. Tennessee Federation of Labor, "Report of the Legislative Committee on the 70th General Assembly" (1937 Regular Session).

58. *Banner*, 23 May 1937.

 5

Quixotic Crusade

GORDON Browning won both the Democratic gubernatorial primary and the general election in 1936 by overwhelming votes. Despite the large turnout for Browning by the Shelby County political machine, Ed Crump had not been the kingmaker. Crump's support had not been solicited—the boss had gone to him. Moreover, it was now apparent that Browning was the most powerful political figure in Tennessee. Nothing better illustrated this power than his control over the General Assembly and the success of his legislative program.

With these developments, perhaps it was inevitable that the governor and the Memphis boss should part political company. Both were strong-willed leaders and neither would subordinate himself to the other. More importantly, they represented conflicting interests, one rural, the other urban. Because his sympathies were with the countryside, Browning entered into an easy alliance with rural leaders in the legislature and the eventual break with Crump was in large part the clash of rural and urban interests. Shortly after the general election in November 1936 the two leaders had met, and it appeared, for the moment at least, that they had entered into a harmonious relationship. Despite the facade of smiling faces and words of unity, it proved impossible for Browning and

Crump to cooperate; smoldering differences between the two flared into the open in the fall of 1937 and led to all-out warfare between the two political leaders.

Although there is little evidence to suggest that Crump tried to dictate policy and appointments, Browning insisted that he was in office but a short time before the Memphis boss became highly irritated because he was not being consulted on appointments. Browning claimed that he finally told Crump that he was not taking instructions from him: "You can ride if you want to but you can't drive. I'm driving this wagon. I'm governor of Tennessee."[1] In reality, the Memphis organization maintained a hands-off policy which was clearly expressed by Mayor Watkins Overton in response to a request for an endorsement for a state job: "We have refrained from endeavoring in any way whatsoever in recommending to our Governor-elect any appointments of this character."[2] Generally, the organization held to the policy of noninterference, with one exception: Crump sent one of his most trusted lieutenants, Will Gerber, to Nashville to protest the appointment of Wallace Edwards as commissioner of the Department of Administration. Crump was displeased because Edwards had served as private secretary to Governor Henry Horton and was, presumably, close to Luke Lea. Gerber reported that Browning "gave us the brush off."[3] The appointment of Edwards is understandable as he had served with Browning in France during World War I and had been the governor's campaign manager in his first try for a seat in Congress. Browning could hardly deny his friend a significant post in his administration, and he probably resented Crump's protest and regarded it as an unnecessary interference.

Inclined to distrust Browning, Crump found it easy to suspect the governor of evil dealings. Crump's biographer demonstrates how the Memphis political leader made much out of certain events which he believed pointed to unethical deals. For example, Crump received a letter signed by a G. K. Rennie soon after the primary in 1936 which seemed to be asking his influence in obtaining favors in distribution of sand asphalt in the state. To Crump, the letter smacked of Luke Lea's old Kyrock firm and he suspected that Browning had some connection with the writer. An investigation which proved little either way did not allay Crump's suspicion.[4] Senator McKellar also began a campaign to convince the Memphis boss that the governor was not sympathetic to TVA and was a tool of the private power trust. McKellar had a personal reason for hostility toward the governor. Browning was a potential opponent, but personality differences may have also been a source of enmity. The governor's flamboyant and free-wheeling manner probably caused the straitlaced McKellar to suspect him of unethical practices. In addition, the problem of federal patronage undoubtedly caused friction between Browning and the senior senator. McKellar controlled federal patronage in Tennessee and his power was demonstrated when he secured the appointment of Burgin Dossett to head the Social Security office in Knoxville over the objections of the Browning administration. Knowing the value of a voice in federal appointments in the state, the governor was incensed because his administration could exercise no influence. Nor could Browning forget that it was McKellar who had blocked his appointment as deputy commissioner of the Farm Credit Administration in 1935.[5] At any rate, the senator kept repeating charges against Browning and was perhaps successful in making Crump uneasy, for the Memphis political boss became more and more uncertain about the governor. Undoubtedly Crump was beginning to rationalize, and actions of the past took on a different meaning because of his growing suspicions.

Crump's greatest fear was a revival of the influence of his political enemy, Colonel Luke Lea. Lea was released from prison in April 1936, after serving an abbreviated term for conspiracy to violate the banking laws. Although Lea took no publicly active part in the primary campaign of 1936, the Memphis boss was still afraid of him and warned Browning about taking Lea into his confidence. Browning told Crump that the colonel was his friend but that if he won the election, no one, not even Lea, would run the governor's office but himself. Browning believed that Lea was innocent of the charges that resulted in imprisonment and that Lea and Rogers Caldwell, his associate in banking enterprises, did nothing more than thousands of others during the financial boom of the 1920s. "My feeling was that he was just a foreigner caught away from home," he said. "He was not guilty in my opinion of anything that called for that kind of punishment."[6] Despite his friendship with Lea, Gordon Browning did not allow his administration to be dominated by his friend, or anyone else. But the governor did have the support of a majority of individuals and factions that had once been a part of Lea's old alliance system. His rural background also led him to an easy alliance with the rural block in the Tennessee legislature. He early established a rapport with the three most powerful members of the General Assembly, Walter "Pete" Haynes of Winchester, James H. Cummings of Woodbury, and I. D. Beasley of Carthage. Thus Browning was allied with a powerful element whose goal was to further the interests of rural Tennessee and to eliminate the power of urban political machines.

Some of Browning's original appointments were members of the Lea alliance system and later appointments demonstrated that he was steadily leaning toward that old organization. Those appointments were disquieting to Crump. His opposition to the appointment of Wallace Edwards to the new Department of Administration has been noted. However, it was well known that Browning intended to name Edwards to the post as early as December 1936. Apparently Crump was not sufficiently displeased at that juncture to intervene, for the Shelby delegation to the General Assembly played an important role in securing passage of the governor's administrative reorganization plan. But the Memphis boss gradually became convinced that the administration was a revival of the Lea organization. For example, John Nolan, state treasurer during Governor Horton's administration and the one responsible for depositing state funds in Lea-Caldwell banks, became director of Budgets and Accounts. Grover Keaton, Horton's campaign manager and alleged go-between in the Kyrock deal, became state treasurer. Eugene Coile, who Crump believed was an insider in the Lea organization, was named state purchasing agent. Finally, Marshall Priest, allegedly an intimate of Lea, became state comptroller during Browning's administration. The appointment that caused Crump the greatest displeasure was probably that of Lewis Pope to head the special commission to investigate state affairs and to collect back taxes. Crump's dislike of the special investigator was understandable. Pope was a candidate for the Democratic gubernatorial nomination in 1932 and lost by only 9,000 votes. He immediately charged that the vote in Memphis was fraudulent, that fictitious voters with addresses in vacant lots were registered, that truckloads of Negroes from Arkansas were hauled to polling places, and that his workers were jailed to keep them inactive. He even filed a protest with the Democratic State Executive Committee, but the protest was disallowed for want of sufficient evidence. Pope then began a speaking tour across the state bitterly repeating his charges at every turn. Insisting that he was the rightful nominee, he eventually campaigned as an independent in a losing effort in the general election in November. The same sequence of events was repeated in the gubernatorial primary and general elections in 1934. Pope repeated his charges of voting fraud in Shelby County so often that they became part of the Crump legend.[7] The Memphis boss was sensitive to accusations of corruption and he came to regard Pope as one of his most unrelenting foes. Although

Governor Browning's reasons for the appointment were not clear, Crump's displeasure was evident. Crump's biographer concludes, "It was obvious that in Crump's view the presence of men in Browning's administration who had formerly been identified with the Caldwell-Lea-Horton group was a fatal disability."[8]

Despite these appointments, the governor and the Memphis boss maintained a pretense of harmony through the meeting of the General Assembly, and the Shelby delegation was prominent in support of some important administration measures. But several events during the meeting of the assembly should have indicated to close observers that all was not well between the two leaders. Rumors flew fast and furious in February that a "break" between the Shelby organization and Governor Browning occurred after the governor made known his intention to name Pope to head the proposed "Probe." Columnist Joe Hatcher denied any such break and pointed out that while members of the Shelby machine opposed the proposed investigation, the county's delegation had done "yeoman" work for the administration' program and that Memphis Senator Blan Maxwell helped push through the merit system. A few days later, however, Hatcher was compelled to report that the Shelby organization objected to Browning's revenue bill.[9] Crump was especially incensed at a proposed one percent gross receipts tax on manufacturers and wholesalers and commented, "If the present tax bill goes through it simply means that taxes assassinated Tennessee and the Governor has pulled the trigger."[10] The Shelby representatives were also vocal in their opposition to Browning's general appropriation bill on several points. Crump was not happy with the governor's debt refinancing proposal. In May, when the General Assembly was debating the measure, the legislators from Shelby County obstructed its passage for a time by attempting to push through a local liquor option bill. Crump opposed the debt measure because he believed that it was intended to aid certain special interests. Apparently he thought, without any definite proof, that Luke Lea was part of a group that would profit by refinancing.

Meanwhile, on 23 April 1937, Senator Nathan Bachman had died of a heart attack. That event had a profound effect upon the relationship between Governor Browning and the leader of the Memphis machine, for the governor was obligated to make an interim appointment to fill the vacancy until the next general election. The senatorial vacancy immediately caused every faction in the state to maneuver for position, and Browning was deluged with suggestions for the post and with visits from those who wanted the appointment. In the days after Bachman's death the governor was hounded almost constantly. Even President Roosevelt was interested in the appointment since his controversial Supreme Court packing plan was then under consideration by Congress and the new senator from Tennessee was expected to play an important role in the passage of the measure. A short time after Bachman's death, the governor visited Washington to attend the Governors' Freight Rate Conference and Roosevelt asked to see Tennessee's chief executive. During the meeting with the president, Browning recalled, Roosevelt said he would not try to tell him whom to appoint, but whom not to appoint. He did not want Secretary of State Cordell Hull taken away from him. "I need him here," Roosevelt said. Roosevelt was undoubtedly aware that Hull was a possible appointee and that the secretary of state was interested in having his old Senate seat back.[11] Browning insisted that Roosevelt did not try to influence him in the appointment, but the Memphis *Commercial Appeal* reported from a "reliable source" that the president and Postmaster General James A. Farley wanted Major George L. Berry, president of the International Pressmen and Assistants Union of North America, named to the post. Berry had endorsed Roosevelt's court reform proposal as the only way to secure sound, progressive social and economic legislation.[12]

Browning kept everyone guessing for two weeks and speculation was rife concerning the vacant Senate seat. Congressman Sam McReynolds was known to be interested in the post and former governor A. H. Roberts formally applied for the appointment. Other possibilities mentioned in the press were Major Berry, Walter Chandler, congressman from Shelby County, and even Crump. The latter two were not considered strong contenders because of their residence in the western section of the state, and most observers thought Berry was disqualified because of a claim he had against TVA for over a million dollars. Constantly harassed by interested parties, an exasperated Browning finally announced that he was going to Huntingdon for a rest. "I want to talk to disinterested friends before I make up my mind finally," he said. "The only thing I am considering is the appointment of a man who will do the people of Tennessee the most good."[13] A few days later, the governor visited Memphis and had a long conference with Crump. The Memphis boss was polite and reserved at the meeting, and Browning had little to say afterwards except that Crump had made no recommendations for the Senate vacancy. Crump's reticence may have helped Browning make up his mind. On 6 May, the governor announced his appointment:

Major George L. Berry. The appointment came as a surprise to most but caused rejoicing in Washington. Reports indicated that the president's legislative leaders believed Berry would provide the margin of victory needed in the court fight. The more conservative element in organized labor was especially gratified. *The Labor Advocate* commented that court reform was needed, and the president needed Berry.[14]

George L. Berry's life was a Horatio Alger story of rags to riches. Reared in poverty, he literally taught himself to read and write. But he quickly acquired wealth and fame. Ultimately, he became president of the Pressman's Union and owner of a large color-label printing plant, allegedly built with union funds. During World War I, he was commissioned an officer in the Corp of Engineers and emerged at the end of the war as a major. President Woodrow Wilson appointed him a labor representative on the European Peace Commission in 1919, and he was sufficiently well known nationally for a minor boom for the Democratic vice-presidential nomination in 1924. President Roosevelt appointed Berry to the post of Coordinator for Industrial Cooperation, an effort to salvage what was left of the National Recovery Act after it was struck down by the Supreme Court. In 1936 Berry was instrumental in forming the Non-Partisan League, an organization whose goal was to help Roosevelt win reelection. Berry was a member of the American Legion and was enthusiastically endorsed for the Senate vacancy by that organization.

Browning's reason for appointing Berry is not clear. He contended that he selected the union leader because he was "the best man for the job."[15] On the other hand, the fact that Berry was a veteran, a friend, and a political supporter were surely important considerations. It remained to be seen whether the appointment was a wise political move. A labor leader had limited political appeal in predominately rural Tennessee, and Berry was probably more of a liability to Browning than an asset. Berry's greatest liability in Tennessee, however, was not his union connection but his claim against TVA. In 1932 Berry was part of a group which purchased extensive mineral rights to 30,000 acres of land in East Tennessee. After TVA was established and construction of Norris Dam was begun, the land was inundated. In 1935 Berry and his associates asked for a settlement, claiming that the water covered marble quarries valued at $5 million despite the insistence by TVA geologists that the marble was commercially worthless. The claim was eventually rejected and TVA Chairman Arthur Morgan considered prosecuting Berry and his associates for making false claims, but Berry was a United States Senator by then, and TVA did not pursue the matter. A few weeks after Berry's appointment, the *Nashville Banner* noted that the senator was going about his work in a quietly efficient manner and making friends in Congress.[16] But the new senator met hostility from his colleague, Kenneth McKellar, and it was apparent from the beginning that the two could not get along. The senior senator was not about to share patronage. After a number of exchanges, Berry complained, and McKellar responded: "There seems to be nothing further that I can add except to reiterate that I cannot agree to any of your proposals concerning patronage in Tennessee."[17]

Crump's biographer contends that the appointment of Berry was not a great issue with the Memphis boss; however, he was surprised because of the appointee's claim against TVA. The biographer asserts that Crump did not want the seat himself because he did not like Washington and would almost certainly have turned it down if offered. Abe Waldauer, a rising member of the Shelby organization and long-time friend of the governor, went to see Browning after Bachman's death to urge the appointment of Crump. The Memphis boss, however, contacted Waldauer when he heard of the mission and had his name withdrawn.[18] Crump may have wanted the offer even though he would have turned it down. The *Banner* reported that it was common knowledge that "Crump would have at least liked the refusal" of the post.[19]

The senatorial appointment and Browning's appointments to state offices, along with other minor if not trivial factors, contributed to Crump's distrust of the governor. Differences over substantial issues had little to do with Crump's uneasiness. Certainly the Memphis boss could not have been greatly disturbed at the governor's legislative program, for Browning had made his goals well known in broad outlines during the campaign, and his measures contained no surprises during the meeting of the General Assembly. The activities of the special investigator, Lewis Pope, could not have antagonized the leader of Memphis, for nothing in the investigation involved his organization. But Crump may well have been displeased by Pope's lucrative fees from collecting back taxes. Governor Browning refused, for some time, to reveal the terms of Pope's contract with the state, insisting that to make public that document would "handicap and obstruct the investigation."[20] The liquor issue was not a major cause of friction between the two political leaders, although they were on opposing sides. After failing to push through repeal of "bone dry" prohibition, the Shelby organization

settled for a compromise referendum on 23 September 1937 to determine the wishes of the electorate concerning prohibition. Governor
Browning announced that if the referendum favored ending prohibition, he would convene the assembly to consider it. He declared that
"I hope that every qualified voter in the State will express his opinion
. . . because I would certainly like to know the sentiment." He added,
"It's not necessary for me to restate my position—I'm voting dry," but,
"we ought to abide by the will of the people and suggest to the legislators
the regulation of the traffic."[21] The governor was safe in his position, for
he realized, as did Crump, that the referendum was a farce. Even if the
wets won, the representatives from the dry rural counties had a sufficient majority in the assembly to defeat repeal, since the referendum
was not binding on the legislature. Thus the Memphis machine, re-
garding the referendum as a "heads I win, tails you lose" proposition,
virtually ignored it, and as expected the electorate voted against repeal
in a light turnout.

The relationship between Browning and Crump continued to dete-
riorate during the summer of 1937. Not until October did the governor
deliberately do anything to antagonize Crump, nor did he actively seek
to destroy the ties that bound them politically. Yet he was determined
that no one would dictate to him. He believed he owed Crump nothing
and remarked that he "never asked for Crump's support back in '36."[22]
Consequently, he did not feel obligated to consult Crump on his appointments or state policy. On the other hand, a little diplomacy might
have soothed Crump's ego and allayed his fears. Browning's course however, was motivated by his desire to go to the Senate, and he wanted
to have a successful administration with some major accomplishments.
He was also a stubborn man.

Why did Crump become antagonistic toward Browning? His biographer suggests two reasons. Crump suspected that Browning was not
in sympathy with TVA and that he was in league with the old Luke Lea
faction. The argument that Browning's attitude toward TVA was heret-
ical is tenuous, for Crump knew of the governor's record on the regional
experiment before he endorsed him in the Democratic primary in 1936.
If Crump came to believe that Browning was an enemy of TVA, it was
because his other suspicions caused him to rationalize. The other reason, that members of the old Lea-Caldwell-Horton regime like Wallace
Edwards were in the Governor's administration, was probably more
significant to Crump. Crump was a rigid puritan, scrupulous in his dealings and standards of morality. The fact that no taint of corruption ever

involved those men seemed to indicate that Crump's fears were imaginary. Browning's estimate that the Memphis boss seized "every piece of evidence, no matter how circumstantial and remote," and magnified "it to damaging proportions," was partially right.[23] The differences that caused friction between the two leaders were small and unimportant. Latter-day representatives of two conflicting classes, their political marriage was an unnatural one from the beginning. Reports that all was not well between the two leaders were prevalent throughout the summer of 1937. They were on the brink of conflict when Joe Hatcher reported in the *Nashville Tennessean*, on 29 September 1937, that the ties that held Crump and Browning together were broken. He gave as the reasons Lewis Pope's activities as a special investigator and the whiskey referendum. Crump denied the report, but the fact that the two were on the verge of open hostilities was soon public knowledge.[24]

Confronted with persistent rumors about Crump's growing antagonism Gordon Browning felt compelled to determine the status of his relationship with the Memphis boss. His overriding concern at that moment was winning reelection and establishing a base from which to challenge for the Senate in 1940. Crump's opposition would have made achieving that goal more difficult. Browning must have realized that a break was inevitable. Steeped in the agrarian myth and the populist dogma that urban centers were dens of iniquity, he was sincerely convinced that the cancer of bossism and the corrupt political machine had to be cut out and the power of cities curbed. But the governor was also a pragmatic politician; as long as Crump did not impede his career, Browning could live with him. Lacking the virtue of patience, and as always restless, Browning resolved to determine Crump's attitude.

On 13 September 1937 the Governor visited Memphis and attended the Mid-South Fair with Crump and some of his lieutenants. Abe Waldauer, apparently at Browning's request, arranged a meeting between the two men in Crump's office. According to Crump's version of their conversation, the governor suggested an alliance that would control state offices for the next three years. Browning said: "I want you to go the United States Senate in 1940. I can send you!" In return for the governor's support in 1940, Crump was to support him for the Senate and Lewis Pope for governor in 1938. Crump replied that he had not asked for anything in return for his support in 1936, but that Browning could have appointed him senator when Bachman died. Now, he said, Browning "was offering me a mere shadow." Memphis Mayor Watkins Overton was also present at the meeting and corroborated the account given by Crump, demonstrating a memory that was extraordinarily sharp for detail.[25] Browning declared that the Memphis boss misinterpreted his offer and gave an exaggerated account of what he had said. He merely "intimated" that he might support Crump for the Senate when the next West Tennessee vacancy came up if he aspired to that post.[26] Both accounts of the conversation were biased. Already inclined to distrust the governor and predisposed to expect something unscrupulous, the imaginations of Crump and his lieutenants magnified Browning's remarks beyond his intent. The governor's version is credible. He must have known that the Memphis boss had no desire to return to Washington and he must also have suspected that Crump had been offended when he was not offered the senatorial appointment the previous April. Browning could not have been seriously offering a trade, but by hint or intimation he hoped to elicit the attitude of the Memphis boss. Perhaps he hoped to flatter Crump into a rapprochement and determine if it was possible to drive a wedge between the Shelby leader and Senator McKellar. At any rate, Browning left Memphis satisfied that the rift in his alliance with Crump was beyond repair.

Exhibiting a natural human trait, Gordon Browning was able to rationalize self-interest with idealism. He resolved to take the initiative and destroy Ed Crump and his urban political machine. His strategy was a bold, sudden, and massive frontal assault. On 1 October 1937 the leading newspapers of the state revealed rumors from the usual authoritative and reliable sources that Browning was considering a special session of the General Assembly to institute a county unit system for primary elections.

Under such a system, each county would have a unit vote based largely on population, but a maximum would be established effectively limiting the vote of the more heavily populated counties. Clearly the large block of votes in Shelby County would be the target of a unit system. The Memphis *Press-Scimitar* stated that Senate Speaker Byron S. Pope and House Speaker Walter Haynes were contacting members of the legislature to determine their attitudes toward a unit system.[27] Browning remained silent, apparently waiting to determine the response of the legislators. Crump was astounded and declared that anyone who tried to put over a unit plan was committing political suicide. "I can't believe it," he said, "for only a crazy man would do it."[28] The Memphis boss decided upon a swift, hard-hitting counterattack. On 6 October he disclosed to Null Adams, city editor of the *Press Scimitar*, his version of the meeting with Browning on 13 September. He told how the governor had proposed a gigantic political trade, and how, when he was refused, he had launched a crusade against Crump. He went on to insist that Browning was untrustworthy and that Lewis Pope and Luke Lea were behind the scheme. Pope may have conceived the idea but very likely the plan evolved in general discussions within the governor's official family.[29]

The war of words continued with a barrage from Browning who denied that he had proposed a trade with Crump He declared that the "fight is on between decent gov't and the forces of corruption." In response to the charge that he proposed a deal, he said:

> The expected has happened. Mr. Crump is running true to form. He has consistently betrayed every Governor he has supported since the late M. R. Patterson. Why I hoped for anything different from him is evidence of a liberal credulity. There is not a truthful statement in his whole harangue. . . .
>
> Mr. Crump's pride was hurt when I failed to appoint him to the United States Senate. Detecting that[,] I intimated to him that there might not be a conflict with any aspiration of his for the next vacancy from West Tennessee, if he wanted to run.
>
> He knew I made no condition whatever in that suggestion. He knew I gave no intimation whatever in that exchange that he was to support me for anything. I have never had any notion of running for the Senate in 1938. I will be elected to succeed myself as Governor that year, and I hereby announce my candidacy. He will live under my administration, whether he likes it or not.[30]

Two days later, 8 October, Browning went on a statewide radio network and made public his plans. He stated that he was calling a special session of the General Assembly to offer a unit plan to be put into effect in the state's primary elections. Devoting most of his speech to an attack on the Memphis organization, the governor never mentioned Crump by name but used such terms as "character assassin," "tsar," and "ruthless overlord." Browning declared, "He shall not hold a deluge of corrupt ballots over the head of the State like a sword of Damocles." The governor also insisted that he had no motive for his action except the "welfare of my State . . . So long as I am Governor no man can dictate my administration."[31] The following night, Mayor Watkins Overton of Memphis went on radio to reply to the governor's assault. He repeated the charge that Browning had offered a deal and that Browning with Luke Lea and Lewis Pope had evolved the unit scheme. He declared that the governor's record was sordid, that he was an ingrate, and that

Browning gladly accepted Crump's support in 1936 but then turned on the Memphis boss when he could not be bought.[32]

Governor Browning had raised an issue that appealed to rural Tennesseans, particularly those who were concerned about the power of the large voting block in Shelby County. Many of those around Browning accepted the conventional wisdom that the growing power of cities was a threat to the countryside, and they did not believe that it was contrary to the principles of democracy to enact a measure that would effectively disfranchise thousands of voters. One of the leaders of the rural block, state senator James H. Cummings of Woodbury, later declared that the principle behind the unit bill had been good, "otherwise you maintain a situation where the centers of wealth and population run the show and rural communities die on the vine." Browning's commissioner of the Department of Labor in 1937 and later a United States Senator, Albert Gore, forty years later conceded that the unit plan may have been undemocratic, but Crump was a ruthless boss, the most corrupting evil of democracy, so the end justified the means. And Browning maintained for the remainder of his life that the unit plan was just and the only way to curb the corrupt power of cities.[33] But he certainly would not have called the General Assembly into special session in 1937 if he had not been reasonably certain of the support necessary to enact such a measure. He had the cooperation of the rural triumverate, sometimes called the "Unholy Trinity," James H. Cummings, Walter Haynes, and I. D. Beasley. The governor also added a lengthy list of local bills to his call for the extraordinary session in order to give him additional bargaining power.

The state's press was almost unanimous in opposition to the plan. The *Nashville Tennessean,* once published by Luke Lea and the chief organ of the anti-Crump forces in the midstate area, attacked the unit scheme in a front-page editorial. Recently purchased by New Deal liberal Silliman Evans, the paper charged that the franchise would mean nothing under the system. The usually reserved *Chattanooga Times* declared that the governor had "committed himself, not to a program but to an act of reprisal which would result in an incalculable amount of harm to the State." The Columbia *Daily Herald* admitted that the people wanted to see Crump's power curbed and that it was desirable to try to clean up elections, but to deliberately disfranchise so many people just to check one man was unjust and undemocratic. Edward J. Meeman's Memphis *Press-Scimitar,* a bitter foe of Crump, declared that the plan was a scheme to build a personal political machine; substituting one machine for another was not progress, the editor maintained. Very few newspapers supported the governor. The *Chattanooga Free Press*, one of the exceptions, considered the unit system the lesser of two evils. The paper believed that the voters would receive a much better deal under a county unit vote because it was important to break Crump's influence in the state. The *Clarksville Leaf-Chronicle*, another exception, commented that the issue had been muddled by the exchange between Crump and Browning, but the fact remained that Shelby County had too great an influence on state affairs. The paper concluded that, if the unit system turned out to be a bad idea, any future legislature could repeal it. It was apparent that the governor, in declaring war on Crump's machine, had caused turmoil in the state and divided the citizenry into two camps. No middle of the road seemed to exist. Moreover, Browning had alienated a number of influential newspapers and individuals. The *Commercial Appeal* commented in an obvious understatement that he could hardly expect enthusiastic support in Shelby County in the governor's race in 1938.[34]

The extraordinary session of the Seventieth General Assembly convened on 11 October 1937 and immediately began to work on the unit scheme. In his message to the legislature, Governor Browning raised the bugbear of dictatorship and characterized the influence of Crump as a shadow of evil falling across the state. Because the governor could not pacify one individual, he said, the whole program of the administration was in danger. An evil shadow was making war "on your program and mine." He insisted that he was not willing for the wicked practices of stuffed ballot boxes and vote stealing to continue in Tennessee and concluded that the unit system was the only fair way to insure a free and honest count in elections. The message contained many references to corrupt elections in Shelby County, and that county's delegation moved to expunge from the record all references to its community, but the motion was tabled.[35] The General Assembly became a bitter battleground as tempers were on edge and both sides used explosive words. The governor's staff and legislative leaders used all the powers available to the chief executive to hold wavering members in line and commissioners Wallace Edwards and Albert Gore lobbied for the measure. One member of the assembly recalled that the pressure got "pretty terrific." After declaring his opposition to the unit bill, he was besieged with visits by members of Browning's staff. Enticements were offered: he would be given more patronage, his indebtedness could be taken care of, and a well-paying state job could be made available. Someone even intimated that his brother, a regional supervisor in the Department of Welfare, might be discharged if he did not conform.[36] The Shelby delegation tried every parliamentary maneuver in a futile attempt to block passage of the measure.[37] Senator McKellar asked for and was granted a hearing before the assembly at which time he pleaded with the legislators to defeat the proposed unit system. He called the bill "treason to the Democratic Party," and "a brazen attempt to disfranchise thousands of honest voters."[38]

Despite the efforts of the Shelby delegation, the governor's legislative leaders controlled enough votes and the unit bill passed on 20 October. The measure repealed the existing primary laws governing nominations for governor, United States senators, and railroad and public utilities commissioners. According to the new bill, each county would have a county unit vote—the number of votes cast for the party nominee for governor in the previous general election, divided by one hundred. The maximum unit vote, regardless of the total vote cast, was one eighth of one percent of the population of the county according to the latest federal census. The candidate carrying the highest number of popular votes in each county would receive the full unit vote. Under the law, Shelby and other metropolitan counties would presumably be equal with counties of average size.[39] The Columbia *Daily Herald* commented after passage of the measure that the governor had won his Pyrrhic victory, but the conflict had just begun.[40] Not content with that victory, the governor's legislative leaders advanced another measure designed to undermine the power of Crump's machine within Shelby County. On the same day that the unit measure passed, a bill calling for a purge of voter registration books was sent to the General Assembly. The measure, which passed eight days later, authorized the governor to make an investigation, upon charges of illegality, of registration lists in each county and to purge names fraudulently placed on the books.[41] Although Shelby was not mentioned by name, the measure was aimed at that county and Browning delegated the probe to the state's special investigator, Lewis Pope.

Meanwhile, the anti-unit forces were not idle. The very day that the system was enacted into law, Crump and his allies began drafting a suit, thereby looking to the courts for recourse. A group of taxpayers headed by Charles A. Gates, Trustee of Shelby County, asked the Davidson Chancery Court for an injunction to prevent the unit act from being enforced. The basis for the contest was the charge that a senator and four representatives had participated in debate and had voted in the assembly while they held state jobs. That violated the constitution, the suit claimed, and the unit act was therefore illegally passed. The constitutionality of the unit system itself was not an issue in the challenge. On 26 October Chancellor R. B. C. Howell of the Davidson Chancery ruled the act invalid, upholding the contention of the challenge, and granted a temporary injunction to prevent the measure from going into effect. More important, Chancellor Howell said in effect that the court had the right of judicial review, and he established ground for taking the case to the state Supreme Court. The opponents of the act were jubilant.

While the governor's opponents waited on the slow process of litigation, Browning remained on the offensive. Early in November, he called the assembly into another extraordinary session for the twofold purpose of creating a state crime commission and increasing the membership of the State Board of Elections. "He'll spew in his own grease," sputtered Crump. "He robbed us, stole our friendship, and then deserted us."[42] Browning went on a statewide radio network to defend his actions. In an extensive report on his legislative program, with special emphasis on accomplishments such as debt reorganization and conservation, he declared that the Shelby crowd had opposed much of his program. He charged that the Memphis machine was a threat to honest government and constructive legislation, but he accepted the challenge:

> Let the threats now being breathed out by the satellites be saved for timid souls. If I had been afraid I would have desisted when the "boss" blew his breath and snorted his vengeance. I have yet asked no quarter, and say now—
> Lay on MacDuff,
> And damned be he who first says Hold enough . . .
> My fellow citizens, a statement by the great apostle I verily believe to be fitting here, when he said: "for we wrestle not against flesh and blood, but against principalities, against powers, against the rulers of the darkness of this world, against spiritual wickedness in high places."
> No, I have no apology to make for an honest attempt to redeem the State from his clutches . . . [43]

The State Board of Elections had three members, one from each of the Grand Divisions of the state, elected by the legislature to serve six-year terms, and no more than two could represent the majority party. In 1937 the membership of the board consisted of Abe Waldauer, chairman; Reed Sharp, of Nashville, a foe of the governor; and Republican Robert T. Johnson, Jr., of Elizabethton. Browning proposed to increase the membership of the board to six, one additional member from each geographical division, and two Democrats and one Republican. Waldauer, the liaison between Crump's organization and the governor, was in a difficult position. Rumors that he would resign were prevalent for several days, but on 9 November Waldauer announced that he would remain on the board. In an emotionally charged radio address he stated that the long friendship with Browning was broken. He declared that the governor, in proposing to increase the membership of the board, had impugned his reputation and thus repudiated his friendship. Waldauer said that he would not be forced out of his position and would, in fact, continue the struggle against the governor's tactics. Browning's war on Crump had destroyed a friendship that began in the dugouts of France during World War I. The *Banner* commented "It is the end of . . . the finest romance known to Tennessee politics. . . . Bonds cut after 20 years of near legendary proportions." Browning's reaction to Waldauer's speech was "I have suffered a great tragedy." The paper noted that "tears ran down his cheeks as he spoke."[44]

The assembly met again that day and the Election Board was the first order of business. Seven days later, the assembly passed the bill, increasing the membership according to the governor's proposal.[45] In effect, the measure restored control of election machinery to the administration because the pro-Browning legislature was certain to elect supporters of the governor. Moreover, it gave Browning indirect power in every county of the state since the State Board was authorized to appoint county elections board members. Two days later, 18 November, the assembly authorized the governor to appoint a commission of three to investigate the whole scope of detection, prosecution, detention, apprehension, punishment, and treatment of persons accused of crime. The commission was given subpoena power to investigate persons, documents, and papers. Yet another weapon was now available to Browning in his war against Crump, the power to investigate alleged corrupt activities in Memphis and Shelby County.[46] Enemies of the administration again went to the courts. In December, they filed a petition with the Davidson Chancery Court asking for an injunction against the act increasing the State Board of Elections for the same reason that the unit system injunction was granted. On the sixteenth, Chancellor Howell granted an injunction against the act, thus assuring that the Tennessee Supreme Court would review the case and blocking temporarily any action taken by the new board. Yet the governor continued the offensive in January 1938 by dismissing James M. McCormack,

Commissioner of Banking and Insurance. McCormack, appointed to please the Crump machine, was the only remaining member of the organization in the administration. Comptroller John W. Britton of Knoxville replaced him, and Marshall Priest of Huntingdon became comptroller. Crump called the removal of McCormack an example of Browning's "brag" merit system for, according to the Memphis boss, Browning had said a short time before that McCormack was doing a good job.[47]

The governor's massive assault on the Memphis machine had caught Crump and Senator McKellar by surprise. Reeling and on the defensive, with the odds seemingly against them, the two were determined to keep up the fight until Browning was defeated. If there had been even the slightest rift between the senator and Crump, the governor's war reunited them and brought the old friends closer together than ever. McKellar apparently never said anything, but he must have felt a sense of satisfaction in the knowledge that he had warned the Memphis boss about Browning. Most certainly McKellar's friends throughout the state were overjoyed by the split between Crump and the governor, for the Memphis boss "had no choice but to turn to them" for help. And it must have been privately rewarding to the senator when Crump was forced to come to him immediately for assistance.[48] At any rate, the two began working as a team in the propaganda war on Browning. Crump urged that they "keep the fire on the 'sneak'—I really think we should keep it up. However, we must not run out of ammunition—keep some of the best stuff in reserve."[49] But Crump did not lose his head and attack wildly, and he shrewdly avoided issues that might have had repercussions. Browning's military service, for example, had been commendable and therefore inviolate. "Lets not move in on Browning's war record," Crump warned.[50] Privately, the Memphis boss and McKellar worked closely to organize all the antiadministration forces to fight the legislative measures as well as to find agreeable candidates for the Democratic primary in August 1938. But Crump would have to depend more on McKellar's contacts than his own; the senator had ties with East Tennessee Republicans and commanded the allegiance of federal employees across the state. It remained to be seen whether the Memphis boss and his ally could put together a political alliance sufficiently strong to win the war with Governor Browning.

It was apparent by early 1938 that Gordon Browning's attack on Ed Crump had caused turmoil and polarized the state. The results were not as he had hoped; signs already indicated that his popularity had declined. The response among moderate to liberal Tennesseans to the governor's sudden offensive had first been surprise and incredulity which gradually changed to anger. Longtime anti-Crump liberals found themselves allied with the Memphis machine. The state's press was almost unanimous in opposing Browning's measures. The *Nashville Tennessean* reflected the bitterness of the opposition when it declared that as long as the county unit system remained on the statute books, the franchise, so far as the primary was concerned, was a mockery. According to that paper, the "county unit act was ill-conceived, ignobly pointed, callously jammed through the Assembly by the most reprehensible of machine tactics." Governor Browning, the *Tennessean* argued, was employing the same dictatorial tactics that he accused the Crump machine of using.[51] Browning realized that he needed to score an important coup to get back into the good graces of the voters. That was the reason why he came forward in January 1938 with a grandiose scheme for the state to cooperate with the federal government in advancing the Tennessee Valley Authority.

By 1938 the massive multipurpose redevelopment program had already begun to fulfill its promises by providing low cost electric power and employment, and it had found favor with Tennesseans. Even so, the agency had yet to become institutionalized. Although the major battle had been won when Congress created the program in 1933, the need for continuing appropriations met stiff resistance. Internal difference concerning the TVA focus had not been settled, and a bitter feud among its directors, A. E. Morgan, David Lilienthal, and H. A. Morgan, still raged. Finally, the legal battles over the constitutionality of TVA were continuing. Early in 1938 there were still more than one hundred suits in litigation challenging the river redevelopment program, and its constitutionality was not firmly established until 1939.[52] Such was the situation when, in January 1938, Browning publicly outlined a proposal that the state of Tennessee and TVA cooperate in the purchase of the facilities of the state's largest private power company, Tennessee Electric Power Company. Wendell Wilkie, president of Commonwealth and Southern, the parent company of TEPCO, had recently proposed the sale of TEPCO properties to TVA. Browning suggested that "the generating and transmission facilities be purchased and operated by one or more power districts of the state of Tenn." In other words, Tennessee would join hands with the federal government to hasten the distribution of power to the people of Tennessee. Shortly thereafter Browning reported that he had talked with the president about the plan, that

Roosevelt had expressed deep interest, and had invited him to the White House for a top level conference with administrative and congressional leaders. However, on 25 January, Roosevelt denied that he had requested a conference. He said that Browning had asked for a meeting and one had been set up but he had no idea what it was about.[53]

Browning's foes, particularly Crump and McKellar, were quick to express opposition to the proposed cooperative purchase. Crump questioned the motives behind the venture and accused Browning of being in league with the power trust. The Memphis boss also wrote to the president voicing his opposition to Browning's plan to purchase TEPCO, but it was McKellar who built opposition to the scheme in Washington. Officials in the nation's capital demonstrated little enthusiasm for the project. David Lilienthal was cold to the plan but declared he would keep an open mind and study it; Senator George W. Norris, father of TVA, expressed his opposition. Only one member of Congress, Representative John Rankin of Mississippi, a staunch supporter of TVA, showed interest in Browning's proposition. On 27 January the governor had a private meeting with President Roosevelt. It was not a high-level conference and accounts of the meeting indicated that Browning's reception was cool and the president polite but unmoved. In a press conference the following day, Roosevelt had "no comment" about the cooperative purchase plan.[54] Senator McKellar had gotten to the president first. "There is no danger at this end of the line," he informed Crump. "Governor Browning's attempt to worm himself into the TVA situation has been a flop. . . . I had a long talk with the President on last Tuesday and acquainted him with every detail of the situation. I think he understands perfectly."[55]

The governor's attempt to score a great coup over his opponents was a failure. Rather than return home after the meeting with the president and admit defeat, Browning distorted the fact that he had been rebuffed and claimed that the conference had been highly satisfactory. In a radio report to the people of Tennessee he insisted that his proposition would insure quick rural electrification and that he had Roosevelt's blessing to pursue the plan. Much of his talk was spent in lashing out at the press coverage of his visit to Washington. The newspapers in the state, he said, had incorrectly reported the president's reaction to the cooperative purchase plan and had consistently misquoted him: "Some papers in the State saw fit to reject the service of the responsible news agencies, and published scurrilous and falsified versions of what took place."[56] In reality, the cooperative purchase plan was a dead letter and a distasteful setback for the man who was struggling to recoup his lost voter appeal.

Browning received an even more stinging defeat when the Tennessee Supreme Court handed down its decision on the constitutionality of the unit system. The decision, based on the suit by Charles A. Gates, Trustee of Shelby County, attacked the constitutionality of the unit act because of alleged illegal service by five members of the General Assembly. In a four to one decision, the court dismissed the question of membership in the legislature by concluding that each house had the right to determine the qualifications of its members. It thus reversed the chancery court's opinion. However, the justices declared that citizens were entitled to the protection of the fourteenth amendment of the Constitution of the United States and that a state could not confer the right of franchise upon one class of voters and deprive another class, unless the discrimination could be justified on some rational basis. The court concluded that in the American form of government a large vote could not be regarded as evil and be dealt with under the police power of the state.[57] The court held in effect that the law was aimed primarily at Memphis and disfranchised the voters of that city. The opinion came as a surprise to many political leaders but the governor's opponents were jubilant; Crump declared that "Sparta perished for want of Spartans. . . . This Jekyll and Hyde government will perish August 4 for want of votes!"[58] The *Commercial Appeal* reported happily that Memphis was still part of the state. The *Nashville Banner* expressed the opinion of most when it stated that the unit system deserved to die and that the court's opinion was a stinging rebuke to the political ambitions of one man.[59] Governor Browning refused to comment. He said later that the decision came as "a bolt out of the blue," because he "had an inside tip that the Court would uphold the law."[60]

The decision by the Tennessee Supreme Court was a stunning blow to Governor Browning's cause and put him on the defensive. He had lost the issue on which he had planned to base his reelection campaign. Moreover, the 1938 governor's race was well under way, and his opponents were on the offensive. Browning's forces groped frantically for some means to recover the lost ground. One alternative considered was to call another extraordinary session of the General Assembly to repeal the poll tax for the primary, a tool effectively used by the Crump machine. However, it appeared that the governor's grip on the legislature was slipping. Although Browning remained silent, the *Tennessean* reported on 15 February, three days after the court's decision on the unit bill, that some of his supporters expressed doubt that he could muster enough strength to get the measure through the House of Representatives. Eleven days later, the same newspaper reported that for the time being the governor had decided to forego plans for a new session of the legislature on the advice of his cabinet. The cabinet recommended a delay to see if a purge of the voting registration books weakened the Shelby organization. If that failed, it recommended calling a special session to repeal the poll tax for the primary.[61] Browning realized that repeal would have been difficult to obtain but that, more important, he could not afford another defeat. Nevertheless, rumors of a special session persisted throughout the spring and early summer of 1938.

The governor's side won an important victory in March when the Tennessee Supreme Court upheld the legislative act of November 1937 which increased the membership of the State Elections Board. Browning was reported to be visibly happy over the decision and immediately announced that Lew Ware would become the chairman of the board. The board met the following week, removed Abe Waldauer as chairman, elected Ware to that post, and held hearings on ouster petitions against three Shelby County elections commissioners charged with fraudulent voter registrations. A few days later the three commissioners were removed and three new members appointed — Galen Tate, an old foe of Crump; Sam Johnson; and David Hanover. Governor Browning's forces were again on the offensive.

Meanwhile, the anti-Browning factions were beginning to coalesce. The chief problem was to present a unified front behind one candidate for governor. On 19 February some antiadministration leaders met in Memphis to discuss possible candidates to oppose the governor and his appointee to the Senate, George L. Berry. The following day, Congressman Walter Chandler of the tenth district, Shelby County, and Browning's World War comrade, announced that he would be a candidate for the gubernatorial nomination and that he had Crump's full support. Browning responded that Crump gave him an additional issue: "The boss is shaping the matter so well for me I don't think I should disturb it."[62] Crump seldom placed one of his own men in a statewide political contest. A few days later state Senator Prentice Cooper of Shelbyville made it known that he would seek the nomination for governor. Although only forty-three at the time, Cooper had adequate credentials. A veteran of the First World War, he had been state commander of the American Legion, was once a district attorney general, had served one term in the state House of Representatives, and in 1936 had been elected state senator. During the regular session of the General Assembly in 1937 he had sponsored the measure calling for the referendum on prohibition and in the extraordinary sessions he had been an outspoken opponent of the governor's measures. Small, dark, and known for an often volatile temper, Cooper was a lawyer, a gentleman farmer, and an "intensely private" man, shunning publicity. His announcement for governor came as something of a surprise. Cooper's reasons for entering the race were not clear. According to one often repeated story, his father, banker William P. Cooper, was being urged to run by some political leaders; the elder Cooper declined but pointed to his son and announced that he would finance his campaign. Cooper may have entered the race only to bargain for a cabinet post.[63] If that was true, it must have been gratifying when anti-Browning forces began to shift to him as the most available man to defeat the governor. Cooper quickly received the endorsement of Silliman Evans, publisher of the *Tennessean*. Now apparently Crump had doubts about Chandler's availability; the most important question was whether a member of the Shelby organization would have statewide drawing power. A canvass of the state indicated that support for one of the machine's own men was only lukewarm and that a candidate outside the county would draw better. McKellar also had reservations about Chandler; he was persuaded by his friends that the anti-Shelby vote would be lost, giving Browning the edge. Undoubtedly the Senator expressed his reservations to Crump, and within a few days Chandler withdrew from the race acknowledging that the antiadministration forces preferred a candidate beyond Memphis. Although Crump may not have been enthusiastic about Cooper, he immediately announced that he would support the Shelbyville attorney. The Memphis boss had never met Cooper and entered into no bargain with him. Cooper did not have the attributes of a vigorous leader, but it appeared that he had a chance of being elected if the anti-Browning factions presented a unified effort. Indeed they did, for all groups opposed to the administration began to rally to Cooper.[64]

The chief problem for the Crump-McKellar alliance at that juncture was to find someone to run against Senator Berry, who had already announced that he was a candidate for the full term. Congressman Sam McReynolds had considered making the race but withdrew leaving those opposed to Berry distressed, for they considered him the strongest and most qualified candiate to unseat the incumbent. But on 21 March Tom Stewart of Winchester, Burgin Dossett's state campaign manager in 1936 and McKellar's friend, officially became a candiate for the Senate. He was not widely known, despite the fact that he had been the attorney general of record in the prosecution of John Thomas Scopes in Dayton's "monkey" trial in 1925.[65] Crump quickly endorsed this second unexciting candidate for statewide post, overlooking two other seekers for the Senate, Congressman J. Ridley Mitchell and Ned Carmack, the son of the late Senator Edward Carmack. In April Cooper, Stewart, and William David Hudson, candidate for one of the posts as Railroad and Public Utilities Commissioner, announced that they would carry on a coalition campaign, a rarity in Tennessee. Following the long established tradition, Browning ran independently of Berry and was well advised to do so; Senator Berry, because of his monetary claims against TVA, was a liability.

Tennessee has witnessed many bitter and hard-fought political campaigns, but few surpassed the intensity of the struggle in the Democratic primary in 1938. And it was not a spotless campaign, for both sides practiced bare-knuckle, no-holds-barred, gutter tactics. None of the candidates left anything to chance, bending every effort both in public and behind the scenes to gain advantages. Browning's forces, in control of the vast state bureaucracy, used every weapon available to the administration to secure support; political assessment of employees was common and hiring, firing, and trading to influence votes was practiced. Senator McKellar used the same techniques to guarantee the support of federal employees for Cooper and Stewart. The state was inundated with campaign posters, banners, pamphlets, and newspaper advertisements, and there was no shortage of oratory.

Browning plunged into his campaign with typical energy. His speeches were a combination of biting humor and satire with eloquence as he unleashed a savage attack on Ed Crump. The governor set the theme of his campaign in his opening speech at Murfreesboro on 4 June. After a lengthy recital of the accomplishments of his administration, he concluded with the assertion that the real issue in the campaign was "bossism." "The question to settle," he said, "is whether the people or a dictator will control Tennessee."[66] The campaign became, in effect, a showdown between Browning and Crump; it was a struggle for political survival in which the other participants were incidental. In the weeks that followed, Browning continued to cite his record of honest leadership and constructive accomplishments: more efficient government, orderly retirement of the state's debt, a merit system in civil service, and better schools. Often he would point out, with some truth, that his opponents distorted his record. Nor was his campaign devoid of con-

structive suggestions. From time to time he advanced the proposition
that the next General Assembly call a constitutional convention to repeal
the prohibition on an income tax. In a state where sources of revenue
were not numerous, the governor saw in an income tax a more equitable
means of revenue than a retail sales tax could provide. Browning also
urged the abolition of the poll tax, although that was part of his attack
on the Crump machine. Although many voters may have been repelled
by the prospect of an income tax, taxation was not an important issue
in the campaign. Neither was education. The governor's critics could
not truthfully say that he was not doing the most any governor could in
the field of public education, for his appropriation measures were as
high as the state's revenue would allow. Browning also endorsed the
Tennessee Education Association's 1938 program for the improvement
of education. But no matter how often he called attention to his accomplishments, he found them ignored, and his fight with Crump remained
the central feature of the campaign. The governor therefore fell back on
the time-honored technique of creating a bugbear. Browning repeatedly
charged that the evil dictatorship in Memphis was trying to extend its
power across the state and assumed the role of a knight in shining armor
fighting for decency and democracy.

Prentice Cooper carried on a comparatively quiet campaign, emphasizing his support for TVA and attacking Governor Browning for his dictatorial measures. Neither a figurehead nor a puppet for the Crump
machine, he was simply an available candidate, and all the antiadministration forces rallied to him. Cooper displayed his independence when
he refused to endorse a platform prepared by Crump, preferring instead
to write his own.[67] More important to Crump, however, was Cooper's
apparent lack of aggressiveness. The candidate simply did not generate
sufficient enthusiasm among the electorate to please the Memphis boss.
With resignation, Crump wrote, "we will have to go on through — make
the best of the matter."[68] But Cooper did not carry the entire burden
of the campaign; Crump and McKellar, in cooperation, conducted their
own attack on the governor. Luke Lea remained the whipping boy, as
Crump charged that Lea was behind every move made by Browning.
The Memphis boss thus raised his own bugbear because Lea did not
play an important role in the administration.

McKellar's organization went all-out to defeat both Berry and Browning. He kept repeating the charge that Browning had not voted for TVA
and was the tool of the private power interests. The anti-TVA theme
quickly became the most effective weapon to use against the governor.

Crump and McKellar agreed that the mass of voters would not get excited over talk of political alliances involving Browning, Luke Lea, and Lewis Pope, but would get worked up over the success of a plan to help the working class.[69] Both repeatedly attacked Browning's record on TVA, and in so doing, raised a false issue. They simply put doubt in the voters' minds by constantly charging that Browning was an enemy of the regional development program, but they utterly failed to demonstrate conclusively that he was a tool of private power interests or an opponent of TVA. Although Crump and McKellar made TVA a leading issue, they did not ignore the legislative acts of October and November 1937 because the electorate was concerned about them. In that respect, the real issue was present in the campaign: should the man who had tried to disfranchise so many voters and who was using the very tactics he accused the Crump machine of using be retained in the governor's office? Browning had in reality created that issue by calling the legislature into special sessions and ramming the unit system, the crime probe, the voter registration purge, and an enlarged State Elections Board through the General Assembly in his war on one man. In the final weeks of the campaign, the citizens of the state were treated to full-page newspaper advertisements written by Crump, which castigated the governor with stinging invectives and appellations such as "hypocrite," "ingrate," and "dictator." The advertisements pointed out that Browning gladly accepted Crump's support in 1936 but then turned on him when he could not be bribed.[70]

Meanwhile, the fireworks continued in the struggle over control of voter registration books in Shelby County. In April, the Chancery Court of Davidson County enjoined the pro-Browning Shelby County Board of Elections from seizing the books, but on 27 May the Tennessee Supreme Court held that the commissioners were entitled to function until controversies over their appointments were settled in court. The court also upheld the act creating the state crime commission. The governor immediately ordered the new Shelby board to seize control of that county's election machinery. Abe Waldauer, however, got possession of the books and began his own purge of the voter lists. Attorney General Roy Beeler ruled that Shelby's books had to be turned over to the pro-Browning board and that they must be kept in the county court house. Waldauer surrendered the books, and early in July the governor's board began an immediate purge of voter registration. How many names were actually removed cannot be known, but the figure of 13,437 given by chairman Galen Tate now appears to be extravagant.[71] At the same time the crime commission moved into Memphis to investigate alleged criminal activities in elections. The hearings turned into a verbal battleground in which accusations of bribery, vote stealing, and stuffed ballot boxes were hurled at the Shelby organization. Despite all that was said about the revelations of criminal activities, all the hearings proved was that the Memphis machine was well organized, registered its supporters, and got them to the polls on election day. Nothing in the way of criminal activity in elections was demonstrated.[72]

Although no criminal activities in the conduct of elections were uncovered by the commission, the Memphis political organization was engaged in illegal and unethical practices all the while. Because of the hotly contested races and because the machine felt threatened by Browning's crusade, efforts to enforce the allegiance of Memphians were stepped up: known and suspected opponents were kept under surveillance by the police, loyalty checks were made on husbands and wives of teachers and city employees, and harassment and intimidation of dissidents were common. The harassment of a mortician, a Browning supporter, was a case in point. Ambulance drivers in his employ were often stopped by the police and given citations for traffic violations.[73] The machine was also accused of assault. Attorney Ben Kohn, a Crump opponent and Browning partisan, charged that he received a beating by a thug or thugs in the hire of Crump's organization. The machine had long been aware of Kohn, regarded him as a troublemaker, and a "disgruntled politician who had supported numerous opposition tickets in our city."[74] The complicity of the organization in the assault was never demonstrated but a newspaper reporter claimed to have located the hideout of the accused attacker, one Sidney Queen, in Oceola, Arkansas, along with evidence of a payoff coming from parties in the Memphis city government.[75]

Browning was quick to use the Kohn incident as proof that dictatorship existed in Memphis and tried to get as much mileage out of it as possible. Hoping, perhaps, to convince some that his charges about the machine were true, the governor announced in late May that he had created a state police force under a 1919 statute. He stated that M. N. Lowry of Memphis had been appointed chief of the force and that between thirty and fifty men were commissioned as members with about the same number to be sworn in later. Members of the force were authorized, he said, to carry badges and arms. He was vague about the force and did not define its duties, but it was assumed that the special unit was to be used in Memphis to preserve law and order. The immediate reaction in Memphis to the formation of the police force was anger. Shelby County Sheriff Guy Joyner threatened to arrest members of the force if they invaded the county, and Memphis police commissioner Clifford Davis remarked that he would defy the force if it tried to operate in Memphis. Crump commented in his usual acrid manner that Browning realized that he was beaten: "He's desperate, The mad dog bites himself." Mayor Watkins Overton, in a less defiant tone, said that the Memphis police force was capable of protecting the citizens of the community. He offered police guard for "any of Gordon Browning's few remaining supporters" in Memphis.[76] Did this special force exist in reality, or was it a bluff by the governor? Only the identity of the appointed chief, M. N. Lowry, was made public; the names of the thirty to fifty officers were never disclosed. In all probability the governor's alleged creation of a state police force was a threat designed to lend credibility to the Kohn attack and to convey to the public the belief that violence was a technique of the Memphis machine. Nothing more was heard concerning the special force. Indeed, Crump was correct in his estimate that Browning was desperate. Nevertheless, the Memphis machine left nothing to chance. A list was compiled of those suspected of being members of the special force.[77] And, according to journalist Clark Porteous, the organization prepared to meet force with force. A large number of men were deputized and a local firm that manufactured ax handles was commissioned to make clubs to use if the special force appeared in Memphis.[78] The city almost became an armed camp and a closed society.

June brought more woes for Governor Browning. On the sixth, his opponents seized the reins of the Democratic party in Tennessee at a meeting of the State Primary Board and immediately installed county boards that were antiadministration. To add to the governor's woes, a truck weight scandal involving the commissioner of the Department of Finance and Taxation, Walter Stokes, was made public. The scandal alleged that large trucking firms made payoffs to allow their overweight trucks to pass over state highways. Moreover, the governor had little press support. The *Tennessean*, once the chief organ of the anti-Crump factions, was on the same side with the Memphis organization. On 31 July the paper editorially summed up Browning's actions during the previous twelve months as "The Year of Disgrace." The paper also sought to compare Governor Browning with the governor commonly regarded as the worst in the state's history, W. G. Brownlow. The *Tennessean* carried a full page Sunday supplement story about this "carpetbag governor," describing how Brownlow resorted to disfranchisement of the electorate and establishment of a police force to maintain his hold on the state. The *Chattanooga Times* opposed the Shelby County machine but supported Prentice Cooper because of its desire to see Browning retired. The *Times* rationalized that Cooper was not owned by Crump and that the Memphis boss supported Cooper only because he seemed to be the most likely instrument to defeat Browning. The *Knoxville News-Sentinel* expressed the sentiments of many when it said that Browning's administration was unsatisfactory but to hope for something better from Cooper was useless. The paper concluded that the only hope was for better candidates two years later. The *Press-Scimitar*, Crump's most vitriolic press foe, refused to endorse either candidate. The *Labor Advocate*, published in Nashville, insisted that the governor's attitude toward labor was negative and that the legislature was controlled by "Browning and Labor haters." The State Non-Partisan Political Campaign Committee of the American Federation of Labor's Trades and Labor Council endorsed Cooper because the working man had "received no consideration whatever from the [Browning] Administration."[79]

In July, Browning committed a tactical error. On the fourth of that month W. T. McLain, District Attorney General for Shelby County and a ranking member of the Shelby organization, died. State law required that the vacancy be filled at the next biennial election occurring thirty days or more after the vacancy occurred but the governor could make an interim appointment. If Browning declared a special election to be held during the regular county general election on 4 August his interim appointee would hold office only until the one chosen in that election took office on 1 September 1938. However, Browning held that the letter of the law required that the vacancy be "more" than thirty days before the biennial election. Therefore the special election would take place in August 1940, and his interim appointee would serve more than two years. Crump immediately denounced Browning for not calling a special election on 4 August, and City Judge Marion Boyd announced that he would be a candidate for the post in the special election that he confidently expected to be held in August 1938. State Attorney Roy Beeler ruled that, according to the state code, the governor had to call a special election in August. He declared that if McLain had lived another forty-eight hours, Browning would have had the right to appoint someone to fill the vacancy until 1940. The governor ignored Beeler's ruling and named Joseph Hanover as interim Shelby County District Attorney until 1 September 1940. Memphis Criminal Judge Phil Wallace refused to administer the oath to Hanover and arbitrarily made an appointment of his own to serve until after the August election. The problem was finally settled on 21 July, when Chancellor L. D. Bejach, a member of the Crump organization, issued a mandatory injunction which required the proadministration Shelby election board to hold a special election on 4 August and to permit the name of Judge Boyd to appear on the ballot. The following day, Supreme Court Justice C. P. McKinney upheld Bejach's ruling.[80] The episode was another embarrasing setback for Browning.

Browning realized that he faced an uphill struggle and possible defeat. His speeches became more strident and lacked the usual humor as he searched for an advantage. In so doing, he began to throw wild punches on the chance that one would land. As the campaign drew to a close, for example, he threatened to send portions of Tennessee's National Guard into Memphis just before the primary to maintain law and order. No immediate announcement was made, but the press got suspicious when the train scheduled to take West Tennessee units of the 117th Infantry of the Guard to summer encampment in Biloxi, Mississippi, was cancelled. Adjutant General R. O. Smith finally confirmed that portions of the Guard would be mobilized and moved into Memphis on 3 August, the eve of the primary. The governor refused to comment, but the move was obviously an attempt to back up his claims of probable violence, intimidations, criminal assaults, and vote stealing in Shelby County on election day. Outbursts of protests came from all over the state. The *Nashville Banner*'s front-page editorial, characteristic of press reaction, censured Browning for his apparent decision to use troops in Memphis, and declared that the people of the state had been humiliated enough by his actions.[81] Crump had learned in June that the use of the Guard was being contemplated and asked Senator McKellar to find out if the governor had the authority. The senator replied that he had checked with the War Department and learned that Browning had that discretion. He then added, "I think it would be best for you to see that there is not the slightest disorder or the slightest pretext for him calling out the troops."[82] Even so, the Shelby forces took quick action after the adjutant general's announcement. A petition was placed before Crump's cousin, Federal Judge John Martin of Memphis, asking him to enjoin the use of troops, and he quickly complied with the restraining order. The governor made his first statement on the matter on the night of 31 July. He denied that he had ordered Guard units to Memphis and said that he would not do so "unless I change my mind." On 1 August he made his first appearance in Memphis at a rally at the Fairgrounds. As he appeared at the speaker's platform, a United States marshal delivered Judge Martin's restraining order. Browning was overheard to say: "I'm not going to listen." In the speech that followed the governor repeated his charges of stuffed ballot boxes and corruption and defended his threat to send troops to Memphis to preserve law and order.[83] Somehow, his words had a hollow sound, and his threat to send troops was an empty one. *Tennessean* reporter John M. Burns, assigned to follow Browning in the campaign, wrote at the end of the year that the biggest news story of 1938 was the one that did not happen. He related how the governor kept telling audiences all over the state that violence would occur in Memphis and reporters came to expect a riot when Browning went to that city on 1 August. Newsmen following the governor were actually surprised, but relieved, when conflict failed to materialize.[84]

The election on 4 August 1938 proved to be calm and peaceful. The electorate spoke in a resounding manner, retiring Governor Browning to private life again. He won only two congressional districts and thirty-three of ninety-five counties, many of them by narrow margins. He lost all the urban areas; his strength was largely rural. Browning's largest number of votes was in West Tennessee where he carried twelve of sixteen counties and the seventh and eighth congressional districts. Prentice Cooper built up a substantial lead in East and Middle Tennessee and crossed the Tennessee River into the western portion comfortably ahead. The margin was cut somewhat in West Tennessee, but he still went into Shelby County with a 31,000 vote margin. Shelby gave Cooper 58,000 votes to a surprising 9,000 for Browning. The final total was 238,000 for Cooper and 150,000 for the incumbent.[85] It was a humiliating defeat for the governor, but even more embarassing was the fact that Cooper would have won under the county unit system by an even more decisive margin had it been in effect. The challenger would have carried 2,270 votes out of a 2,991–unit total. The unit system had been designed to reduce the influence of urban centers, however, it was not only ill conceived but hastily drawn. The voting power of the five largest counties in Tennessee would have been reduced, but the great majority of small, rural counties would also have lost enough to balance what the heavily populated counties lost.

Governor Browning's appointee to the Senate, George L. Berry, was also decisively defeated. Berry, a supporter of the New Deal and allegedly appointed so that President Roosevelt could have more support for his court reform bill, changed his theme during the campaign and charged the New Deal with extravagant waste in government spending. The senatorial primary produced a scandal of assessments, shakedowns, and coercion of state and federal employees which was not separate from the governor's race. So widespread were those tactics that Chairman Morris Shepherd of the United States Senate's Campaign Expenditures Committee began an investigation in July. The committee's report revealed that the Cooper, Stewart, and Hudson group assessed and collected campaign funds from postal, Internal Revenue, and other federal employees having civil service status, and from some individuals in relief classification. The committee also found that similar contributions were solicited and obtained by the Browning-Berry forces from state employees whose salaries were derived in part from federal sources and from persons working on Works Progress Administration projects.[86] No further action was taken beyond filing the report.

In 1936 Gordon Browning was elected governor by the largest majority in Tennessee's history. His defeat in 1938 was not because he lost the support of Crump's machine; it was because he lost the support of the people of Tennessee. In 1936 he won outside of Shelby County, and in 1938 he lost outside of Shelby. Browning's unit system, the purge, the increase in the members of the Elections Board, the establishment of a crime commission, and his arbitrary use of power—the same power he accused Crump of using—were all causes of his defeat. Memphis *Press-Scimitar* Editor, Edward J. Meeman, suggested that Browning's ambition to be elected to the Senate in 1940 was the reason for his defeat. "Had he 'flung away ambition'and concentrated on the job of being governor,"asserted Meeman, "the headlines today would read: 'Browning Renominated by Immense Majority, Exceeding That of 1936.'"[87] After the primary, there were rumors that Browning would be an independent candidate in the general election but he conceded the loss, congratulated Cooper, and stated that he would abide by the primary results.

Early in January 1939 Browning sent his last report to the General Assembly. He pointed with pride to the accomplishments of his administration, putting special emphasis on the debt retirement plan and the effective budgetary controls he had instituted.[88] His achievements were not ignored by the press. The *Tennessean* commented that the governor had made inexcusable mistakes and outraged the electorate, but that he had advanced the welfare of the state in material ways, and those advances should be appreciated and maintained.[89] Browning's successor, Prentice Cooper, saw no reason to repudiate the reforms of 1937, although he recommended some modifications in the Administrative Reorganization Act of 1937. Cooper was, in later years at least, openly complimentary of his predecessor's achievements, especially the debt retirement plan.[90] In his farewell address in January, Gordon Browning declared that the fight against dictatorship had just begun. He hinted, in effect, that he would be heard from again in the political wars of the future.[91] For a man who repeatedly demonstrated his political resilience, he probably meant it. He told a reporter years later, "I didn't feel as if I were through. I felt than as I feel now—that the election was stolen from me."[92] He would be back.

NOTES

1. George Barker, "Of War, Peace, and Politics," *Nashville Tennessean Magazine* (23 September 1962), p. 19; repeated almost verbatim in Gordon Browning, interview with the author, Huntingdon, 28 December 1965.

2. Watkins Overton to Henry Dickinson, copy, 1 December 1936, Gordon Browning Papers, Tennessee State Library and Archives.

3. William D. Miller, *Mr. Crump of Memphis* (Baton Rouge: Louisiana State University Press, 1964), p. 238.

4. Ibid., pp. 237–238.

5. *Nashville Banner*, 24 July 1937; D. W. McKellar to Watkins Overton, 11 October 1937, Political Correspondence, Box 35, D. W. McKellar to Harry S. Berry, 25 Sept. 1937, Kenneth Douglas McKellar Papers, Memphis-Shelby County Public Library and Information Center.

6. Barker, "Of War, Peace, and Politics," p. 19; Miller, *Mr. Crump*, p. 239; Gordon Browning, "Gordon Browning: An Oral Memoir," ed. Joseph H. Riggs (Memphis Public Library, 1966), pp. 28–29, 113–114.

7. Joe Hatcher, "Lewis Pope Big in Crump's Fall," *Nashville Tennessean*, 16 May 1972; Hugh Walker, "No Regrets—Lew Pope," Ibid., 28 February 1971.

8. William D. Miller, "The Browning-Crump Battle: The Crump Side," *The East Tennessee Historical Society's Publications* 37 (1965), p. 84.

9. Joe Hatcher, "Politics," *Tennessean*, 11, 21 February 1937.

10. *Banner*, 19 February 1937.

11. Browning, interview, 28 December 1965.

12. Memphis *Commercial Appeal*, 1 May 1937; *The Labor Advocate*, 11 March 1937.

13. Quoted in *Banner*, 29 April 1937.

14. *Tennessean*, 8 May 1937; *Labor Advocate*, 13 May 1937.

15. Browning, interview, 28 December 1965.

16. *Banner,* 15 July 1937.

17. Berry to McKellar, 15 July 1937, McKellar to Berry, 16 July 1937, Political Correspondence, Box 35, McKellar Papers; see also Robert Dean Pope, "Senatorial Baron: The Long Political Career of Kenneth D. McKellar"(unpublished Ph. D. dissertation, Yale University, 1976), pp. 261–263.

18. Miller, "The Browning-Crump Battle,"p. 87; Miller, *Mr. Crump,* p. 245.

19. *Banner,* 15 July 1937.

20. Ibid., 4 August 1937.

21. Quoted in Ibid., 1 September 1937.

22. George Barker, "Victory, Defeat, Victory,"*Nashville Tennessean Magazine* (30 September 1962), p. 8.

23. Miller, *Mr. Crump,* p. 260; Miller, "The Browning Crump Battle," p. 87–88.

24. *Tennessean,* 29 September 1937; Memphis *Press-Scimitar,* 29 September 1937.

25. Miller, *Mr. Crump,* p. 243–244; Miller, "The Browning-Crump Battle," p. 86.

26. *Banner,* 6 October 1937.

27. *Tennessean,* 1 October 1937; *Press-Scimitar,* 2 October 1937.

28. Quoted in *Press-Scimitar,* 1, 2 October 1937.

29. Ibid., 6 October 1937. Lewis Pope denied that he sponsored the idea, *Tennessean,* 1 October 1937.

30. Quoted in *Banner,* 6 October 1937.

31. Quoted in Ibid., 9 October 1937.

32. *Commercial Appeal,* 10 October 1937.

33. Jim Cummings, interview with the author, Woodbury, 8 June 1976; Albert Gore, interview with the author, Nashville, 15 May 1977; Browning, "Oral Memoir,"pp. 70–71.

34. *Tennessean,* 9 October 1937; *Chattanooga Times,* 11 October 1937; Columbia *Daily Herald,* 5 October 1937; *Press-Scimitar,* 9 October 1937; *Chattanooga Free Press,* 11 October 1937; *Clarksville Leaf-Chronicle,* 9 October 1937; *Commercial Appeal,* 10 October 1937.

35. *Senate and House Journals of the Second and Third Extraordinary Sessions of the Seventieth General Assembly of the State of Tennessee* (Jackson, 1938), pp. 18–25.

36. Basil McMahan, interview with the author, Manchester, 14 June 1972.

37. *Senate and House Journals, 70th GA,* pp. 398–400.

38. *Commercial Appeal,* 20 October 1937. Senator George Berry spoke in favor of the bill.

39. *Senate and House Journals, 70th GA,* pp. 56, 405; *Public and Private Acts of the State of Tennessee Passed by the Seventieth General Assembly, Extra Sessions, 1937* (Nashville, 1937), pp. 44–63.

40. *Daily Herald,* 21 October 1937.

41. *Public and Private Acts, 70th GA*, pp. 85–93.

42. Quoted in *Press-Scimitar*, 8 November 1937.

43. Quoted in *Banner*, 10 November 1937.

44. Quoted in Ibid; see also Miller, *Mr. Crump*, pp. 247–248.

45. *Public and Private Acts, 70th GA*, pp. 324–328.

46. Ibid., pp. 343–348.

47. *Tennessean*, 5 January 1938.

48. McKellar to Crump, 30 November 1937, Crump-McKellar Correspondence Box 3, McKellar Papers; Pope, "Senatorial Baron," 264–268. McKellar was aboard ship returning to the States from Europe when the Governor issued the call for the first special session. Crump contacted McKellar by radiogram requesting his help and the senator quickly responded by issuing a statement denouncing the unit plan.

49. Crump to McKellar, 8 December 1937, Crump-McKellar Correspondence, Box 3, McKellar Papers.

50. Crump to Don W. McKellar, 30 December 1937, Ibid.

51. *Tennessean*, 2 January 1938.

52. Wilmon H. Droze, *High Dams and Slack Waters: TVA Rebuilds a River* (Baton Rouge: Louisiana State University Press, 1965); Thomas K. McGraw, *TVA And The Power Fight, 1933–1939* (New York: J. B. Lippincott, 1971); for a brief treatment, see also George B. Tindall, *The Emergence of the New South, 1913–1945*, vol. 10, *A History of the South* (Baton Rouge: Louisiana State University Press, 1967), pp. 446–457.

53. *Tennessean*, 22, 23, 26 January 1938.

54. Ibid., 27, 28, 29 January 1938; *Commercial Appeal*, 25 January 1938.

55. McKellar to Crump, 27 January 1938, Crump-McKellar Correspondence, Box 3, McKellar Papers; see also Pope, "Senatorial Baron," pp. 269–270.

56. Quoted in *Banner*, 5 February 1938.

57. *Gates et al. v. Long et al.* 113 S. W. 2d 388.

58. Quoted in *Tennessean*, 13 February 1938.

59. *Commercial Appeal*, 13 February 1938; *Banner*, 12 February 1938.

60. Browning, interview, 28 December 1965.

61. *Tennessean*, 15, 26 February 1938; James H. Cummings, interview, agreed that Browning would have had difficulty in getting anything through the legislature.

62. Quoted in *Tennessean*, 21 February 1938.

63. Frick Stewart, interview with the author, Winchester, 25 May 1977; Pope, "Senatorial Baron," pp. 271–272.

64. Miller, *Mr. Crump*, pp. 250–251; Harry Berry to McKellar, 28 February 1938, Political Correspondence, Box 36, McKellar Papers; Pope, "Senatorial Baron," p. 271; James H. S. Cooper, "Boss Crump and Governor Prentice Cooper: Study of a Relationship, 1938–1944" (unpublished history honors paper, University of North Carolina, 1975), pp. v–viii, 8–9.

65. Frick Stewart, interview, indicated that Tom Stewart had seriously considered the governor's race in 1938.

66. Quoted in *Banner*, 4 June 1938.

67. Miller, *Mr. Crump*, p. 251; Cooper ("Boss Crump," p. 18,) declared that the platform was sent unsigned to Cooper and returned, also unsigned to Crump.

68. Crump to McKellar, 2 May 1938, Crump-McKellar Correspondence, Box 3, McKellar Papers.

69. McKellar to Crump, 18 November, McKellar to Crump, 20 November 1937, Ibid.

70. *Commercial Appeal*, 26 July 1938.

71. *Tennessean*, 28 May 1938; *Press-Scimitar*, 26 July 1938; Miller, *Mr. Crump*, p. 254.

72. Miller, *Mr. Crump*, pp. 255–257.

73. A file labeled "1937–1938 — Browning Campaign, Police Reports," Box 1, Watkins Overton Papers, Memphis State University Library, indicates that Mayor Overton was kept fully informed of all the police political activity.

74. Overton to H. A. Taylor, 30 November 1934, Box 3, Ibid.; *Tennessean*, 24 May 1938.

75. Clark Porteous, in an interview with the author (Memphis, 22 June 1977) recalled that on one visit to the Oceola hideout he came face to face with a shotgun which forced a hasty retreat.

76. Quoted in *Tennessean*, 28 May, 2 June 1938.

77. Box 1, Overton Papers.

78. Clark Porteous, interview.

79. *Tennessean*, 24, 31 July 1938; *Chattanooga Times*, 29 July 1938; *Knoxville News-Sentinel*, 31 July 1938; *Labor Advocate*, 14 July 1938; *Trades and Labor News*, 28 July 1938. The Political Campaign Committee also preferred Stewart to Berry in the Senate race.

80. *Tennessean*, 5, 6, 7, 24 July 1938.

81. *Banner*, 30 July 1938.

82. McKellar to Crump, 17 June 1938, Crump-McKellar Correspondence, Box 3, McKellar Papers.

83. Miller, *Mr. Crump*, p. 258; *Press-Scimitar*, 2 August 1938; *Tennessean*, 1 August 1938; *Commercial Appeal*, 2 August 1938.

84. *Tennessean*, 1 January 1939.

85. Alexander Heard and Donald S. Strong, *Southern Primaries and Elections, 1920–1948* (Tuscaloosa: University of Alabama Press, 1950), p. 118.

86. U. S. Congress, Senate, Committee on Senatorial Campaign Expenditures, *Report of the Special Committee to Investigate Senatorial Campaign Expenditures and the Use of Governmental Funds in 1938*, 76th Cong., 1st Sess. (Washington, 1939), pp. 18–19; see also Pope, "Senatorial Baron," pp. 273–275.

87. *Press-Scimitar* 5 August 1938.

88. *House Journal of the Seventy-First General Assembly of the State of Tennessee, 1939* (Nashville, 1939), pp. 30–46.

89. *Tennessean,* 6 January 1939.

90. Mrs. Prentice Cooper, interview with the author, Shelbyville, 10 October 1976.

91. *House Journal, 71st GA,* pp. 156–161.

92. Quoted in Barker, "Victory, Defeat, Victory," p. 20.

The Interim

IN THE weeks following the Democratic primary of 1938 Gordon Browning was, for the moment at least, dejected about his overwhelming defeat. His relegation to the darkness of private life involved an unpleasant adjustment because of his total commitment to public service. Moreover, it appeared that his retirement was permanent, for he had been thoroughly repudiated by the voters. Few who suffered such a resounding defeat could ever expect to return to the good graces of the electorate. Browning did indeed appear to be a dead politician, and his dreams of going to the United States Senate seemed to have evaporated. But those who believed that his political career was over were not aware of his perseverance. In any event, the decade after 1938 belonged to Crump and McKellar.

The Crump-McKellar axis became the dominant political force in Tennessee following Gordon Browning's forced retirement from the political scene. From 1938 to 1949, the alliance had allies in the governor's office, achieved rapport with East Tennessee Republicans, and cooperated with other local political machines for the mutual exchange of legislative favors in the General Assembly. Even a truce was achieved in the continuing struggle between the forces of rural and urban Tennessee. But opposition was not entirely eliminated as a significant portion of the press kept up a continuous attack on machine politics, and leaders of the rural block remained ever alert to prevent cities from gaining advantages.

Ed Crump's power in Tennessee resulted from his control of Memphis and Shelby County, the largest urban area in the state, and his ability to deliver from forty-five to fifty thousand votes to the candidate of his choice in a statewide race. Crump was in many ways typical of urban bosses, but he was in some respects unique. He was generally honest in both his political and business deals, and he avoided situations that might have caused suspicion of dishonesty. For example, his insurance firm refused to bid for coverage of any of the city's insurance needs.[1] No scandal ever touched the machine although it is likely that minor figures in the organization participated in petty graft. Crump, like other political bosses, enhanced his image in Memphis through benevolence. He contributed to individuals in need as well as to organized charities, and financed well-publicized boat trips and circus visits for orphans, cripples, and the elderly. The success of the Memphis machine was the result of efficient organization. There may have been occasions when vote fraud was perpetrated but that was not a normal exercise; the Memphis organization knew their supporters, registered them, paid their poll taxes, and got them to the polling places on election day. The machine did indeed truck large numbers of blacks to voting places, but not from Arkansas and Mississippi as alleged. They did not have to, for there were enough in Memphis legitimately registered to keep trucks busy transporting blacks from various industries or businesses where they worked. The machine was so well organized that the number of votes in each precinct could be predicted with considerable accuracy.

Honest, benevolent, and with an efficient organization that turned out the vote, Ed Crump could therefore remain aloof from the more sordid aspects of his machine which exhibited features of a typical ruthless, despotic, and absolute rule. Memphis was a closed society, and signs of disloyalty were dealt with quickly and efficiently. A merchant, for example, who showed signs of disaffection would be threatened with an increase in his assessment, or perhaps the sidewalk and street in front of his establishment would be torn up for months on end by water or sewer repair crews; health department inspectors could find the most minute violations in business establishments; and police harassment was common. There were times when no action was necessary to enforce conformity. A black minister once invited Gordon Browning to speak to his congregation, but the elders of the church quickly cancelled the engagement. Crump and his lieutenants denied that pressure had been applied to rescind the invitation, and quite likely none had been necessary. The machine often intimidated blacks without actually doing anything; the elders quickly perceived that wisdom was the better part of valor.

Vice also continued to flourish in Memphis and quite possibly was an important source of revenue to the machine. Like Wyatt Earp, the famous frontier marshal in Dodge City, Crump set up a "deadline," a red-light district where drinking, gambling, and prostitution went on with little official interference. The Memphis boss therefore did not clean up the city; he simply swept the dirt into a corner. But Crump could piously proclaim that Memphis was a clean city. With the military build-up just prior to World War II, vice in the Bluff City was finally curbed. Crump's biographer asserts that, with the establishment of military stations in the area and the appearance of soldiers on the city's streets, the Memphis boss became concerned about the morals of the young men in uniform. Another observer suggests that Crump's motive in cleaning up Memphis was to forestall a cleanup initiated by the Justice Department of the federal government.[3] In any case, the homicide rate remained high in the city that had long been called the murder capital of the nation. Crump claimed that many of the acts of homicide were committed in nearby Arkansas and Mississippi; the victims were brought to Memphis hospitals where they died and the city was credited with the killings. But one reporter at the time contended that the murders were committed in the black sections of Memphis and the boss only deceived himself.[4]

The black community in Memphis was a vital component of the political machine headed by Ed Crump. Scholars have held that the organization had a "sincere although patronizing sympathy for the Negro's welfare" and that under Crump he got "a fairer break than usual in public services."[5] Thus two writers concluded that the Memphis boss "accomplished a genuine rarity in the South, an effective biracial urban machine."[6] The black population in the Bluff City was large, almost two-fifths of the total and certainly large enough to be decisive in elections. In the early years, when Crump needed black votes to establish his control, black leaders were treated with deference and the black community was rewarded with just enough in the way of parks and services to garner its support. As time passed, the machine gradually became more repressive and black leaders were reduced to total subservience, or as David Tucker put it, became "Brown screws in the Crump machine."[7] According to Ralph Bunche, the black population was "beaten into submission by police nightsticks and guns" and were voting with the machine out of fear.[8] By the 1940s, the rewards to blacks for voting with the organization were so minimal as to be nonexistent. Only a few menial city jobs were available to them; there were no black firemen or policemen; expenditures for Negro parks, playgrounds, schools, health care, and welfare were far out of proportion to numbers. Even black participation in the commercial and business life of the city had declined sharply from the early years in the century.[9] In short, the black community in Memphis was no longer getting a "fairer break" and blacks had been reduced to voting cattle.

While Memphis may have been controlled by a ruthless, authoritarian regime, the Bluff City was governed efficiently. The police and fire departments were effective; the streets were well paved and clean; health and other municipal services were good; fire insurance rates were low; and, most important, the taxes were low. As one observer put it, Memphis had benevolent government but at the cost of freedom of choice.[10] Thomas Harrison Baker writes, "Crump's political success was based ultimately upon the easy assumption of most Memphians that boss rule was a fair price to pay for an admittedly clean and efficient city government."[11]

Contemporaries and scholars in later years assume that Ed Crump became in fact boss of Tennessee after the primary of 1938. The Memphis boss did indeed exercise considerable influence in state affairs because he was able to deliver from twelve to fifteen percent of the total vote in a Democratic primary for governor. And, after 1938, he had an ally in the governor's office, the relatively youthful Prentice Cooper of Shelbyville. A scion of the Bourbon aristocracy, Cooper was a lawyer by trade and a gentleman farmer by avocation; he was quiet and reserved but occasionally revealed an explosive temper. His gubernatorial administration was characterized by solid but unspectacular achievement with emphasis on efficiency in government. Tennessee Democrats traditionally rewarded their governor with a second term and in 1940 Cooper defeated a token opponent in what the Memphis *Commercial Appeal* called one of the quietest primaries ever.[12]

The relationship between the Memphis boss and Cooper was not an easy one. Cooper respected Crump and often called upon him for advice and the leader in Shelby County just as often tendered his counsel. No doubt Governor Cooper was irritated by Crump's continually looking over his shoulder and he sometimes displayed irritation and independence. The Memphis boss was not enthusiastic about the governor. A poor speaker and "formal and reserved on the hustings," Cooper was not the forceful and dynamic leader that Crump preferred.[13] More important to Crump, however, was that fact that the man in the governor's office did not constitute a threat to his hegemony in Memphis and Shelby County. Moreover, the Memphis boss had a voice in state patronage and in the establishment of election machinery in his own community. In addition, he had the power to bargain for legislative favors with other leaders across the state. By strict definition, Crump was not boss of Tennessee, for he had no lieutenants or organization across the state. In the final analysis, his power in the Volunteer State stemmed from his alliance with Governor Cooper and the senior United States Senator, Kenneth McKellar.

Many Tennesseans in the 1930s and 1940s mistakenly believed that Senator McKellar was merely Crump's lieutenant and errand boy in Washington, if not his lackey.[14] A man with McKellar's temperment and personality could not accept second place to anyone. Invariably dressed in cutaway coat, stiff white shirt with often a bow tie, the senator gave the appearance of dignity, and was, in the Bourbon tradition, a courtly man. Yet he had an explosive temper, regarded differences in policy and ideology as personal affronts, and was fully capable of resorting to physical violence when involved in an argument. McKellar became something of a legend in Washington because of his outbursts in committee hearing rooms and even on the floor of the United States Senate. One oft-repeated tale of questionable truth was of his striking publisher Silliman Evans over the head with a cane. On at least one occasion he came close to assaulting Ed Crump.[15] Senator McKellar was a magnetic and vital man held in high regard, but his contemporaries both in Washington and Tennessee respected him with an awe bordering on fear.

The relationship between the senator and Crump was not based simply on political expedience. They admired each other, were close personal friends, had similar interests, and shared political, social, and economic philosophies; since they agreed on basic issues, there was little reason for them to clash. When they did differ, it was over petty matters, for both were acutely sensitive in personal relations and easily hurt over some unintentional slight. Crump would sometimes petulantly chide the senator for some oversight or action that had offended him.[16] The Memphis boss was a master at writing vituperative letters, but McKellar never received one from Crump. Once Senator Tom Stewart infuriated the Shelby leader by his votes in the Senate and

Crump fired off a blistering letter that concluded with a warning that the Memphis organization might not support him in the next election. To McKellar, who cast identical votes, he merely wrote, "We were a little surprised at your vote."[17] Probably the reason McKellar never received one of Crump's caustic letters was that he would have replied in kind. When the Memphis boss hurt his feelings, the senator did not hesitate to say so, but his response to Crump's petty harangues tended to be measured.[18] McKellar was always more direct with Crump than other members of the Shelby organization or allies were, and he could express himself freely without retaliation. The senator had a statewide organization independent of Crump's Memphis machine. He did not clear state appointments with the Memphis boss and often retained on his staff those who had offended Crump. Moreover, there were those within Memphis, such as federal marshal Bert Bates, who owed allegiance to McKellar first and to the machine second. Certainly Crump had no desire to break with the senator who had a power base as vital to him as his own Shelby organization.

Already a power in Washington as the chairman of the Senate's Post Office Committee and senior member under the chairman of the Committee on Appropriations, McKellar's position was enhanced by the election of a Democratic president in 1932, Franklin D. Roosevelt, and the advent of the New Deal. The senator supported the New Deal in principle and his voting record behind the president was as consistent as any member of Congress. But because he often clashed with heads of New Deal agencies, he was never regarded as a New Dealer. Even so, with his tenacious ability to get what he wanted, perhaps more than any congressman or senator, he was able to obtain for Tennessee more than its share of government projects. One legend in particular illustrates the power exercised by Tennessee's senior senator. During the build-up prior to World War II, the military chiefs in Washington developed plans for new bases and stations across the nation. McKellar obtained a copy of the plans and when he discovered that none were to be located in Tennessee, he called the chiefs to give an explanation. The reasons given were unsatisfactory, and the senator exploded and stalked out. Conscious of McKellar's power in the Senate and in the Appropriations Committee, the military leaders submitted revised plans a few days later which included the establishing of Camp Forrest near Tullahoma. There were a number of versions of the story, differing in detail, but all containing the essential point: McKellar got what he wanted, a plum for Tennessee.[19]

But there was one agency in Tennessee that the senator was unable to control: The Tennessee Valley Authority. Even so, he had a wealth of patronage to dispense, and, never apologizing for favoring his friends, built a strong organization based on the rewards at his command. As his power increased in Tennessee, he grew stronger in Washington and that in turn improved his position in the state. Although McKellar did not have a highly structured organization across Tennessee, it was sufficient to keep him in office; and not until his very last race was he seriously challenged at the polls. Moreover, at no time was the Memphis machine the difference between victory and defeat; McKellar always won handily outside of Shelby County. Scholars have assumed that it was Crump who established the alliance with East Tennessee Republicans, but it was in reality McKellar who cemented the working relationship with the Grand Old Party in the eastern section. Although disagreeing over policy and on traditional issues, the senator exchanged favors with long-time Congressman B. Carroll Reece of the first district and J. Will Taylor of the second district. The two Republican congressmen remained unchallenged leaders in their districts and McKellar often got the votes of their constituents.[20] The primary victories of Prentice Cooper in the governor's race and Tom Stewart for the Senate were as much McKellar's responsibility as Crump's. And with Cooper as the state's chief executive, the senior senator had an important voice in election machinery and party organization. McKellar had an ideal colleague in Stewart for the junior senator was quiet, inoffensive, pliant, and willing to follow the senior senator's lead.[21]

In the Democratic primary of 1942, Senator McKellar played a more important role than Crump. After seriously considering making a race for the Senate, Governor Cooper declared for a third term while Stewart stood for renomination. Probably Cooper declined to make the Senate race because he could not obtain McKellar's support. Ed Crump had little enthusiasm for Cooper and even less for Stewart; of the junior senator, he wrote: "Really the appraisal of Stewart's value to Tennessee is more or less nil." Again he wrote concerning both Cooper and Stewart: "There isn't a thing about Cooper and Stewart to make any fellow feel as though he would like to throw his hat sky high with enthusiasm for them." But following McKellar's lead, Crump went along by endorsing Cooper and Stewart, largely because he feared a revival of the "Browning Crowd."[23] And he had some cause for concern. Cooper's opponent was former Congressman J. Ridley Mitchell, and E. W. Carmack, the son of the crusading editor-politician, Senator Edward Ward Carmack, challenged Stewart.

Gordon Browning broke four years of political silence when he consented to introduce Mitchell at a rally in McKenzie. In the introduction, Browning appeared to be in old political form, using forceful language and the same colorful invectives against Crump.[24] Apparently he did not intend to do more for Mitchell's cause, but a month later the Memphis boss placed an advertisement in the major dailies of the state which assailed Mitchell and charged that Browning and the *Nashville Tennessean* had duped Mitchell to run on their platform and "misrepresent me." Stung by Crump's advertisement, Browning agreed to make a statewide radio talk in Mitchell's behalf. He presented a ringing appeal for the candidate and called Governor Cooper "Little Lord Fauntleroy." Then he turned his fury upon the Memphis boss and characterized those running with Crump's support as "trained seals."[25] Obviously the old fire was not gone.

Both the Senate and governor's races were close. Cooper challenged Tennessee's two-term tradition, and the less than colorful Stewart was threatened by a famous and popular name as well as a dynamic speaker. Both incumbents won, Cooper by 47,000 votes and Stewart by less than 20,000. Cooper and Stewart won the first three congressional districts in East Tennessee by good majorities, though the senator's was by a smaller figure. Thus, they polled well in an area where McKellar had considerable influence. The challengers carried Middle Tennessee by a good margin and a similar voting pattern. In West Tennessee, Cooper did well, carrying thirteen counties outside of Shelby County while Stewart won only five. Across the state outside of Crump's own county, Cooper won by a bare 3,000 votes; his 47,000 in Shelby gave him a much larger margin of victory. Carmack won the Senate race outside of Shelby by 16,000 votes; thus Stewart's 42,000 in Crump's hometown enabled him to retain his seat in the Senate.[26] The vote in Shelby County alone did not mean the difference between victory and defeat for Cooper and Stewart; the senior senator's influence in East Tennessee was just as vital to the Crump-McKellar axis as the votes produced by the Memphis boss. As Robert Dean Pope concludes, Crump and McKellar had separate power bases that complemented rather than threatened each other. "When they worked together they repeatedly demonstrated that no one in Tennessee could beat them."[27]

Although the enemies of the Crump-McKellar axis were disorganized and perhaps demoralized, a significant portion of the state's press kept opposition alive through the 1940s. One of Crump's most caustic critics was in Memphis, Edward J. Meeman, editor of the *Press-Scimitar*. The city's only evening paper, the *Press* had been owned since 1926 by the Scripps-Howard syndicate and Meeman had been brought in as editor in 1931. The syndicate dictated editorial policy on national issues but gave its local editor freedom to determine the paper's position on local matters, and the new editor placed emphasis on local news. Meeman had a flair for sensational journalism, and he was a champion of causes; above all, he was concerned with conservation of natural resources. But the Memphis editor was also an idealist committed to progressive dem-ocratic government, and it was not long before he launched an attack on Crump's repressive and undemocratic regime.[28] Over the years, Meeman became one of the most strident critics of what he called "Shelby's hydra-headed organization." He conceded that Crump had done much good in Memphis. In response to a complaint made by Crump's son, he declared that he was "not without admiration of many of your father's activities."[29] But committed as he was to the concept of freedom and democracy, the machine had to be broken, and Meeman began in 1932 an editorial crusade aimed at just that. The *Press* invari-ably supported anti-Crump candidates in Memphis and in statewide political races. Meeman's editorials directed at the Memphis boss and his organization were always sharp, sometimes petty, and often grasped at straws. The hypersensitive Crump refused to ignore the criticism and the editor often received letters of protest over what the Memphis boss regarded as unwarranted criticism of himself and his organization. "I read your low, cowardly editorial," he would write, "you have enjoyed the cowardly privilege of writing lying, misleading and colored stuff in your sheet." Or, "I have warned you before to stop lying about me in your paper." And again, "Oh! how you do hate me. . . . Your paper has written many lies about me."[30] Memphians looked upon the running battle between the editor and the boss with some amusement because it kept politics interesting in an otherwise dull atmosphere. Meeman probably had little influence on attitudes in the Bluff City but he kept opposition alive in Memphis.

There was a contrast between the evening paper in Memphis and the morning *Commercial Appeal*. For years the morning paper, under the editorship of C. P. J. Mooney, had been Crump's press gadfly and that tradition was continued after its purchase by Luke Lea in 1927. But the paper went into receivership in 1930 with the fall of the Lea-Caldwell regime. Finally in 1936 Scripps-Howard purchased the *Commercial*

Appeal and made conservative Frank Ahlgren editor. Reflecting the philosophical bias of its editor, the morning paper became sedate, with "old fashioned dignity and restraint." Although the *Commercial* could be mildly critical of the Memphis boss, after 1936 the paper "maintained an attitude of nonpartisan detachment" toward Crump.[31] The paper with the largest circulation of any newspaper published in the state, the *Commercial* also served the tri-state area that included eastern Arkansas and northern Mississippi. It was not aligned with any faction in Tennessee, although more often than not Ahlgren endorsed candidates supported by the Memphis boss.

Neither of the two Chattanooga newspapers were attached to any state political faction. The *Chattanooga News-Free Press*, published by the ultraconservative Roy McDonald, had little sympathy for Ed Crump. An advocate of classical *laissez-faire* government and economy, McDonald's editorial stances in regard to issues and political candidates was invariably based on his philosophical biases. Affording a contrast, the *Chattanooga Times* was, as Hugh Davis Graham notes, "generally more progressive by Southern standards." The *Times* was still in the family of Adolph Ochs who had purchased the paper for a mere $250 in 1878 and built it into a prosperous paper before going on to greater fame as publisher of the *New York Times*. Similar in format to the New York paper, the *Chattanooga Times* was sedate and restrained on issues. Always measured in its criticism of the Memphis boss and his influence in state affairs, the *Times* tended toward political independence but invariably endorsed the more liberal of candidates for local and state offices.[32]

In Knoxville, the evening *News-Sentinel*, another member of the Scripps-Howard chain, was like the Memphis *Press-Scimitar* in style and expressed similar political convictions on the editorial page. Perhaps because of sectional antagonism, the *News-Sentinel* considered Crump anathema and was often shrill in its criticism of the Memphis boss. The morning *Knoxville Journal* was edited by a conservative Republican, Guy L. Smith. Allied with B. Carroll Reese, first district congressman, Smith was a power in the Republican party in Tennessee and influential at the national level. Because of the unique relationship between East Tennessee Republicans and the Crump-McKellar alliance, and perhaps because any disruption in the status quo might cost him his preeminence in the party, Smith saw no reason to attack the Memphis boss. Editorially, the *Journal* took an abstract party stance without attacking personalities.[33]

More than any of Tennessee's major dailies, the two Nashville papers, the *Nashville Banner* and the *Nashville Tennessean*, reflected political conflict in the state. The senior *Banner* had been founded in 1876 and was acquired nine years later by Major Edward Bushrod Stahlman. Stahlman was born in Germany in 1843, and his family migrated to the United States in 1854 but, for some reason, Edward never formally applied for citizenship. After a successful career in railroading, he turned to journalism which became his passion after he took over the *Banner* in 1885. The *Banner's* editorials reflected the personality of the publisher. The paper was merciless in attacking political opponents and vigorous in promoting causes Stahlman believed in. Allied with the political machine headed by Nashville Mayor Hilary House, the evening daily also became, in effect, the voice of the city's conservative business community. E. B. Stahlman died in 1930 and his grandson, James G. Stahlman, soon became publisher and continued the tradition established by his grandfather. The Stahlmans were close friends with Senator McKellar, and the *Banner* was the only major daily in the state to express sympathy for Ed Crump. The rival *Tennessean* was founded in 1907 as the personal organ of the flamboyant Luke Lea. The papers were in competition for circulation and Lea and Stahlman also became bitter political enemies. During World War I, for example, Lea urged that Stahlman be declared an enemy alien, which would have required confiscation of the *Banner* by the Alien Property Custodian of the United States government and possible deportment for the publisher. That was probably a publicity stunt to boost circulation, but it turned the rivalry into a bitter feud unsurpassed for acid invectives. Legend had it that reporters on both papers carried revolvers for protection from each other.[34] With the support of Rogers Caldwell, Lea expanded his holdings by purchasing the *Commercial Appeal* and *Knoxville Journal*. But when Caldwell's financial empire collapsed in 1930, Lea lost his papers and the *Tennessean* went into receivership.[35]

A new era began for the *Tennessean* in 1937 when Silliman Evans, a native of Texas, gained controlling interest in the paper. Evans learned the newspaper business while working as a reporter under Amon Carter, well-known publisher of the Fort Worth *Star-Telegram*. A liberal Democrat, Evans went to Washington as a political reporter and eventually became fourth assistant to Post Master General Jim Farley, and then chairman of the board of the Maryland Casualty Company. Evans was an ardent New Dealer, but his first love was publishing and the chance to purchase the *Tennessean* provided the opportunity to return to the newspaper business. The short, stocky, well-dressed Texan made significant changes in short order. To ease the financial burdens of both papers, the *Tennessean* and *Banner* put aside their hostilities and formed the Newspaper Printing Corporation, thus combining their physical facilities and advertising offices into one plant. The dailies remained poles apart philosophically but the financial strain on both eased as a result of the arrangement. And Nashville remained one of the few cities across the nation with two home-owned newspapers. Evans also insisted on responsible journalism and the *Tennessean* soon became an influential paper with the largest circulation within the state and the only large daily in the state that declared its affiliation with the Democratic party. Vain, ambitious, but politically astute, Evans soon became embroiled in Tennessee politics.[36]

Early in the 1940s, Silliman Evans began a crusade against Ed Crump, and the point of attack was Tennessee's poll tax requirement. Evans sought to demonstrate that Crump's dictatorship profited by the poll tax because it kept voter registration at a controllable level. The issue soon resulted in a bitter political feud between the publisher and the Memphis boss. Crump opposed repeal unless a system of permanent registration was established, for he did not believe that elections could be purified until such a system was put into effect.[37] Clearly, Crump would have been able to control elections just as well under a system of permanent registration as under the poll tax. Senator McKellar was even more adamant than Crump and opposed repeal of the tax without qualification. He declared that repeal was contrary to the best interests of the state and people and that it would injure the Democratic party, perhaps even threaten its supremacy, in Tennessee.[38] In spite of Crump and McKellar, Governor Cooper made repeal of the poll tax an administration measure when the General Assembly convened in January 1941. Repeal failed to pass in that session and the *Tennessean*, with its crusade against Crump well under way, blamed the Memphis boss for the defeat. In 1943 Cooper again pressed for repeal against strong opposition but the legislators responded positively and the poll tax was abolished. Sheriff Burch Biggs of Polk County quickly contested the constitutionality of repeal in a suit in Chancery Court. Chancellor T. L. Stewart, father of Senator Tom Stewart, upheld the challenge and declared that because the Tennessee constitution required a poll tax, the legislature could not repeal its own act of 1891 implementing the requirement. The Tennessee Supreme Court, in a three to two decision, sustained the chancellor's ruling. Justice Frank

Gaylor, a stalwart in Crump's organization and recently appointed to the bench by Governor Cooper, voted with the majority. Opponents of the poll tax immediately charged that the decision was purely political and some even suggested that Gaylor's appointment was made deliberately to secure rejection by the court.[39] But James H. S. Cooper notes that Gaylor was the logical choice for the appointment at the time and "it is unreasonable to assume that [Governor] Cooper wanted to alter the court's balance" to overturn a measure he had long sought. Moreover, "not even a Crump political maneuver would be so baldfaced. . . . Those who really knew the issue were disappointed, but not surprised, at the court's decision."[40]

Nevertheless, the ruling by the Supreme Court gave the *Tennessean* additional ammunition for its attack on the Memphis boss. In 1944 Jennings Perry, a *Tennessean* writer, published an exaggerated account of the paper's crusade against Crump and the poll tax in a little volume entitled *Democracy Begins at Home: The Tennessee Fight Against the Poll Tax*. Crump was described irreverently as "arrogant," "vain," "vindictive," "self-righteous," and a despotic "semi-literate" old man.[41] And in editorial columns of Nashville's morning daily, Crump's machine was regularly depicted as undemocratic and totalitarian. Although editor Meeman was always serious in his challenges to the Memphis boss, the *Tennessean*'s attack, led by political writer Joe Hatcher, was often laced with humor. Crump was never able to take criticism calmly and found it even more difficult to accept personal abuse in the form of humor. He always responded in writing as expected. He called Evans a "puffed up foreign frog," and Hatcher and Perry were described as conscienceless liars, scoundrels, perverts, and degenerates. The *Tennessean* tended to ignore Crump's shrill response. Finally, in 1945, frustrated at his inability to gain some satisfaction, the Memphis boss wrote a classic letter villifying Evans, Perry, and Hatcher as "3 Slimy, Mangy, Bubonic Rats." The letter was widely circulated and Senator McKellar had it inserted in the *Congressional Record*.[42] Perhaps Crump's only satisfaction was in having expressed his frustration openly because the *Tennessean* once again chose not to respond in kind. Evans' motives for challenging the Memphis boss were mixed. Most certainly the attendant publicity surrounding the Crump-*Tennessean* feud must have helped circulation. And it is likely that Evans realized that if he could in some way break Crump's political influence in the state he would move into a position as one of the power brokers in the Democratic party. At any rate, Tennesseans were entertained by the struggle between the publisher and the Memphis boss. It provided an interesting and fascinating sideshow during the years when political battles were relatively dull and Crump-endorsed candidates were routinely victorious at election time.

The struggle between the Crump-McKellar alliance and its opponents has, of course, been examined and interpreted by scholars who have long attempted to find order and continuity in political structures. Thus, V. O. Key, Jr., in his extensive study of political institutions in the South found bifactionalism in Tennessee's Democratic party. Each faction was a coalition resembling a holding company and Key identified the one controlled by Crump as the "organization" and the opponents of the Memphis boss as the "anti-organization." He also traced historical continuity in the antiorganization from Luke Lea through Lewis Pope to Gordon Browning. Key oversimplified political patterns in Tennessee, however, and weakened his case by making exceptions to his generalization. He wrote that the factions were "shifting alliances" that resulted from "frequent alterations" in the alliance systems; moreover, "the line of political descent has . . . been blurred by movements both ways across factional lines."[43] In reality, there were many factions in Tennessee built around local and regional leaders. The dual factional pattern makes sense only in terms of the "ins," the Crump-McKellar axis, and the "outs," all of whom were presumably anti-Crump. But even that is too simple a parallel, for there were those friendly with McKellar but hostile to the Memphis boss. V. O. Key fails to acknowledge the most realistic bifactional pattern in Tennessee, the continuing rural-urban cleavage. Much of the opposition across the state to Crump, but not necessarily to Senator McKellar, was based on the traditional hostility in the countryside toward cities and urban political machines. To rural Tennesseans the Memphis boss, controlling a repressive and undemocratic machine, remained the epitome of urban evils. It was especially galling to rural white Tennesseans that blacks voted in Memphis. As Ralph Bunche observed in 1939, "It is common to hear responsible white Southerners point to Memphis as a horrible example of what would happen if the Negro is given the vote in the South."[44] Although the countryside viewed the continued growth of urban areas with alarm, rural and small-town Tennessee retained a numerical majority in population as well as representation in the legislature and was not without strong and effective leadership.

For almost forty years, the interests of rural and small-town Tennessee were upheld by three dominant personalities in the General Assembly, James H. "Mr. Jim" Cummings, I. D. Beasley, and Walter M.

"Pete" Haynes. Known inelegantly but affectionately as the "Unholy Trinity," the trio controlled Tennessee's legislature. Cummings had the longest tenure of the threesome. Born in Woodbury in Cannon County in 1890, Cummings was educated at Cumberland University, began the practice of law in his home town in 1922, and was first elected to the House of Representatives in 1928. All told, he served fourteen terms in the House and four in the Senate for a total of thirty-six years, longer than any representative in the state's history. A small man with a high-pitched voice, Cummings was always cheerful but shrewd, alert, and unmatched as a floor leader.[45] I. D. Beasley of Carthage in Smith County teamed with Cummings as a floor leader. Born in 1895, and also educated at Cumberland University, Beasley was a lawyer, and won his first seat in the state House of Representatives in 1920. He served thirteen terms in the General Assembly, eight in the Senate and five in the House for a total of twenty-six years; Beasley and Cummings actually rotated between the Senate and House for many years. A bachelor, fond of good food, grossly overweight—he carried 230 pounds on a five-foot, three-inch frame—Beasley was perhaps the most colorful character to serve in the state legislature. Known as the "Mockingbird of Capitol Hill," Beasley could mimic anyone he heard speak and he became a legend for using his talent to play practical jokes on governors, visiting dignitaries, and other political leaders.[46] The third member of the trio, "Pete" Haynes, was a skillful trial attorney from Winchester in Franklin County, and, like the other two, was educated at Cumberland University. According to legend, Haynes participated in a football game that set a scoring record. In 1916, a "pick up" team from Cumberland journeyed to Atlanta, Georgia, to play Georgia Institute of Technology and was defeated by the score of 222 to 0. During the course of the game, a Cumberland player fumbled the ball and shouted to Haynes to pick it up. Haynes allegedly replied: "Hell, you dropped it! You pick it up! I don't want it!" Haynes won his first race for the General Assembly in 1928 and served nine terms in the House and three terms in the Senate for a total of twenty-four years; he was Speaker of the House three terms and Speaker of the Senate two terms. Although missing from Capitol Hill for several years in the 1940s, Haynes served as the master parliamentarian and cloakroom intriguer when the "Unholy Trinity" worked together.[47]

Cummings, Beasley, and Haynes played practical jokes, and often wrecked the dignity of the legislature. Yet working together the trio was one of the most skillful teams in the annals of parliamentary bodies.

They were adept in interpreting bills, at parliamentary procedure, debate, cloakroom maneuvering, and persuasion; and they could milk lobbies and vested interests for all they were worth. They could obtain passage of any measure they supported or by using all the techniques at their disposal kill a measure, if necessary, by tying up the legislature in red tape. Governors were forced to cooperate or see their legislative programs destroyed by the "Unholy Trinity." Other legislators were often frustrated in the General Assembly controlled by Cummings, Beasley, and Haynes. One freshman representative recalled that he went to Capitol Hill with visions of great achievements and had carefully studied Roberts Rules of Order in preparation to do battle with the trio only to be outmaneuvered; one measure he introduced was killed by the simple procedure of sending it to the wrong committee.[48] For more than a generation, the "Unholy Trinity," sometimes singly, more often in concert, ruled the Tennessee General Assembly with iron hands.

The Cummings-Beasley-Haynes team played a vital role in protecting the interests of rural and small-town Tennessee. As Cummings noted, "We were three country lawyers connected by our interest in rural Tennessee." The sage of Woodbury voiced the rationale for protecting the countryside against the urban threat: "We must not," he declared, "allow numerical concentrations of people" to have too great a voice in government. "It's not healthy . . . . I believe in collecting the taxes where the money is—in the cities—and spending it where it's needed—in the country."[49] Cummings claimed to have waged many battles with Ed Crump but he was at the same time a friend and gave support to Senator McKellar. Moreover, as often as not the trio worked with governors endorsed by the Memphis boss. They were effective in obtaining for the countryside perhaps more than its proportionate share in allocations for schools and roads and other state services. But the most vital issue that concerned the three leaders was legislative apportionment. Despite a constitutional provision requiring reapportionment every ten years, any move in the General Assembly to do just that was effectively blocked by Cummings, Haynes, and Beasley. The task of looking out for the interests of rural Tennessee was not overly difficult because the membership of the legislature was predominantly rural and small-town, and Tennessee's governors were rural in outlook.

The years that Memphis political boss Ed Crump had his greatest degree of influence in state politics were therefore years in which the rural bloc continued to dominate Tennessee. Thus Crump would not have been able to press successfully for urban interests, even if he had been philosophically inclined to do so. And it could hardly be said that the great majority of the residents of Tennessee's cities were urban in outlook. As Richard Hofstadter notes, "The United States was born in the country and has moved to the city."[50] Many, if not most, of the residents of Tennessee's urban areas were migrants from the countryside. Retaining their rural values, they had little inclination to support any massive effort to press for urban interests. Ed Crump's position in the conflict between the cities and the countryside was defensive. By endorsing a rural gubernatorial candidate, and usually one from Middle Tennessee, he was in a position to prevent attacks on his bastion. The period of Crump's greatest influence in Tennessee was therefore an era of stalemate in the struggle between rural and urban interests, and in the mid-1940s the Tennessee Democratic party also reached the nadir of factionalism. Nothing better illustrates the achieving of consensus in the Democratic party than the gubernatorial primary of 1944. The constitutional provision limiting a governor to three consecutive two-year terms forced Governor Cooper to retire, and Jim Nance McCord of Lewisburg, possibly with Senator McKellar's blessing, announced for governor. Born in Unionville in Bedford County in 1879, McCord had worked as a traveling salesman before becoming publisher of Lewisburg's *Marshall Gazette* in 1910. He also became a well-known auctioneer of livestock and real estate. At the same time he served simultaneously for more than a quarter of a century as mayor of Lewisburg and as a member of the Marshall County Court. In 1942 he had been elected without opposition as congressman from the fifth district. McCord's chief asset was his speaking ability although the standard comment was that, while he spoke beautifully, he never said anything worthwhile. Following McKellar's lead, Crump's Shelby organization endorsed McCord for governor, as did Silliman Evans. Normally a primary without an incumbent attracted a number of hopefuls, but McCord won the contest almost by default for he had no opposition. Apparently no one was willing to challenge the hegemony of the Crump-McKellar axis.

Gordon Browning was not, for several years at least, available for leadership among the anti-Crump forces in Tennessee. Some of the bitterness of his humiliating defeat in 1938 was reflected in his farewell address to the General Assembly in January 1939. He said that while his tour as governor was abbreviated, he would be protected in private life from attacks by "unscrupulous persecutors" who impeded his efforts to serve the people.[51] Rationalization came easy for Browning. Shortly after he left office he was quoted as saying, perhaps sincerely at the time, "I'm glad to get rid of the responsibilities and worries." His wife, Miss Ida, was more direct. She declared, "I'm satisfied. I'll be glad when we can settle down. I would much prefer a quiet life to a political one."[52] She was being completely honest. She had not liked the fast pace of Washington or the limelight of the executive mansion in Nashville. Years later Browning reminded a reporter that his wife was never a social butterfly: "One night she just refused to attend some social function we had been invited to and I accused her of being a terrible wife for a Congressman to have. 'That's all right, Sonny . . . . I'll be a mighty fine wife to settle down with after you get beat!'"[53] On a more serious note, he declared:

> The thing I most regret about my life in public service was my inability to have my wife happy about the work I was doing. And even though she did her best to be a governor's wife, she never did like it. She felt every-thing about politics was dirty and a sham and a scandal. She didn't believe that the people in politics believed in anything they were doing. She thought the whole business was full of tricks, largely because she saw me double-crossed several times. Public life was distasteful to her but she had too much courage to let anybody find it out except me. . . . Her life re-minded me of a poem which ends something like this: "She did exactly what she did not want to do." She did it because of her love for me and for the respect she had for my success. There'll never be another woman that suffered like she did without talking about it.[54]

Within a few days after he left office, Browning and his wife departed with friends for a vacation in Mexico. Upon his return home to Hun-tingdon, he entered the uneventful routine of law practice in the firm of Lassiter and Browning. During the years after his defeat, Browning was a frequent guest speaker before church groups, at veterans' meet-ings, school graduations, picnics, and the like. He was one of the most sought-after banquet speakers in West Tennessee, not only because he was a former governor, but because he was a delightful story teller. He could hold the interest of an audience for hours with his off-the-cuff humor, homilies, and anecdotes. Always cheerful, he was the center of attention at every affair. And Browning's robust appearance indicated that he also enjoyed the food served at picnics and banquets. Private life gave him more time for fishing and hunting expeditions—always with a group of friends, for Browning was an extrovert and happy only when he was in a crowd. Requests for his presence at functions and for his service as a speaker helped to soothe the feelings of a man who had been repudiated at the polls.

Yet while that was satisfying to an extent, Browning began casting about for a measure of recognition. Early in 1940 he became involved with several others in a plan, on which he worked for many months, to establish a firm to manufacture newsprint. Browning was to be the president of a $6 million enterprise, and a plant was to be erected on the Tennessee River near Savannah. Subsequently the Tennessee Department of Insurance and Banking approved the establishment of the firm and the federal Securities and Exchange Commission allowed the sale of stock. Various manufacturing and transportation interests were then approached and pledges to purchase up to fifty percent of the stock were obtained. It therefore became necessary to apply to the Reconstruction Finance Corporation in Washington for a loan to cover the remaining fifty percent of the original investment. Once again Browning found it difficult to evade Ed Crump and Senator McKellar. Bob Guinn, a Savannah contractor and friend to both Browning and the senator, was dispatched to Washington to get McKellar's assistance in obtaining the loan from the RFC. Apparently unaware that the former governor was involved, the senator, as always coming to the aid of his constitutents, interceded and won approval for the loan.[55] Shortly after word of the venture became public knowledge, Crump wrote to McKellar admonishing him "not to take under our wing these unworthy fellows, whom we know will expect something." An embarrassed senator could only respond that he was afraid the paper " 'deal' will be a costly one for the government if it goes through."[56] But the paper mill never came to fruition because, according to Guinn, the original backers did not live up to their commitments.[57] Whether Crump or McKellar had anything to do with that is unknown. The United States was beginning to mobilize for war in 1940 and undoubtedly that was one reason why the mill failed to materialize; newsprint had a very low priority in a nation gearing for war. At any rate, Browning soon turned to other interests.

A few months later Gordon Browning began quietly seeking a modest elective post, chancellor of the Eighth Chancery Division, which included many of the counties of his old congressional district. Chancery Courts reflect the complexity of Tennessee's judicial system. Vestigial remnants of the old English judicial system, they are in some instances courts of original jurisdiction for equity cases, or cases which can not be settled by strict application of the law. In other matters Chancery Courts have concurrent as well as local and personal jurisdiction. Browning recalled that he originally did not want the post but former governor Tom Rye, chancellor of the Eighth Chancery, was anxious to retire and asked him to run. He said he told Rye that he did not want the job, but was informed that he had already been qualified. At any rate, he finally agreed to make the race, Chancellor Rye announced his retirement, and J. B. Avery of Alamo (who had qualified to run earlier) withdrew, leaving Browning without opposition. The Democratic primary board decided to go ahead and hold a primary since the machinery had already been set up. In the primary in August 1941 Browning received a complimentary vote of more than 12,000, and in the general election the following year he was elected to the eight-year term without opposition.[58] Browning declared that he enjoyed his service on the bench. It paid well, he did not have to fight the battles of an administrator, and it was the "best job a country lawyer could ask for."[59] It could hardly be said, however, that in seeking the chancery post Browning was beginning a comeback in state politics, because chancellors gained little publicity. However, the United States had just become involved in a national emergency that would have a major impact on the political career of Gordon Browning.

World War II had a profound effect on Tennessee. The build-up for conflict had begun well before the Japanese attacked Pearl Harbor in December 1941, and Tennesseans were already caught up in mobilization when war actually came. The state became an armed camp with the establishment of United States Army posts at Tullahoma, Paris, and Clarksville; air bases at Halls and Smyrna; the largest inland naval training station at Millington; and the activation of military hospitals at Memphis and Nashville. Important defense industries were built in Tennessee at Millington, Nashville, and Milan; and the project to build the atomic bomb led to the establishment of an entirely new city, Oak Ridge. The military bases and new defense industries caused an economic boom in the state, unemployment became negligible, and wages soared. The rapid industrialization caused by the war effort also accelerated urbanization in the state as rural Tennesseans were attracted to the increased wages paid by defense contractors. Despite the loss of labor, farmers prospered as farm prices soared. World War II therefore brought prosperity to Tennessee despite the loss of manpower to the armed forces. One of the 315,000 Tennesseans in uniform was former governor Gordon Browning.

Inclined as he was to martial zeal, Browning was quick to volunteer his services to the United States Army soon after war broke out. But an appointment was slow in coming. In his "Oral Memoir," Browning described how Senator McKellar almost prevented him from receiving a commission:

> In the second World War they wanted me to come into the military government as a lieutenant colonel. As soon as my name went in, McKellar commenced raising hell. He wouldn't let the General have charge of my commission—wouldn't let him put me in school. He was afraid to, because he knew what the wrath of God was, and the circumstances before McKellar even got started. I didn't blame him. Then, he wanted to know if I'd become a major and I said I would. McKellar blocked that, too. Then I said to old John Henry Ulio, the Adjutant General: "You've got a record of mine here from the first World War. I don't even know what's in it, but I'll stand on it, and I want you to look at it." So he sent out and got it and said: "Damned if you haven't. I can't give you anything other than present rank, and that's captain. Do you want that?" I said, "Yes, I do: swear me in." And he did. After that, McKellar couldn't do one thing about it.[60]

Browning's account may have been exaggerated. On the other hand, the senior senator jealously guarded his domain, and Browning, despite his defeat in 1938, was still a political enemy and military service might give the former governor an opportunity to regain public esteem. When, in 1947, Browning's charge was aired in the state's press and nationally by columnist Drew Pearson, the senator's office denied that McKellar had attempted to block the commission.[61] Very likely the senator did not deliberately interfere with the former governor's application for a commission. But McKellar's power in Washington was such that in some instances he did not have to take action on an issue. Army chiefs were undoubtedly cognizant of the emnity between the two men and did not deliver the commission for fear of provoking the senator's wrath. At any rate, Browning was eventually given a commission as captain and subsequently reported for active duty on 4 March 1943. "I feel like I have another good fight in me," he declared when he left.[62]

Captain Browning was first assigned to the antiaircraft section of the artillery and went through intensive training at Camp Wallace, Texas, before being sent to the West Coast area. He was soon reassigned to military government and given a three-month course at the University of Virginia in preparation to accompany forces invading Europe. His task was to help establish occupation procedures in the conquered territories, and by March 1944 he was with the preinvasion army in England. In June he was made deputy head of a mission in G-5, the civil affairs section, a quasi-diplomatic office of the Supreme Allied Headquarters Mission to Belgium and Luxemborg. After the conquest of

Belgium, he set up headquarters in Brussels and began restoring normal governmental functions. Browning's account of his experiences in Europe were spiced with humor, and he always emerged as something of a hero in every encounter with adversity. He delighted in describing his improvisation when faced with shortages of food and other needs of the Belgians in their efforts to recover from the ravages of war. Army regulations required a full colonel in the position he held. He took some pleasure in the fact that, as a captain, he could issue orders to officers superior in rank.[63] Browning was eventually promoted to the rank of lieutenant colonel, however. The belief was widely held that his promotions were blocked by Senator McKellar for political reasons, but the senator denied the charge and Browning later conceded that he was promoted on every eligible date.[64]

In January 1946 Lieutenant Colonel Browning was assigned to the military government in Germany and was made director of military government in the Bremen Enclave. His position carried a great deal of responsibility and he lived in considerable luxury. He recalled that he tried to get his wife to join him: "I told her about the big house and servants and other comforts but she wouldn't come. She just said I had better make well of it because I wouldn't have it that good any more."[65] Apparently Miss Ida was more interested in her husband's returning home to Huntingdon. After nearly a year in Bremen, he asked for his release, which was granted, and he returned to Huntingdon on terminal leave. For his services, Browning received the United States Legion of Merit for exceptionally meritorious service, the Order of the British Empire, the Order of the Crown of Belgium, the Order of Adolph of Nassau of Luxembourg, and the Order of Orange Nassau of the Netherlands.

Although still in uniform overseas, Gordon Browning became involved in Tennessee politics in 1946 through what appears to have been a spontaneous development. Anti-Crump forces were desperately searching for someone to run for governor against Governor McCord. No well-known individual was available to challenge the Crump-McKellar axis except E. W. Carmack, who was campaigning against Senator McKellar. In May 1946 some five hundred voters signed a petition qualifying Browning as a candidate for the Democratic gubernatorial primary in August. Joe Hatcher, political writer for the *Tennessean*, described how it came about. A group of citizens in Marshall County, the home of Governor McCord, formed a "Carmack for Senate" club which embarrassed McCord and he strenuously objected. His protest rankled members of the club and they responded by drafting the petition to place Browning's name in the race for governor.[66] The enthusiasm for the former governor gained such momentum that in June it was united with Carmack's senatorial campaign to form a coalition ticket and a joint campaign manager was named. Rumors were prevalent that Browning would return from Germany a few days before the election for a whirlwind campaign. Browning remained silent concerning his intentions, however, and caused consternations within the ranks of the forces of both McCord and McKellar. Late in June he announced from Germany that he would stay at his post, but would allow his name to remain on the ballot and his race in the hands of the people. Browning recalled that he tried to get his "friends" to remove his name from the ballot "but they begged so hard" that he gave his permission to leave it on.[67] Actually, it was a good test of his popularity at no cost or effort.

Meanwhile, Carmack carried on a spirited drive, and Wally Fowler and his country music band toured the state in behalf of Browning. The forces of both McKellar and McCord were sufficiently concerned to launch a vigorous fund raising drive and to conduct more aggressive campaigns.[68] A number of major daily newspapers come out for the candidate *in absentia*. The *Tennessean* supported Browning and declared that the state needed a patriot like the man who was presently serving his country. The *Chattanooga Times* came out in support of the former governor, as did the Memphis *Press-Scimitar*, although the latter endorsed McKellar in preference to the inexperienced Carmack. The *Times* admitted that Crump had given good government in Memphis but declared that he had been bad for the state. The people must end bossism, concluded the paper, and a vote for Browning would be a vote for good government in Tennessee. The *Press-Scimitar* urged the voters to look to Browning, for according to editor Meeman, his one term as governor had been the finest since Austin Peay.[69] Newspapers that supported McCord were reluctant to criticize a man in uniform. Morris Cunningham, political writer for the *Commercial Appeal*, attacked Browning indirectly. He simply suggested that the former governor was not interested in making the race. He admitted that the incumbent administration had not been spectacular but McCord demonstrated more concern than Lieutenant Colonel Browning who refused to return home and campaign.[70] Rumors spread that the former governor was really not interested in the race and Miss Ida went on the air to refute the charge. It was a grueling task for a woman who hated the limelight, but she felt she had to defend her husband. Browning recalled that she told him, "I just got tired of sitting around and hearing your enemies try to tell the people what you thought. I decided that somebody that knew what you had been saying all the time was going to tell them to their faces."[71] On 21 July Mrs. Browning made a radio talk in which she denounced rumors that he was not interested in being governor. She stated that the false reports were unfair; that Browning had never entered a race with that attitude, and that he was in the governor's race to win[72] The only effect of her talk was to add a little drama to an otherwise dull campaign. No one really expected Browning to win, but the vote for the absentee candidate was surprising.

The final count in the primary gave McCord 187,119 votes to 120,535 for Browning. The former governor polled almost thirty-nine percent of the total, and he actually won thirty-six counties and the fourth, seventh, and eighth congressional districts. Shelby County cast 45,543 votes for Governor McCord to 5,625 for Browning. Without Shelby's vote, the governor's margin was only 27,000. McKellar defeated Carmack by 81,000 votes, the closest he had been pressed since entering the United States Senate in 1917.[73] The turnout in the primary was light. Fewer than one in ten eligible voters cast ballots and Joe Hatcher suggested that the number of workers on the state payroll could easily have been the difference.[74] Browning demonstrated drawing power even though he ran *in absentia*. More important, the results of the primary seemed to indicate that the electorate was becoming restive under the Crump-McKellar regime.

In December 1946 Browning returned to Huntingdon on terminal leave and was discharged soon thereafter with the rank of colonel. He declined to discuss politics and stated that he would resume his duties as chancellor of the Eighth Chancery Court.[75] But he had unquestionably become the leader of the anti-Crump forces in Tennessee. He had received a great deal of publicity in the campaign and had returned home a hero in uniform, having regained much of the public esteem he had lost in 1938. The forces opposed to the Crump-McKellar axis rallied to him as a colorful, well-known figure who could lead them to success in 1948.

NOTES

1. William D. Miller, *Mr. Crump of Memphis* (Baton Rouge: Louisiana State University Press, 1964), p. 167.

2. File labeled "1937–1938—Browning Campaign, Police Reports," Box 1, Watkins Overton Papers, Memphis State University Library.

3. Miller, *Mr. Crump*, p. 276; Clark Porteous, interview with the author, Memphis, 22 June 1977.

4. Clark Porteous, interview.

5. Lee S. Greene and Jack E. Holmes, "Tennessee: A Politics of Peaceful Change," *The Changing Politics of the South*, ed. William C. Havard (Baton Rouge: Louisiana State University Press, 1972), pp. 167–168; V. O. Key, Jr., *Southern Politics in State and Nation* (New York: Alfred A. Knopf, 1949), p. 74.

6. Numan V. Bartley and Hugh D. Graham, *Southern Politics and the Second Reconstruction* (Baltimore: The Johns Hopkins University Press, 1975), p. 44.

7. David M. Tucker, *Lieutenant Lee of Beale Street* (Nashville: Vanderbilt University Press, 1971), pp. 120–154.

8. Ralph J. Bunche, *The Political Status of the Negro in the Age of FDR*, ed. Dewey W. Grantham (Chicago: University of Chicago Press, 1973), p. 500; see also Tucker, *Lieutenant Lee*, pp. 120–154; David M. Tucker, *Black Pastors and Leaders: The Memphis Clergy, 1819–1972* (Memphis: Memphis State University Press, 1975), pp. 103–106.

9. Bunche, *The Political Status*, pp. 493–502; Robert L. Taylor, interview with the author, Memphis, 10 August 1976; William W. Farris, interview with the author, Memphis, 22 June 1977.

10. Gerald Capers, "Memphis, Satrapy of a Benevolent Despot," *Our Fair City*, ed. Robert S. Allen (New York: Vanguard Press, Inc., 1949), pp. 211–234.

11. Thomas Harrison Baker, *The Memphis Commercial Appeal: History of A Southern Newspaper* (Baton Rouge: Louisiana State University Press, 1971) p. 262.

12. *Commercial Appeal*, 28 July 1940.

13. James H. S. Cooper, "Boss Crump and Governor Prentice Cooper: Study of A Relationship, 1938–1944" (unpublished history honors paper, University of North Carolina, 1975), pp. 29–36; Miller, *Mr. Crump*, p. 289.

14. Key (*Southern Politics*, pp. 63, 65) stated that "Crump's Memphis votes and tactical skill converted the senior Senator into a junior partner" and "after some essays toward independence, he [McKellar] accepted a role as number-two man in Tennessee."

15. W. R. Davidson, interview with the author, Tullahoma, 1 September 1977.

16. Crump to McKellar, 17 January 1931, Crump to McKellar, 20 January 1932, Crump-McKellar Correspondence, Box 2, Crump to McKellar, 11 April 1937, Crump to McKellar, 7 June 1937, Crump-McKellar Correspondence, Box 3, Kenneth Douglas McKellar Papers, Memphis-Shelby County Library and Information Center.

17. Crump to Stewart, 20 February 1942 (copy), Crump to McKellar, 21 February 1942, Crump-McKellar Correspondence, Box 5, Ibid.

18. McKellar to Crump, 20 January 1932, Crump-McKellar Correspondence, Box 2, McKellar to Crump, 9 June 1937, Crump-McKellar Correspondence, McKellar to Crump, 23 February 1942, Crump-McKellar Correspondence, Box 5, Ibid.

19. T. Arthur Jenkins, interview with the author, Manchester, 8 June 1976; Frick Stewart, interview with the author, Winchester, 25 May 1977.

20. Robert Dean Pope, "Senatorial Baron: The Long Political Career of Kenneth D. McKellar"(unpublished Ph. D. dissertation, Yale University, 1976), pp. 282–283.

21. Ibid., p. 281.

22. Cooper, "Boss Crump and Governor Prentice Cooper,"pp. 77–78.

23. Crump to McKellar, 21 January 1942, Crump to McKellar 21 February 1942, Crump to McKellar, 15 July 1942, Crump-McKellar Correspondence, Box 5, McKellar Papers.

24. *Carroll County Democrat*, 26 June 1942.

25. *Nashville Tennessean*, 23 July, 2 August 1942.

26. *Tennessee Blue Book* (Nashville, 1943), pp. 83–84.

27. Pope, "Senatorial Baron,"p. 287.

28. Miller, *Mr. Crump*, pp. 191–192; Clark Porteous, interview.

29. Edward J. Meeman to E. H. Crump, Jr., 14 March 1933, Box 6, No. 21, Edward J. Meeman Papers, Memphis State University Library.

30. Crump to Meeman, 23 October 1939, 6 March 1943, 10 November 1946, Ibid.

31. Baker, *Commercial Appeal*, pp. 272–284, 303–310, 317–319.

32. Hugh Davis Graham, *Crisis in Print: Desegregation and the Press in Tennessee* (Nashville: Vanderbilt University Press, 1967), pp. 32–33, 46–47.

33. Ibid., pp. 31, 48.

34. Ibid., pp. 34–36, 41–42; Baker, *Commercial Appeal*, pp. 272–273; Ralph McGill, "Boss Crump's Town: A Cub Reporter's First Campaign,"*The Atlantic* (January 1960), pp. 63–66; Ralph McGill, *The South and the Southerner* (Boston: Little, Brown, 1964), pp. 90–91.

35. Graham, *Crisis*, pp. 34–36; Baker, *Commercial Appeal*, pp. 272–285; John Berry McFerrin, *Caldwell and Company: A Southern Financial Empire* (Nashville: Vanderbilt University Press, 1969), pp. 87–98.

36. Graham, *Crisis*, pp. 30–31n, 34–36; Miller, *Mr. Crump*, p. 193.

37. Miller, *Mr. Crump*, p. 295.

38. McKellar to Lipe Henslee, copy of telegram to Crump, 24 January 1941, Box 4, Crump-McKellar Correspondence, McKellar Papers.

39. Frederick D. Ogden, *The Poll Tax In The South* (University, AL: University of Alabama Press, 1958), pp. 193–197.

40. Cooper, "Boss Crump and Governor Prentice Cooper," p. 100; see also Miller, *Mr. Crump*, p. 297.

41. Jennings Perry, *Democracy Begins at Home: The Tennessee Fight Against The Poll Tax* (New York: J. B. Lippincott, 1944).

42. Miller, *Mr. Crump*, pp. 294–300.

43. Key, *Southern Politics*, pp. 62, 67, 70, 71.

44. Bunche, *Political Status of the Negro*, p. 55.

45. George Barker, "The Biggest Gun in Cannon County, "*Nashville Tennessean Magazine* (12 April 1964), pp. 8–9, 11; James H. Cummings, interview with the author, Woodbury, 8 June 1976.

46. George Barker, "The Mockingbird of Capitol Hill," *Tennessean Magazine* (19 April 1964), pp. 14–16.

47. George Barker, "Trials of a Country Lawyer," *Tennessean Magazine* (26 April 1964), pp. 8–9, 13; Elizabeth Haynes, interview with the author, Decherd, 14 November 1976; J. L. Haynes, interview with the author, Decherd, 14 November 1976.

48. Joe Bean, interview with the author, Winchester, 6 November 1976.

49. *Tennessean*, 24 May 1972; Barker, "Biggest Gun in Cannon Country," p. 11.

50. Richard Hofstadter, *The Age of Reform: From Bryan to F. D. R.* (New York: Vintage Books, 1955), p. 23.

51. *House Journal of the Seventy-First General Assembly of the State of Tennessee, 1939* (Nashville, 1939), pp. 156–161.

52. Quoted in *Carroll County Democrat*, 20 January 1939.

53. George Barker, "Three Times and You're Out," *Tennessean Magazine* (7 October 1962), p. 12.

54. Gordon Browning, "Gordon Browning: An Oral Memoir," ed. Joseph H. Riggs (Memphis Public Library, 1966), pp. 14–15.

55. Bob Guinn, interviews with the author, Savannah, 23 June 1977, 10 September 1977; *Carroll County Democrat*, 19 January, 12 April, 31 May 1940.

56. Crump to McKellar, 19 April 1940, McKellar to Crump, 22 April 1940, Crump-McKellar Correspondence, Box 4, McKellar Papers.

57. Bob Guinn, interview, 23 June 1977.

58. Browning, "Oral Memoir," p. 20; *Carroll County Democrat*, 6 June, 4, 25 July, 8 August 1941, 14 August 1942.

59. George Barker, "Victory, Defeat, Victory," *Tennessean Magazine*, 30 September 1962), p. 20.

60. Browning, "Oral Memoir," p. 117.

61. *Press-Scimitar*, 26 April, 6 June 1947; McKellar to Meeman, 4 June 1947, Political Correspondence, Box 58, McKellar Papers.

62. *Tennessean*, 21 February 1943.

63. Browning, "Oral Memoir," pp. 117–118.

64. *Tennessean*, 6 May 1946; Gordon Browning, interview with the author, Huntingdon, 23 June 1966.

65. Browning, "Oral Memoir," p. 14.

66. Joe Hatcher, "Politics," *Tennessean*, 6, 9 May 1946.

67. *Carroll County Democrat*, 28 June 1946; Joe Hatcher later acknowledged that his newspaper, the *Tennessean*, sent him to Germany to try to persuade Browning to make the race; see Hatcher, "Gordon Browning is still a Democrat," *Tennessean*, 20 April 1972; Browning, "Oral Memoir," p. 121.

68. Hatcher, "Politics, " 28 July 1946.

69. *Tennessean*, 21 July 1946; *Chattanooga Times*, 28 July 1946; *Press-Scimitar*, 29 July 1946.

70. *Commercial Appeal*, 28 July 1946. Browning's actions in 1937 and 1938 were not raised against him in 1946.

71. Browning, "Oral Memoir," p. 121.

72. *Press-Scimitar*, 30 July 1946.

73. *Tennessee Blue Book, 1947–1948* (Nashville, 1948), pp. 248–250.

74. Hatcher, "Politiccs," 4 Aug. 1946.

75. *Carroll County Democrat*, 3 Jan. 1947.

7

The Restoration

"RECENT observers have offered evidence that social and economic change is coming to the South more rapidly than to other sections of the country," wrote an authority on the American scene in 1949.[1] Sociologist Howard W. Odum described some of the changes in the South: increased income and wealth; a higher level of living, even in rural areas, bringing about a more equitable balance between city and country and between agriculture and industry; more public works and social services; and increased efforts in public education. In addition, public issues were discussed more openly and freely than before. Progress was also being made in civil rights as the black began to assert his desire to a larger role in the life of the South. The most obvious change, however, was the region's rapid industrialization and urbanization.[2] In short, the South was beginning to experience what has been labeled the "bulldozer revolution."[3] Urbanization and industrialization also contributed to the development of a new middle class whose thinking was more oriented toward the culture of the rest of the nation than to that of the old South. Organized labor was also emerging as a political force. In earlier years, labor had played only a nominal role in the electoral process, in part because rural areas were hostile to unions; but by the end of World War II, labor was asserting itself. In contrast to the lack of concern in the past, business and professional leaders were anxious to participate in public life and speak out boldly on issues. Finally, but certainly not least, veterans of World War II were eager to play a role in political affairs. When they returned from war to find the internal paths to power choked by the vested interests of machine politics, many of those young men drifted into the opposition and began to speak out boldly against political bossism. Southern political leaders of the postwar years were forced to adjust to the new politics produced by socioeconomic changes. The older leaders who advocated the negative concept of states' rights retrenchment were being replaced by a new breed more committed to the public service concept of government.[4]

Tennessee was also caught up in the "bulldozer revolution." During the ten years between 1938 and 1948, industry developed rapidly and was increasingly diversified in the Volunteer State, in part because of cheap electricity generated by the Tennessee Valley Authority. Like the other southern states, Tennessee saw a strong population shift from rural areas to the city. From 1937 to 1948, the state's urban population increased by a little more than nine percent. Although its urban population in 1950 was still only about thirty-eight percent, the urban growth rate from 1940 to 1950 was twenty-three percent, while rural areas grew at a rate of less than eight percent. All the major cities grew rapidly: Memphis, for example, increased by more than a hundred thousand in the decade and one city, Oak Ridge, which had not existed in 1940, boasted of a population of more than thirty thousand in 1950.[5] But industrialization and urbanization were mixed blessings as enormous problems with political implications resulted from the economic changes. Cities desperately needed expensive services, and the countryside demanded more and improved highways. Tennessee's educational system was in a state of near chaos because both rural and urban school buildings were dilapidated and teacher salaries were woefully inadequate. Moreover, higher education was strained to provide facilities for training veterans of World War II who were attending school under the G.I. Bill. To complicate matters, Tennessee's sources of revenue were inadequate to meet the needs for more and better services.

In 1947, after a careful study of the educational needs of the state, Governor Jim McCord was convinced that the system had "deteriorated to the core" and that only massive appropriations could remedy the situation. Because sources of revenue were limited in the main to property and privilege taxes, he concluded that only a sales tax could produce the needed funds. Therefore, the governor and his commissioner of education, Burgin Dossett, girded for battle. Although Ed Crump had long opposed a sales tax, a motorcade carrying McCord and his official family visited Memphis to win Crump's support for such a tax. Finally convinced of the need for such a tax, Crump agreed not to join the opposition and this helped pave the way for the governor to obtain legislative enactment in 1947 of a two-percent levy on all general retail sales in Tennessee. Although the tax produced revenue that enabled the state to improve its educational system significantly, it caused a bitter public debate over taxation in principle and became an issue for the next gubernatorial election.[6] The General Assembly in 1947 also took action that angered a small but increasingly active minority in Tennessee. Responding to a national reaction against organized labor, the United States Congress had passed the Taft-Hartley Act in 1947 and one provision of that measure enabled states to pass open shop or "right-to-work" laws. The General Assembly, still dominated by rural legislators, quickly enacted such a measure. Organized labor's influence in Tennessee was still minimal, but passage of the act angered union leaders and insured that they would be active during the next election.

Tennessee's electorate became increasingly restive after the close of World War II and opposition to machine rule became more active. Two East Tennessee machines, one controlled by Burch Biggs in Polk County and Paul Cantrell's McMinn County machine, came under direct attack by reformers. In 1946 returning veterans sought to end the iron-handed control by Biggs and Cantrell and, organizing in secret for the most part, put up a nonpartisan slate of candidates for county offices. Intimidation by the machines led the veterans to arm themselves, and by election day that year both counties were armed camps. Violence erupted in Athens in McMinn County as veterans laid siege to Cantrell's deputies in the county jail. In the end, the Biggs and Cantrell machines were broken, although peace and tranquility did not immediately return to those two strife-torn communities.[7] The challenges to those organizations was a forecast of eventual attacks on other machines across the state, including one on Crump's own Shelby County organization. Sensing the mood of the electorate and realizing that the establishment would likely face a stiff challenge at the polls in 1948, Crump and his allies searched for ways at least to mitigate, if not arrest, the trend. Late in 1946 an ally of the Crump-McKellar axis conceived of one tactic: separate county elections from the state primaries. County general elections had long been held in August in conjunction with the biennial party primaries. Local elections tended to generate more interest and resulted in a larger turnout in the statewide primaries than might have been otherwise, and an exciting primary contest could bring out a larger vote in a relatively dull county election. The Democratic primary in 1948 included a senatorial contest along with the gubernatorial race and the general elections included virtually all county offices. The motive for separating the two elections was clear: political machines could more easily control the results of an election if the voter turnout was light. The scheme was quietly brought out when the General Assembly convened in January 1947, but antimachine forces were quickly alerted to the threat. Fourth district Congressman Albert Gore made a hurried trip to Nashville to help organize opposition and the move was defeated. Thus, after nearly a decade of dominance by the Crump-McKellar axis and relative quiescence in Tennessee politics, antimachine forces in Tennessee were becoming assertive and it was apparent that the establishment would be seriously challenged in the elections of 1948.[8]

The three most available antimachine challengers for both statewide offices to be determined in 1948 were the congressmen from the fourth and third districts, Albert Gore and Estes Kefauver, and former governor Gordon Browning. Born at Granville in Jackson County, Gore attended college and taught school for several years before becoming superintendent of Smith County schools in 1933. In the meantime he attended YMCA law classes at night in Nashville. In 1934, he managed Browning's race for the Senate and became commissioner of the Department of Labor in Browning's cabinet in 1937. When fourth district Congressman J. Ridley Mitchell resigned to run for the Senate in 1938, Gore entered the congressional race and won the first of five terms in Congress. He represented a relatively safe district, once served by one of Tennessee's most beloved sons, Cordell Hull, but Gore was ambitious to move up to the Senate. He admitted privately, "No sooner had I won my spurs in Congress, than I began to build, slowly but surely, a foundation upon which to seek, come the proper time, a promotion to the United States Senate." However, 1948 was not the proper time because "my financial circumstance was quite strained due to a business adventure and expansion, making it then impossible for me to finance any part of a campaign." Although declining to run, Gore still had a vested interest in the races in 1948.[9]

Equally ambitious to move up to the Senate was Estes Kefauver of Chattanooga. Born near Madisonville in Monroe County, Kefauver was educated at the University of Tennessee and the Yale University law school. He served briefly as commissioner of finance and taxation under Governor Prentice Cooper in 1939 and then won a special election to fill a vacancy in Congress from the third district later that same year. Charming, magnetic, and a master of the personal touch, Kefauver was also anxiously awaiting the proper time to run for the Senate. The third district congressman was urged to run against Senator McKellar in 1946, and he gave serious thought to making the race, but decided that the old senator was still too entrenched to beat. Looking back, he believed "that conditions were more favorable in 1948."[10] Reporter Pugh Moore believed that Gordon Browning was instrumental in persuading Kefauver to make the senatorial race in 1948. Moore recalled that, hoping to get some idea about Browning's future political plans, shortly after the end of World War II he visited with the former governor in Europe where he was still serving in the army. In discussing the Senate, Browning told the reporter, "I'm not the man for the Senate"; he believed that what Tennessee needed was a younger man who could stay long enough to gain seniority. "Now Estes Kefauver, there is a young man . . . whom I could support all the way." Moore returned to the States and related his conversation to the Chattanooga congressman. According to Moore's story, Kefauver, with Browning's blessing and with the potential support of the former governor's loyalists, committed himself to the senatorial race in 1948.[11] If Browning was indeed encouraging Kefauver to run for the Senate, he probably had in mind a race against McKellar in 1946. At any rate, the Chattanooga congressman began to build an organization and eventually announced, in November 1947, his candidacy for the seat occupied by Tom Stewart.

The most available of the potential antiestablishment candidates for either the Senate or the governorship was Gordon Browning. He had name recognition, was well known as an opponent of the Crump machine, and had a hard core of support across the state. Certainly he would have preferred the Senate race because he had not given up his ambition for that office, but the choice was not easy. If he made the race for Stewart's seat, he would once again challenge the unwritten rule that no one of the Grand Divisions of the state should have a monopoly in the United States Senate; moreover, his wife was adamantly opposed to returning to Washington. On the other hand, the governor's race was attractive because it offered an opportunity to avenge himself and break the influence of his arch enemy, E. H. Crump. Browning was pressured both ways as various interests and individuals sought to influence his decision.

Especially anxious for him to enter the Senate race was Albert Gore. The long-time friends and allies had often discussed state politics and their own future prospects. Once, for example, Gore visited with Browning in Europe where they had a lengthy discussion and they met on several occasions upon Browning's return to the States. Gore tried his best to persuade Browning to run for the Senate in 1948 and made no attempt to hide his motive: he did not want their similar ambitions to come into conflict at some point in the future, presumably 1952. Meeting at Gore's home in Carthage sometime in late 1947, the congressman finally advised Browning that he would support him for either the Senate or the gubernatorial race. But if Browning chose to run for governor, he must not use that office as a stepping stone for a move up to the Senate; "you must have the consent of your mind that that would be an end unto itself." However, the friends left the meeting in Carthage with different interpretations concerning the substance of their conversation: Gore believed that Browning had agreed that the governorship would be the extent of his ambition whereas Browning apparently felt he had made no such commitment. That misunderstanding was the beginning of a rift between the two that would gradually widen over the next four years. [12] But for the time being, they shared one common goal, the end of machine rule in Tennessee.

Other influential leaders across the state encouraged Browning to try for the governor's office. Conscious of the value of his name in the campaign against the establishment, Kefauver's advisors wanted the ex-governor in the gubernatorial contest. [13] Browning also appealed to individual leaders such as Edward Meeman and Silliman Evans because he was the best known anti-Crump politico in the state and stood a good chance to defeat any gubernatorial candidate endorsed by the Memphis boss. [14] Machine forces may have preferred the former governor in the Senate race. Browning once intimated that he received word that he would have only token opposition for the Senate if he would "lay off the Governor's race." [15] Despite intense pressure both ways, Browning kept his own council and the state guessing. In January 1948 he made one last tour of Tennessee to study conditions and feel out sentiment. Finally, on 20 March, Browning officially tossed his hat into the gubernatorial contest. His brief announcement was to the point:

> In response to widespread and persistent urging that I make my political intentions known, it is hereby announced that I will be a candidate for governor of Tennessee this year, subject to the action of the August

Democratic Primary. Quite soon I shall set out my ideas of a constructive
program proposed for the consideration of the people.

Those people who have tired of domination from one source in Tennessee
comprise the vast majority of our voters and while I propose to stand or fall
on the quality of service offered to all, it is nothing but fair to also offer a
leadership which is unfettered and possessed of a free mind.[16]

Three factors undoubtedly influenced Browning to commit himself to
the governor's race rather than the Senate: first, he had an old score to
settle with Ed Crump; second, he discovered that many of his old
friends were commited to Senator Tom Stewart's candidacy for renomination but would support him for the governor's office; and third, he
came to the realization that the electorate thought of him more as the
state's chief executive than as a senator. Once the commitment was
made, Browning began to build an organization to do battle with the
Crump-McKellar establishment. Gore recommended that he widen his
base of support and specifically urged him to approach attorney Robert
L. Taylor of Johnson City, the son of the late Governor Alf Taylor.[17]
Browning took the advice, contacted Taylor, persuaded him to serve as
his state campaign manager, and in so doing made what was probably
the most important acquisition to his campaign. Taylor (distantly related
to Browning's Shelby County campaign manager) had a highly
respected name, was influential in East Tennessee, and had been a
McCord supporter in 1946.[18]

There had never been any doubt that Governor McCord would be
a candidate to succeed himself for a third term and that he would have
the support of Crump's Memphis orgnization. Support for Tom Stewart
was another matter. The junior senator's lackluster career had excited
little enthusiasm and only the large block of votes in Shelby County
returned him to the Senate in 1942. Yet he had made friends, performed
individual service for constituents, and had gone out of his way to do
favors for his loyalists. It was generally conceded, however, that a strong
candidate could unseat him in 1948. Crump had never been pleased
with Stewart's lack of aggressive leadership and advised the senator well
before 1948 that he could not expect the backing of the Shelby organization.[19] The Memphis boss probably deserted the junior senator because he believed Stewart would have difficulty in securing renomination
and Senator McKellar went along with Crump's decision. Why the senior senator agreed to dump Stewart was not entirely clear because the
junior senator had been an ideal colleague. McKellar wrote: "Mr.
Crump advised me that he could not support Senator Stewart this time

as he did not believe he could be elected. . . . I tried to get him to support Senator Stewart but without success and under the circumstances, of course, I am obligated to go along with Mr. Crump because of the great help that he has been to me for so long."[20] Very likely the senior senator bent to Crump's will because of age and declining health. McKellar was far less active than before, saw fewer visitors, and was often under the care of a doctor. The Memphis boss could see no reason to support Kefauver whose alleged liberal voting record in Congress disturbed many conservative Tennesseans. Instead, surprisingly, on the recommendation of Memphis utility executive Colonel Roane Waring, Crump endorsed a man he did not know and had never met, Judge John Mitchell of Cookeville.[21] Senator Stewart, however, did not withdraw and announced for renomination; thus the senatorial contest became a three-way race among Kefauver, Mitchell, and Stewart. The gubernatorial contest settled into a duel between Browning and McCord.

Conforming to tradition, no coalition tickets were formed between senatorial and gubernatorial candidates and in some instances great pains were taken to avoid any entanglement. Browning's manager for the seventh congressional district, E. W. Eggleston, for example, was emphatic in advising county leaders that "there is no line-up between Governor Browning and *any other candidate* . . . and there positively will not be any alignment or line-up in the Seventh Congressional District."[22] There were efforts in some instances to maintain old factional alignments, but because of the confusing nature of the races, old alliances broke down. Stewart's candidacy caused much of the confusion. His loyalists had expected Crump's endorsement and were surprised and angered when the Memphis boss came out for Mitchell. Although some vacillated and thus hurt Stewart's cause, many had already made a commitment to the junior senator and refused to consider Mitchell. Others abandoned McCord in retaliation and supported Browning instead. McKellar was unable to hold his followers for Mitchell and McCord. Most of the members of Browning's hierarchy—Robert L. Taylor, Pete Haynes, Rube McKinney, Jim Cummings, and I. D. Beasley—were indebted to the incumbent senator and gave him their support. And across the state there were pockets of common support for McCord and Mitchell, and for McCord and Kefauver, as well as for Browning and Kefauver. Nevertheless, there was an informal alliance, perhaps the most important of all, between Browning and Kefauver because both were committed to destroying the influence in Tennessee of Boss Ed Crump.[23]

Machine rule in Tennessee became the leading issue in both the gubernatorial and senatorial primaries. Browning made it clear in his opening address in June at Murfreesboro that he would pursue the theme of dictatorship by the Memphis boss. He declared, "When I left office in 1939, notice was expressly given that this fight for free and decent government in Tennessee had only begun." If there had been no Crump, Browning suggested, he would not have returned to the political wars and he did so reluctantly. "The people were determined that a fight should be made. It is not boasting to say that they demanded this race of me as the one they believe can drive this dictatorship from sinister domination of our fair state."[24] If indeed he was reluctant to take the lead, it did not take much urging for the old war horse to heed the call to the post. His drive was waged on a limited budget since Browning's forces possessed scant financial resources. He later claimed that he had pledges totaling $100,000, but the money never materialized.[25] Funds were so short that a small group around the candidate took turns paying for the outgoing mail, and all the secretarial and stenographical help in the state headquarters in Nashville was voluntary.[26] Browning also did some of the actual driving in his tours around the state. Most of the large contributors across Tennessee were already committed to the incumbent governor, but one contractor, an old Browning friend, admitted to the purchase of insurance by making a $1,500 donation to the challenger's cause.[27] Despite the lack of funds, Browning's campaign was spirited and optimistic and, sensing the mood of the state, pursued the theme that would most likely produce victory.

Estes Kefauver also made machine rule the central issue in his senatorial drive. Conducting a vigorous and unorthodox campaign, the congressman, instead of trying to elicit the support of professionals and county organizations, gathered about him prominent and influential citizens who had never been involved in politics before. Thus one of the myths emerging from Kefauver's campaign was that he involved citizens who became active with no motive other than to help restore good government in Tennessee. Perhaps that was partly true, but there were many others, shut out by vested machine politics, who recognized a rising star and boarded the bandwagon for the spoils and power. Memphis was especially important to the senatorial candidate. Shortly after he made his official announcement, a group of influential Memphians braved the wrath of the machine and formed an organization to promote Kefauver's cause in Shelby County. From that point, enthusiasm for the candidate gathered momentum and encouraged others across the state

to wage political war against the Crump-McKellar axis.[28] Kefauver prob-
ably had more money in his campaign treasury than Browning did.
There were common contributors such as Meeman and Evans, but
Kefauver could also draw on benefactors such as Memphis businessman
Edmund Orgill and M. M. Bullard, an enigmatic Newport contractor.[29]
It should be emphasized, however, that Browning and Kefauver did not
form a coalition ticket except that both were fighting the organization.
The candidacy of one complemented the other. Their campaigns appeared to be a great mass movement to overthrow the Memphis political
boss. Browning received some support from Kefauver's liberal backing
in the urban areas, and Browning's rural support helped the Congressman's drive for the senatorial nomination.

　　Although both the gubernatorial and senatorial races had the common
issue of bossism, each contest had particular issues. The senatorial race
involved the Tennessee Valley Authority, the spector of Communism
and the intimidating activities of the so-called 100 percent American
groups, antilynching legislation, a federal proposal to end the poll tax,
and federal aid to education. The governor's race included such issues
as the sales tax adopted under McCord, state finances and retirement
of the state's debt, previous political records of both candidates, pardons
and reprives, highways, and education. Browning ignored Governor
McCord for the most part except to say that he was "owned body and
soul by the dictator" in Memphis. He insisted that the campaign was a
"fight between me and Crump." Browning's foes reminded the electorate of the unit system he had rammed through the General Assembly
in 1937 but the challenger responded that he could defeat McCord
"without a Unit Bill." He insisted, "there is no need for such a bill now"
for the electorate was aroused to the menace of dictatorship.[30] Browning
also ignored the sales tax issue except to indicate his willingness to maintain it until another source of revenue could be found. The tax was bitterly opposed by many, especially *Tennessean* publisher Silliman Evans.
Morris Cunningham, political writer for the Memphis *Commercial Appeal*, commented that Browning's refusal to advocate repeal of the hated
tax caused some unhappiness among his supporters.[31] Browning had
always opposed a sales tax but he was realistic enough to accept it because of the state's need for revenue. He did, however, call for a larger
proportion from the sales tax revenue to go to education. Besides the
promise of a thorough housecleaning in state government, the two principle planks in Browning's platform included the pledge to build hard
surfaced rural roads and to improve the educational system.

By midsummer, the campaigns for Browning and Kefauver were gaining in enthusiasm. Both anti-Crump candidates received the support
of organized labor. The Political Action Committee of the Congress of
Industrial Organizations was especially eager to assist Kefauver, largely
because he had opposed the Taft-Hartley Act and, although Browning
was "no hero to the working man," he was endorsed because of Mc-
Cord's record on the sales tax and the open shop law. The chief organ
of labor, *The Trades and Labor News*, endorsed both anti-Crump candidates and launched an aggressive "get-out-the-vote" campaign among
the workers.[32] Both Browning and Kefauver won considerable support
in the press. The *Chattanooga Times* held to the theme that the only
way for Tennessee to get the "Old man of the Mississippi Bluffs and his
army of henchmen, high and low, off its back" was to nominate Browning
and Kefauver. Some papers, like the *Johnson City Press-Chronicle*,
backed the ex-governor because they contended that he proved himself
in 1937 by getting Tennessee out of a financial hole and setting the standard of financial soundness. Pro-Browning papers in East Tennessee like
the *Knoxville News-Sentinel* kept alive a charge that McCord would split
the University of Tennessee at Knoxville and move half to "Crumpville."
Papers that opposed Browning included the *Chattanooga News Free-
Press*, the Columbia *Daily Herald*, the Dyersburg *State Gazette*, and
the *Commercial Appeal*. The opposition press attacked the former governor's record, especially for the county unit system he tried to install
in 1937 and the threat to send National Guard troops to Memphis in
1938. Several of the pro-Browning papers split their support in the
three-way senatorial contest. For some publishers, the governor's race
clearly took second place in interest. The *Nashville Banner* virtually
ignored the gubernatorial race and most of the paper's editorial space
and caustic cartoons were devoted to an attack on Congressman
Kefauver. The *Banner* supported Stewart in preference to Mitchell.
Edward Meeman's Memphis *Press-Scimitar* focused most of its attention on Kefauver's efforts, although the editor left no doubt of his support for Browning.[33]

The enigma in the Browning camp was Congressman Albert Gore.
Although quietly working behind the scenes for the gubernatorial challenger, Gore refused to make an open endorsement and that irritated
members of Browning's inner circle. The congressman later explained
his reluctance to participate actively in the campaigns of others: "I do
not think . . . that a public official . . . has the freedom of action enjoyed
by the citizens without such responsibilities." He concluded, however,

"there are circumstances in which action is justified." Such a circumstance occurred in the campaign of 1948 when a full page advertisement, paid for by Crump forces, appeared in the newspapers in his district questioning his integrity and veracity. Having therefore no "honorable choice," he publicly espoused the cause of Gordon Browning.[34] But his initial unwillingness for open participation left some Browning partisans bitter toward the congressman.

Crump's biographer suggests that the Memphis boss was primarily concerned with the senatorial contest and would have avoided the governor's race had it not been for the fact that Browning was in it; the fight ten years earlier "was still fresh in his mind."[35] Crump, therefore, conducted his own campaign against the former governor. His plan of attack was simply to describe the record and repeat everything Browning had done in the past, including his proposition to the Memphis boss in 1937, the unit system, the voter purge, the establishment of a police force, and the threat to use troops in Memphis. Crump also raised the issue of Browning's pardon and reprieve record, pointing out that a number of murderers, rapists, and robbers whom the ex-governor had pardoned had been returned to prison for committing additional crimes. In order to get across his charges, Crump purchased full-page advertisements and on 21 July the first of two appeared in the state's leading newspapers. Crump declared, "I am, as usual, the 'whipping boy.' " He then described Browning as a "wolf in sheep's clothing, righteousness of voice but venom in heart." He stated that "we are against Browning" because he was the biggest hypocrite who ever ran for a state office and probably the trickiest and most unreliable. The advertisement cited as evidence of the ex-governor's hypocrisy Browning's offer to send Crump to the Senate and his telegram in 1936 in which he said that there were 60,000 reasons why he loved Memphis. Crump also noted that the *Nashville Tennessean* had once opposed Browning but now was his mentor and sponsor. The advertisement concluded:

> I have said it before, and I repeat it now, that in the art galleries of Paris there are twenty-seven pictures of Judas Iscariot—none which look alike but all resemble Gordon Browning; that neither his head, heart, nor hand can be trusted; that he would milk his neighbor's cow through a crack in the fence; that of the two hundred and six bones in his body there isn't one that is genuine; that his heart had beaten over two billion times without a single sincere beat.[36]

A week later a second full-page advertisement appeared in the papers entitled "The *Nashville Tennessean* Told the Truth Once—In 1938!" Five of the paper's editorials that had attacked Browning for the unit system, the purge, the police force, and the threat to use troops in Memphis were reprinted. Crump concluded the second advertisement with the statement, "Browning has about as much chance to beat Jim McCord on August 5th as a one legged grasshopper has in a turkey field."[37] Silliman Evans was embarrassed. On the date the first advertisement appeared, the *Tennessean* carried a front-page statement apologizing for carrying Crump's ad but declared that a responsible newspaper was required to do so; "we can take no pride," the statement continued, in carrying such a tirade. An editorial stated: "The *Nashville Tennessean* strongly espouses the causes for which Gordon Browning now fights. It does not, however, contend that he has, in the past, never made mistakes. This newspaper was quick to oppose him on the unit bill, for the passage of which an extra session of the legislature was called in 1937 . . . [but now] this newspaper welcomes the opportunity to lend its aid and encouragement as he leads a crusade against established forces of political venality."[38]

Edward Meeman saw no reason for an apology for opposing Browning in the past. On 23 July the *Press-Scimitar* carried an editorial entitled "We Vote For Gordon Browning." Meeman declared:

> The *Press-Scimitar's* choice is Gordon Browning. Browning, serving as governor in 1937 and 1938, gave Tennessee a superb administration. He put into effect a financial program for the state so good and so essential that his successors have had to follow it. In the general quality of his administration Browning set a mark for his successors to shoot at. . . .
>
> A great deal has been said about Browning's unit plan. The *Press-Scimitar* opposed that plan. But let us not forget that Browning was fighting fire with fire. He proposed this unit plan only because there had long existed in Shelby County a "unit plan" of voting which humiliated the citizenship of this county and disfranchised the rest of the state.

Meeman's editorial concluded that the unit system was no longer necessary for the people were ready to remove the dictator.[39]

Both Browning and Kefauver replied to Crump's advertisements. The congressman was mild in his assault on the Memphis boss. When Crump called him a pet coon, the candidate replied that he was not Crump's pet coon and, capitalizing on the charge, made the coonskin cap the symbol of his fight against bossism.[40] Browning used humor in rebuttal and related to audiences across the state how Crump and his organization stalwart, Will Gerber, had been observed in a cemetery one night. Gerber was on his knees reading names from the tombstones while Crump recorded the names in a notebook. "He came to one he couldn't read because the moss had grown up all over it. 'Just put down any name,' he said, 'I know there's a name here but I just can't read it.' 'No Willie,' replied Crump, 'you've got to read it. We've got to have the right name. This has got to be an honest election.' "⁴¹ Browning's bit of satire was designed to emphasize his charge of fraudulent methods of voter registration and ballot box stuffing in Shelby County. According to Crump's biographer, the story hurt him deeply, because he had a "strait-laced reverence for the dead." Moreover, he did not like being made the butt of a joke.⁴²

It became increasingly apparent as the campaign progressed that the alliance system built around the Crump-McKellar axis was disintegrating. East Tennessee Republicans, for example, ignored the Democratic primary because they were having their own factional fight. Crump's decision to abandon Stewart was a more important factor in the breakdown of the system. As noted, many of the senator's friends were angry at Crump's switch to Mitchell, and some local factions refused to go along. Late in the campaign, rumors were prevalent that Crump considered transferring his support from Mitchell back to Stewart. If indeed he did consider such a switch, it probably would not have helped at such a late date.

Crump's inability to suppress opposition in Memphis was indicative of his troubles. Relatively youthful people, many of them veterans of World War II just beginning their professional and business careers, were especially active in their opposition to the boss. It took courage for those who were trying to establish themselves to challenge the machine. Two participants in Browning's campaign in Shelby County recalled that it was a frightening experience to go against the machine and friends warned them that their activities would lead to retaliation. They were reminded of the tales of earlier rebels who were run out of town. Although there was some intimidation, both admitted in retrospect that their worst fears did not materialize.⁴³ An underlying discontent existed in Memphis which partially explains why the machine was unable to strike back as harshly as it might have in the past. For example, Browning's Shelby County campaign manager, Robert L. Taylor, obtained a sound truck, plastered the side with campaign posters, and applied for a permit to use the vehicle on the city's streets. The permit was denied but, hoping to be arrested to create an issue, Taylor used the truck anyway. He drove around the courthouse and Crump's office playing a popular song of a few years earlier, "I'm Looking For the Bully of the Town." Memphis police made no attempt to interfere and even gave signs of approval when they were away from the courthouse.[44] Memphis police and firemen, as it turns out, were disgruntled because salaries and fringe benefits had not kept pace with inflation. Browning's forces in Memphis operated with very little money although there were plenty of volunteers at campaign headquarters. According to Taylor, workers tended to disappear, however, when newspaper photographers arrived on the scene. Taylor also recalled that he tried to get agents of the Federal Bureau of Investigation to be present at polling places on election day but was advised by the Justice Department that they lacked jurisdiction. Nevertheless, in an effort to intimidate the machine, he spread the word that FBI agents would be present and then arranged for a number of well-dressed young men to visit polling places to give the story the appearance of legitimacy.[45] Whether the effort had the desired effect is not clear, but antimachine forces believed that, because they had a large number of poll watchers, Memphis had its first honest vote count in many years. The relatively large number of votes cast in Shelby County for both the gubernatorial and senatorial challengers demonstrated that Memphians were more willing to oppose the machine than was expected and they reflected the statewide mood for change.

Gordon Browning won the Democratic primary by a landslide on 5 August and it was the most satisfying victory in his political career. He carried every congressional district except the tenth which was Shelby County. The final count was 240,676 votes or fifty-six percent of the total for the former governor, to 183,938 or forty-three percent for the incumbent, McCord. Browning even won the Republican strongholds, the first and second districts, albeit by only a few thousand votes. His victory in East Tennessee indicated that the McKellar influence there had declined and the alliance with Republicans had broken down. Browning polled extremely well in Middle Tennessee and went into Shelby with a lead of 85,000 votes. Although Crump's stronghold gave Governor McCord slightly over 48,000, a surprising 20,000 votes were cast for Browning. Kefauver won a plurality in the three-way senatorial contest by polling 152,000 votes or forty-four percent of the total. Stewart received only thirty-two percent of the vote, and Mitchell (endorsed by Crump and McKellar) came in a poor third with only 78,000 votes or twenty-two percent of the total. Browning polled almost 70,000 more votes than the nominee for the Senate, although Kefauver was ahead of Browning's total in Shelby County by about 7,000 votes.[46]

Browning gave Kefauver a great deal of credit for his victory. He contended that the congressman helped him in Shelby County and other urban areas, but that he helped Kefauver in the rural areas.[47]

The most obvious result of the Democratic primary in 1948 was that the Crump-McKellar axis controlling state politics had been broken. The destruction of the alliance system was achieved by a combination much like the Crump-McKellar system: two separate organizations held together by their opposition to the Crump machine. The Memphis boss, stunned by his first statewide defeat in twenty years, blamed the results of the election on the sales tax and the labor vote.[48] The estimate was partially correct. There was widespread opposition to the sales tax, the rank and file of organized labor was hostile to the machine, and the labor turnout was high in 1948. Despite rumors that he would support a Republican or an independent in the general election in November, Crump acquiesced to the desires of the electorate and agreed to support the nominees of the Democratic party.

Why did the Crump-McKellar organization go down to such a decisive defeat? Crump's biographer makes several suggestions. The Memphis boss lost touch with the mood of the electorate and some disaffection existed in Memphis itself. His old style of campaigning did not go over well and his advertisements misfired. He alienated the labor vote and tried to dump Senator Stewart for an unknown. Finally, returning veterans wanted to take a more active part in state policy making.[49] But other factors were equally important. Senator McKellar played only a minimal role and was clearly unable to hold his forces for Mitchell and McCord. Moreover, it appeared that a majority of the electorate in Tennessee simply wanted to end the Crump-McKellar rule in the state. It has also been suggested that Crump spread himself too thin by attempting to defeat two strong opponents at the same time,[50] although the Crump-McKellar axis would likely have been defeated regardless of the number of opponents the Shelby leader sought to defeat. The more sophisticated electorate wanted a new generation of leadership that was responsive to the changed social and economic environment of postwar America. That Browning was reelected at a time when a new breed was being voted into office was an anomaly, for he was a states' rights conservative whose sympathies were with rural Tennessee. In reality, the Crump-McKellar axis was broken by the anti-Crump rural block working together with the new urban-oriented middle class. Browning was a popular figure who represented the desire to end bossism in the state, and had there been no Crump, there would not have been a Browning return in 1948. But Crump's control in his own back yard was not completely gone. He was still strong in Memphis, and no one was naive enough to claim that he did not still have some influence over the state. Nevertheless, the organization would never be the same.

For the first time in years, the Republican party in Tennessee took life and caused some concern among Democrats by placing candidates in the races for governor and United States senator in the general election in November 1948. The party put up a good fight, albeit in comic opera fashion. Conservative Republican B. Carroll Reece, former congressman from the first district, perhaps hoping to capitalize on Kefauver's image as a liberal, ran for the Senate. The Republican candidate for governor, nominated in the party's primary in August, was Roy Acuff, leader of a country music band, the "Smoky Mountain Boys," and star of Nashville's famous radio program, the "Grand Ole Opry." Acuff had qualified for the primary without authorization, and much to his surprise, won the nomination. Perhaps the Republicans realized that the only way to win the gubernatorial race was to present a colorful and popular personality to the electorate. Acuff's chief interest in politics, as he publicly stated on several occasions, was to see Crump's power broken. During the Democratic primary campaign, he entertained Browning at his Dunbar Cave retreat near Clarksville, Tennessee. After winning the nomination, Acuff suddenly found himself besieged and perhaps a bit bewildered as Republicans from across the state flocked to his support.[51] Nevertheless, he carried on a spirited campaign as he and his band toured the state playing popular song hits such as "Night Train to Memphis," and "Great Speckled Bird." Because his campaign was high in entertainment value and drew large crowds, the Democrats were sufficiently concerned to conduct a more active campaign than normal for the general election. Party leadership also believed that the national Republican party was "pouring" money into the party's campaign in Tennessee, especially for the senatorial nominee.[52]

Democrats, however, had other reasons for apprehension. Kefauver was genuinely worried because he carried the liberal label in a state whose constituency tended toward conservatism. Some Democrats urged Browning to wage a separate campaign but he rejected the suggestion and he and the senatorial nominee conducted a joint canvass.[53] There was also a rupture in the national Democratic party over civil rights, and the presidential hopeful, Harry Truman, was expected to run poorly in Tennessee and be defeated nationwide by the Republican candidate, Thomas E. Dewey. Browning and Kefauver, interested primarily in their own campaigns, gave only passive support to the national ticket. Although Crump defected to the "Dixiecrat" party and its candidate, J. Strom Thurmond of South Carolina, Senator McKellar remained loyal to the Democracy, and his organization was active in behalf of Truman. Republicans were disappointed if they expected to be helped by the split in the Democratic party resulting from the bitter primary campaign; Crump was apparently unwilling to have the state governed by an entertainer and refused to endorse the Republican candidate. Acuff won the first congressional district, but Browning carried the state by the very comfortable margin of 364,000 votes to Acuff's 180,000 while Kefauver defeated Reece 326,000 to 167,000. Browning also ran well ahead of the Democratic presidential candidate who won the state narrowly.[54] Beset with their own internal quarrels, Republicans were unable in 1948 to break the Democratic habit in Tennessee.

NOTES

1. Joseph M. Ray, "American Government and Politics: The Influence of the Tennessee Valley Authority on Government in the South," *The American Political Science Review* 63 (October 1949): 922.

2. Howard W. Odum, "Social Change in the South," *The Journal of Politics* 10 (May 1948): pp. 242–258, reprinted in Taylor Cole and John H. Hallowell, eds., *The Southern Political Scene, 1938–1948* (Gainesville: University of Florida Press, 1948), pp. 242–258.

3. Hugh Davis Graham, *Crisis in Print: Desegregation and the Press in Tennessee* (Nashville: Vanderbilt University Press, 1967), p. 271.

4. Dewey Grantham, Jr., *The Democratic South* (Athens: University of Georgia Press, 1963), p. 76.

5. U. S., Bureau of the Census, *Census of Population, 1950: A Report of the Seventeenth Decennial Census of the United States*, vol. 1 (Washington: Government Printing Office, 1952): 1–21; see also B. U. Ratchford, "Recent Economic Developments in the South," *The Journal of Politics*, 10 (May 1948): 259–281, reprinted in Cole and Hallowell, *Southern Political Scene*, pp. 259–281.

6. Frank B. Williams, Jr., "Tennessee Schools and The Sales Tax," *Southern Observer* 4 (November 1956): 291–300; William D. Miller, *Mr. Crump of Memphis* (Baton Route: Louisiana State University Press, 1964), p. 332.

7. Theodore H. White, "The Battle of Athens, Tennessee," *Harper's Magazine*, (January 1947), pp. 54–61.

8. Robert G. Everett in "The 1948 Senatorial Primary in Tennessee: A His-

tory and an Analysis" [(unpublished M. A. thesis, Memphis State University, 1962), pp. i, 1] suggested that the 1948 primary was a watershed in Tennessee politics; that for the first time in many years progressive democracy and conservatism were clearly delineated; and that the forces of rural Tennessee and urban Tennessee were in a contest for dominance.

9. Albert Gore to Gordon Browning, 28 June 1950, copy, Box 9, No. 31, Edward Meeman Papers, Memphis State University; see also Albert Gore, *Let The Glory Out: My South and Its Politics* (New York: The Viking Press, 1972), p. 58.

10. Joseph B. Gorman, *Kefauver: A Political Biography* (New York: Oxford University Press, 1971), pp. 3–5, 14–16, 36.

11. Pugh Moore, "How Browning Launched Kefauver On His Career as a U. S. Senator," Memphis *Press-Scimitar,* 26 May 1976; Pugh Moore, interview with the author, Memphis, 10 August 1976.

12. Gore to Browning, 28 June 1950, copy, Box 9, No. 31, Meeman Papers.

13. Charles G. Neese to Kefauver, n.d., 5ᵈ Box 14, The Estes Kefauver Collection, University of Tennessee Library.

14. Ed Meeman to Gore, 19 May 1947, Box 9, No. 31, Meeman Papers.

15. Gore to Browning, 28 June 1950, copy, Box 9, No. 31, Ibid.

16. *Nashville Tennessean,* 21 March 1948.

17. Gore to Browning, 28 June 1950, copy, Box 9, No. 31, Meeman Papers.

18. Robert L. Taylor, interview with the author, Knoxville, 27 July 1976; Marshall F. Priest, Jr., "Politics in Tennessee: The 1948 Democratic Gubernatorial Primary" (unpublished M. A. thesis, Memphis State University, 1963), pp. 50–51.

19. Frick Stewart, interview with the author, Winchester, 25 May 1977. Stewart declared that the real reason for Crump's hostility was that Tom Stewart never "reported" to the Memphis boss.

20. McKellar to Thad A. Cox, 14 November 1947, Political Correspondence, Box 58, Kenneth Douglas McKellar Papers, Memphis-Shelby County Public Library and Information Center.

21. Miller, *Mr. Crump,* pp. 324–325.

22. E. W. Eggleston to county managers, et al., 2 August 1948, copy, 5ᵈ, Box 8, Kefauver Collection.

23. Robert L. Taylor, interview, Knoxville; T. Arthur Jenkins, interview with the author, Manchester, 8 June 1976; Robert L. Taylor, interview with the author, Memphis, 10 August 1976; Charles G. Neese, interview with the author, Winchester, 24 January 1978; Gorman, *Kefauver,* p. 43; Howard F. Butler to Kefauver, 27 April 1949, Charles Fontenay to Kefauver, 14 February 1950, 4ᶜ Box 7, N. R. Wilson to Kefauver, 5 April 1948, 5ᵈ Box 10, Kefauver Collection.

24. *Nashville Banner,* 5 June 1948.

25. Gordon Browning, "Gordon Browning: An Oral Memoir," ed. Joseph H. Riggs (Memphis Public Library, 1966), p. 127.

26. Robert L. Taylor, interview, Knoxville; W. R. Jarrell, interview with author, Springfield, 21 June 1966; Priestly Miller, interview with the author, Nashville, 23 June 1966.

27. Bob Guinn, interview with the author, Savannah, 23 June 1977.

28. Allen H. Kitchens, "Political Upheaval in Tennessee: Boss Crump and the Senatorial Election of 1948," *The West Tennessee Historical Society Papers* 16 (1962): 104–126; Gorman, *Kefauver*, pp. 35–63.

29. William Buchanan and Agnes Bird, *Money as A Campaign Resource: Tennessee Primaries, 1948–1964* (Princeton: Citizens Research Foundation, n.d.), p. 19.

30. *Tennessean*, 17 June 1948; Memphis *Commercial Appeal*, 18 July 1948; *Banner*, 23 June 1948.

31. *Commercial Appeal*, 4 July 1948.

32. Matthew Lynch, interview with the author, Nashville, 7 July 1977; Dan Powell, interview with the author, Memphis, 10 August 1976; *Trades and Labor News*, 22 April, 1, 15, 29 July 1948.

33. *Chattanooga Times*, 1 August 1948; *Johnson City Press-Chronicle*, 1 August 1948; *Knoxville News-Sentinel*, 12 July 1948; *Commercial Appeal*, 18 July 1948.

34. Albert Gore to Ed Meeman, 17 July 1954, Box 9, No. 21, Meeman Papers.

35. Miller, *Mr. Crump*, p. 327.

36. *Commercial Appeal*, 21 July 1948.

37. Ibid., 28 July 1948.

38. *Tennessean*, 21 July 1948.

39. *Press-Scimitar*, 23 July 1948.

40. Gorman, *Kefauver*, pp. 47–48.

41. *Press-Scimitar*, 3 August 1948; Clark Porteous, interview with the author, Memphis, 22 June 1977.

42. Miller, *Mr. Crump*, pp. 329–330.

43. Robert L. Taylor, interview, Memphis; William W. Farris, interview with the author, Memphis, 22 June 1977.

44. Robert L. Taylor, interview, Memphis. Taylor recalled that away from the courthouse, police in patrol cars would extend their arms and form the "OK" sign, an open hand with the thumb and forefinger forming a circle.

45. Ibid.

46. *Tennessee Blue Book, 1949–1950* (Nashville, 1950), pp. 273–274, 277–278.

47. Gordon Browning, interview with the author, Huntingdon, 28 December 1965; Browning, "Oral Memoir," p. 124.

48. *Tennessean*, 8 August 1948; Miller *Mr. Crump*, p. 332.

49. Miller, *Mr. Crump*, pp. 331–332.

50. Ibid.

51. *Banner*, 8 June 1948; Joe Hatcher, "Politics," *Tennessean*, 9 August 1948.

52. Kefauver to Leslie Biffle, 27 September 1948, 5ᵈ Box 8, Kefauver Collection.

53. Kefauver to Mrs. Oliver Sabin, 30 September 1948, Browning to Kefauver, 28 August 1948, Ibid.

54. *Tennessee Blue Book, 1949–1950*, pp. 296–299.

8

The Governorship II

O N 17 JANUARY 1949, Gordon Browning was inaugurated governor of Tennessee ten years to the day from his departure from that office in 1939. In his inaugural address he reviewed the accomplishments of his first administration as "living testimonials supporting a justified pride in human accomplishment." Displaying pleasure at returning as chief executive, he referred to his defeat in 1938 as the work of sinister forces and to his election in 1948 as vindication of his efforts ten years earlier to crush dictatorship.[1]

In 1937 Tennessee had faced a crisis that required imaginative and forceful leadership. Because the state was much better off financially in 1949 than it had been in 1937, Browning entered his second term with fewer major proposals. Nevertheless he launched his new administration with characteristic enthusiasm and his program included pledges to improve the state's economy and educational system, the democratization of the electoral process, and the construction of hard surfaced rural roads. Returning as chief executive in 1949, Governor Browning enjoyed the usual advantages of patronage and a supportive General Assembly. He made a deliberate attempt to fill cabinet posts and executive departments with qualified personnel, but he had some difficulty in putting together a competent official family. In 1949 the salary of a commissioner was only $6,000 a year and Governor Browning had five refusals from his first choices for cabinet posts.[2] Most of those with good credentials for administrative offices were unwilling to leave their more lucrative jobs for the poor pay of public servants, and some of those who accepted did so with reluctance.[3] There was no shortage of applicants, but few had the qualities desired by Browning. The governor's official family was, however, respectable, if not outstanding. As was customary, the General Assembly elected Browning's choices for the constitutional offices: James H. Cummings of Woodbury, stepped out of the legislature and became Secretary of State; W. N. Estes of Jackson, who had served in Browning's first administration by assisting in the debt reorganization and by organizing the Department of Local Finance, was elected Treasurer; and Cederic Hunt of Nashville, a veteran of the First World War, became Comptroller. Those appointed to statutory departments included John F. Nolan to the Department of Accounts, a post he had held during Browning's first administration; W. R. Jarrell of Springfield, a veteran of the First World War and active in the American Legion, was named State Purchasing Agent; and James A. Barksdale of McKenzie appointed Director of Personnel. Barksdale, a prominent educator, was named commissioner of the Department of Education in 1950. Appointments to cabinet posts included James C. Evans of Nashville, commissioner of the Department of Finance and Taxation; E. W. "Ned" Eggleston of Franklin, commissioner of the Department of Highways and Public Works; Sam K. Neal, a publisher from Carthage, was named commissioner of the Department of Safety; and in contrast to his first administration, Browning appointed a labor union officer, James Lee Case, commissioner of the Department of Labor. There were fewer veterans of World War I in the official family but most of those who were not members of the original American Legion clique were veterans of World War II.

Browning's most valuable advisor was his brother, F. L. Browning, who was named administrative assistant. F. L. had had adequate administrative experience for the post. After attending college briefly at Valapraiso in Indiana with his brother and then Union University in Jackson, Tennessee, F. L. taught school for several years and served as superintendent of education in both Gibson and Chester counties. He was Browning's secretary briefly in 1937 before becoming secretary to Senator George L. Berry. After holding positions in industry during World War II, F. L. returned to serve his brother in 1948. To mild charges of nepotism, the governor responded,"I can't do without F. L.

and I won't do without him if I can help it—and I can help it!"[4] The
governor's brother was certainly his key confidant and most trusted advisor and the one who probably wrote and pushed through the assembly
most of the administration policies. He played a leading role in patronage and his influence was such that he was called Tennessee's "unofficial
governor." Quiet and unassuming, F. L. was, more than anyone else,
able to restrain his more impetuous brother. As one supporter noted,
Governor Browning had "a certain impetuosity about him . . . being
too quick and glib about every little issue that comes up."[5] But more
important, Browning would often take action or adopt a policy in haste,
and without considering ramifications. F. L. was the restraining influence. Loyalists who believed that the governor was taking an unwise
action would appeal to F. L. who in turn was able to convince Browning
to abandon his course.[6] However, tragedy struck the Browning family
when F. L., after a brief illness, died in July 1949 and eight days later
the governor's father, James H. Browning, also passed away. Browning
was probably correct when he said of his brother's death: "I lost the
biggest concentration of information and advice that a man had when
I lost him."[7] After the death of F. L., Browning's control over his own
administration and organization was not as effective as it might have
been. One observer asserted that "Browning had to start watching over
his shoulder for increasing instances of financial chicanery among some
people who took advantage of his trust in them."[8] Charles Wayland of
Knoxville succeeded F. L. as administrative assistant and remained in
that post until he became commissioner of the Department of Highways
and Public Works in August 1950. Robert A. "Fats" Everett of Obion
County, former administrative assistant to Senator Tom Stewart, assumed the post for Browning after Wayland accepted a cabinet office.

As an administrator Governor Browning was conscious that certain
functions of government required highly technical and skilled personnel
who could operate best without political interference. In the Department of Education, for example, he did not attempt to dictate appointments or policy on political considerations.[9] On the other hand, Browning
realized that he should reward his supporters. Other departments, especially those purchasing a great volume of materials or awarding contracts, were more appropriate agencies for rewarding friends. But even
there the governor called for some restraint. His policy on purchasing
materials was simple: first, contracts and purchases should go to the
citizens of the state whenever possible, and second, to "our friends" if
the cost was not unreasonable.[10] There were those who served Browning

loyally and with integrity and efficiency but there were others who took advantage of their position for selfish reasons. The latter would prove to be troublesome to the Governor before his tenure was over.[11] Perhaps recalling a classic remark attributed to President Warren G. Harding, Browning declared on several occasions that his friends caused more problems than his enemies.[12]

Governor Browning had an inner circle of friends and cronies such as Nashville attorneys Jack Norman and John Hooker, Sr., Nashville Mayor Tom Cummings, Sam Neal of Carthage, Nashville minister Priestly Miller, and Silliman Evans, publisher of the *Tennessean*. How much influence the "kitchen cabinet" had on the governor is impossible to measure but Browning was not inclined to consult a group, official or otherwise, and make decisions according to consensus. Instead, he made individual decisions, often against the advice of friends and allies. Of the inner circle, Silliman Evans was the most prominent figure. He had played an important role in keeping the anti-Crump forces in the state alive during the 1940s, and when Browning took the oath of office in 1949, political control of Tennessee passed into his orbit. Evans's *Tennessean* was the leading press supporter of both Browning and Senator Estes Kefauver and the publisher delighted in having power and influence.

Gordon Browning was once again the dominant political leader in Tennessee and, as governor, was able to control the legislature. By any measure, the meeting of the General Assembly in 1949 was a great success for the governor as his program sailed through with only minor changes. Holding top priority were measures designed to upgrade the public school system in Tennessee. Education was the largest enterprise in the state, and it behooved the governor to devote attention to its advancement. A week before he took office he announced a program that guaranteed a minimum salary of $2,000 a year for teachers with a bachelor's degree, more adequate appropriation for building construction, significant increases for higher education, and an annual increase of $1,000,000 for the retirement system. Browning had not campaigned against the retail sales tax enacted under Governor Jim McCord; he had pledged, however, to increase the percentage of the tax allocated to teachers' salaries. With more revenue, funds for increased appropriations for schools were available and the General Assembly enacted his education package without change.[13]

Next to the education program, the chief accomplishment of Browning's second administration was the construction and improve-

ment of rural roads. Late in January, he sent a message to the Assembly
which outlined a program for the construction, improvement, and main-
tenance of farm to market roads. It was, as the *Tennessean* reported, a
very popular measure, for the $48 million appropriation passed the leg-
islature with unusual speed and was sent to the governor for his signature less than two weeks after its proposal.[14] A year later, Browning
could claim that under his administration more than three times as many
roads had been built than in any comparable period before, and more
highway construction contracts were in force in 1949 than in any state
except New York. Moreover, the Highway Department had begun to
build roadside parks.[15]

Perhaps Gordon Browning's greatest desire when he took office in
1949 was to reform the state's election laws. Indeed, he seemed to take
up where he left off in 1937, but any fears of a revived unit system were
soon dispelled. His object, he declared, was to eliminate election
frauds, vote buying, and machine control by organizations such as the
one in Memphis. Browning was sincere in his desire for clean elections,
but he was also politically motivated in seeking reform legislation. He
did not intend to let the issue of bossism die—it was still a potent political theme. At any rate, he outlined an election reform package that
included the end of the poll tax and a system of permanent voter registration. The General Assembly went to work at once, and, before it
adjourned, passed a long list of measures on elections. The first was the
repeal of the Crump-backed measure, passed during the previous session of the legislature, that separated state elections from national elections if Congress should repeal the poll tax for federal elections. When
the governor also asked that the State Board of Elections be expanded
from five to six members, the assembly granted his request. Because
that measure was obviously intended to break control of the board by
the Crump-McKellar axis, the delegation from Shelby County put up
a stiff fight against the increase. A few days later, the assembly enacted
another administration bill which abolished the poll tax as a prerequisite
to voting in primary elections for gubernatorial nominees, United States
senators, members of Congress, members of the legislature, and Railroad and Public Utilities commissioners. In addition, the assembly exempted women and veterans from the poll tax requirement in general
elections. The Tennessee constitution required a poll tax and an amendment was necessary to abolish it altogether, but the number of citizens
compelled to pay the fee was drastically reduced. The most important
election reform was one which established a permanent system of voter

registration in all civil districts, wards, and voting precincts which had
a population of 50,000 or more, and in all cities, towns, and metropolitan
areas having a population of 25,000 or more. Permanent registration
was therefore limited to heavily populated areas and small rural counties
were exempted. The measure was a significant change nevertheless.
Another measure prohibited city, state, county, and federal employees,
and candidates for political office from serving as election commissioners
or as election officials. Still another act required that all State Elections
Board meetings and county primary board meetings be open to the public and records kept of such meetings. Other measures required the use
of metal ballot boxes, except where voting machines were used, and
established more adequate machinery to handle absentee voting. The
assembly also sent to the governor a bill that would require employers
to give time off to employees to vote, but Browning held that it should
not be necessary to legislate such a requirement and vetoed it. [16]
Governor Browning believed that these election reforms would hasten
the downfall of his arch enemy, Ed Crump, and prevent the rise of other
political bosses.

The governor's election reforms were opposed by members of the
Shelby County organization even though some of the measures had
been advocated by Crump in the past. The fact that they were sponsored
by the Browning administration accounted for the opposition of the
Crump machine. During the primary campaign the following year, a
group of Shelby County citizens filed suit in court seeking an injunction
to prevent the permanent registration law from being implemented,
but in the face of vigorous opposition, the suit was dropped. [17]

Most of Governor Browning's proposals passed the assembly with little change, but on one occasion he had to use all the power and influence
of his office to block a measure he considered to be contrary to the public
interest. The trucking industry had emerged as one of the most powerful
lobbies, and, in 1949, sponsored a measure that would increase the
maximum weight limit of trucks on Tennessee's highways. Coming from
an area well served by railroads, the governor had little sympathy for
trucking and was also persuaded by Commissioner of Highways Ned
Eggleston that heavier trucks would damage roads in the state. Although Browning announced his opposition to the increase, observers
expected the weight bill to pass. In opposing the measure, the governor
came into conflict with several members of the rural block, including
Secretary of State Jim Cummings. From rural Cannon County, an area
not served by rail, Cummings had several heated discussions with

Browning as he tried to persuade the governor that the weight increase would aid the economic development of his county by providing better freight service. Browning remained adamant and appeared before the House to express his opposition to the increase, pointing out that many highways were already in a sad state of disrepair and funds for repair were limited. An increase in weights, he argued, would put a greater burden on the state. Browning's appearance may have been the decisive factor in the defeat of the measure. Columnist Joe Hatcher commented that the governor won what was probably his greatest victory as "The truck lobby was perhaps the most potent that has hit the capitol in years."[18]

In a move contrary to the wishes of most of his rural constituents, Browning took the lead in a futile effort to amend the state's fundamental law. Tennessee's constitution had not been amended for over half a century and representation in the legislature was malapportioned. Moreover, that document severely limited the state's sources of revenue. As usual, there was resistance to change, but Browning, characteristically, strongly urged that the constitution be modernized. Consequently, he placed the prestige of his office behind a measure which would allow voters to determine by referendum whether there should be a constitutional convention. The General Assembly passed a resolution to that effect and the subjects specified for consideration included item veto power for the governor, repeal of the poll tax, a simplified method of amending the constitution, reapportionment by population, a four-year governor's term, and classification of property for assessment. The assembly set November 1949 as the date for the referendum. The people, however, voted down the proposed convention by only 3,000 votes out of a few more than 120,000 cast.[19] Three factors determined the outcome: the fear that taxes would be increased, rural opposition to reapportionment, and the light turnout because no other issue was involved. Those who opposed the limited convention carried the day, and constitutional reform was defeated for the time being.

Governor Browning also ran afoul of a small but increasingly vocal lobby, the Tennessee Municipal League. Drawing its membership from mayors and other city officials across the state, the TML was organized shortly before World War II to promote the interests of the state's cities and its most immediate goal was to secure a larger share of state revenues for municipalities. During the general election campaign, the league obtained a promise from Browning, or so the members believed, to support a return to the cities of one cent of the gasoline tax for street repairs, a proposal that would have produced four million dollars for municipalities. During the legislative session, the governor advised William D. Baird, Mayor of Lebanon and president of the TML, that he endorsed "the proposal to allocate one cent of the gasoline tax" for cities to use for street construction and repair.[20] He did not, however, follow through and near the end of the session advised Herbert Bingham, the league's executive secretary, that he needed the funds for his rural roads program. Bingham bitterly drafted a fifteen-page statement outlining Browning's promises and his failure to keep them and forwarded it to the mayors across the state.[21] The governor could possibly afford to alienate one small lobby in 1949 in order to please his larger rural constituency, but the TML was becoming more active and influential in state politics as the urban areas grew. The forces of organized labor were also upset by Browning's failure to press harder for repeal of the state's open shop law. Having supported Browning in 1948, union leaders had expected greater effort on his part. Although Matthew Lynch, legislative representative for the Tennessee State Industrial Union Council, believed that the governor sincerely wanted repeal, organized labor in general was beginning to have doubts about Browning.[22] Despite these bad omens, when the General Assembly adjourned in 1949, Governor Browning believed that he had not alienated any important interest group vital to his own interests and that his position remained secure for the foreseeable future.

Although he was the leader of the Democratic party in Tennessee and was able to dominate the General Assembly, Browning still had to deal with Crump. The statewide coalition revolving around the Crump-McKellar axis had been broken and no longer controlled state political machinery, but its defeat in 1948 did not mean that Crump was politically dead or that his influence had dissipated. He was still a power to be reckoned with in state affairs, and within his own county he was still master of the scene, although his control was slipping.[23] To Browning, Crump remained the epitome of all the evils in politics. He was upset when one of his supporters in Memphis, Lucius Burch, publicly praised the Memphis government for its efficiency. "I had just as soon extol the virtues of the Nazis as to claim any for Ed Crump," Browning wrote. He continued that some of his friends failed "to understand that he tried to mix enough public appeal with his nefarious gestapo rule to hold it together. I refuse to subscribe to the doctrine that Ed Crump is anything except public enemy number 1. He has done more to destroy the liberties of people in Tennessee than any other man since its history began. I have no compromise to make with him or any disciple of his."[24]

Indeed, Browning regarded it as his duty to rid the state of the Crump influence, and that was the only reason "I am back in politics, other than the satisfaction I get trying to serve my people."[25] Above all, Browning was insistent upon removing from the state payroll all those connected with the machine and he complained when he was unable to have some who had "sinister connections directly with Memphis" discharged from state jobs.[26] On the other hand, Crump was politically useful to the governor. The Memphis boss was Browning's bugbear, and he intended to get as much mileage out of the Crump issue as possible. In reply to a friend's suggestion that he keep the issue of bossism alive, Browning wrote: "I am fortunate as long as I can keep Ed Crump a live issue in politics, and I certainly want him that way as long as I stay in it."[27] Unfortunately for Browning, he used the bossism issue long after it lost its popular appeal.

Memphis remained one of the most vexing political problems to Browning's regime. Opposition to Crump flared in Memphis in 1948 when several prominent citizens dared to support Estes Kefauver in his bid for the United States Senate, and that nucleus of opposition encouraged the anti-Crump forces over the state. The hometown opposition probably helped to secure victory for Browning and Kefauver and to end control of the state by the Crump-McKellar axis. However, jealousy and discord wracked the anti-Crump forces in Memphis after the election and made establishing a cohesive organization difficult. A major problem was the lack of harmony between Kefauver loyalists and Browning's partisans. One of the governor's supporters wrote a few weeks after the 1948 primary that, while hostility had been suppressed during the campaign, the various factions opposing the machine had not achieved harmony or coordination and had begun to look askance at each other out of jealousy and fear.[28] Browning was aware of the need for a strong organization in Memphis and he had a hard core of friends among prominent Memphians who might have been the nucleus of a good organization: Tom Robinson, restaurant owner, and attorneys Lucius Burch, Gilmer Richardson, and Robert L. Taylor. Some of his friends were also Kefauver loyalists while others regarded the senator with antipathy. The governor also enjoyed an intimate relationship with Edward J. Meeman, editor of the Memphis *Press-Scimitar*.[29] But unlike Silliman Evans, Meeman was not the type to become involved in a political organization. An idealist, he regarded the governor as the hero in the battle to destroy the Crump machine and as the means to achieve good government in Memphis and the rest of Tennessee.

Browning's policy toward the factions in Memphis was cautious. Indeed, it was almost a hands-off policy. He wrote that he would like to see a good political organization get out the vote in free elections but opposed the creation of what he termed a "machine." He warned his friends in Memphis against using Crump's tactics in establishing harmony.[30] The contrast he made between organization and machine is not clear. Apparently he meant that a machine would pad the ballot boxes and steal votes. He also thought it wise, if not necessary, in the interest of harmony among the anti-Crump factions in Memphis, for him not to be actively identified with any one candidate for either city or county offices. However, he let it be known that he and his "friends" would support candidates who seemed to have the best chance of success and hoped that the opponents of Crump could agree on candidates so as to prevent a split of the vote.[31] Browning was reluctant to dictate to his allies in Memphis and was ambivalent about discipline. To an inquiry as to whether state employees in Shelby County should get involved in the anti-Crump movement, he responded: "It is my purpose to make any contribution I can toward the complete restoration of government in the state to the people to be governed." He would not deny state employees the right to participate, but neither would he recommend that they do so.[32] Browning may have erred in his failure to take a hand in trying to help create a strong antimachine organization in Memphis, for lack of harmony among his enemies was a factor in Crump's continued strength. In the elections of 1950, for example, the Memphis boss appeared to be as powerful as ever when the anti-Crump "Citizens Committee" ticket was decisively beaten in contests for local and state offices. And the Crump forces won again in the local elections of 1952. But as one observer suggested, the machine was unable to regain its full power after being successfully challenged.[33] Moreover, Ed Crump was getting old, and "the old zest for attack seemed to have left him."[34]

Governor Browning's statewide organization, if indeed it could have been called that, was based largely on friendships. A system of rigid discipline was lacking and no real chain of command existed. Browning was unwilling and therefore unable to create a strong and cohesive machine. Furthermore, he lacked the killer instinct either to destroy rival organizations or to absorb them. Repelled by the prospect of power, Browning shrank from its use and sought only to contain the opposition. The governor realized the necessity of using the weapons at his disposal, such as patronage and purchasing, to maintain political control, but he failed to act aggressively and was not ruthless enough to establish and maintain political control of his party. His efforts were often inconsistent and therefore not as effective as they might have been. On one occasion, for instance, a woman was discharged from state employment and Senator Kefauver wrote requesting that she be reinstated, noting that she was a friend of his. Browning responded that the woman's husband had led a public campaign for his opponent in the previous election, and that he had to consider those who supported his cause before those who opposed him. On another occasion, however, he demonstrated little concern when a foe was appointed to the elections board in Johnson City. He noted that the individual was active for his opponent in the primary campaign in 1952 but stated that he did not care, except to insure an honest count and proper conduct in the election.[35] Browning also acted without sufficient resolution in making appointments agreeable to all interested parties. At times he made a genuine effort to select elections commissioners at both the state and county levels who would conform to the interests of Senator Kefauver, congressmen, members of the legislature, local city and county organizations, and other interested parties. At other times, he angered allies by his appointments to elections commissions. In order to maintain his position, the governor also had to establish an alliance with local leaders, but he was only partially successful in that. His greatest disadvantage was that his chief support came from small, rural county organizations. Unlike Crump, he did not control an urban machine commanding a large voting population which could determine the outcome of a statewide election. Establishment of rapport with East Tennessee Republicans through patronage was also desirable, but unfortunately Browning was unable to achieve and maintain a good system of interparty trading.

Governor Browning was even unable to establish a firm alliance with Senator Kefauver's organization. Although the governor and Kefauver became associated in the anti-Crump movement during the campaign of 1948, there was no real alliance between the senator's supporters and Browning's organization; they were merely allied in common cause. Browning and Kefauver remained personal friends and tried to maintain harmony between their forces; nevertheless tension existed as the followers on both sides viewed each other with suspicion—and with good reason.

Part of the problem was undoubtedly ideological, because some of Browning's more conservative following viewed the more liberal senator with some hostility. But the conflict mainly involved control of the Democratic party and could be traced initially to the primary campaign in 1948 and the lack of unity among the regional and local supporters of both the senator and Browning. The two forces emerged from that campaign already disposed to view each other with suspicion. In short, the governor and those close to him tried to prevent the senator from gaining state control of the party. The result was a series of controversies. A dispute raged when Browning blocked a move in 1949 to hold the national convention of the Young Democratic organization in Knoxville largely because a meeting in that city would have been dominated by those who had worked for McCord in 1948 although many of them were Kefauver loyalists. The following year another conflict developed over the presidency of the Young Democrats. Browning was reluctant to place known Kefauver loyalists in positions of responsibility in the party. Then in 1952 he withheld the appointment of Martha Ragland as National Democratic Committeewoman from Tennessee until pressure was exerted upon him from all over the state. Finally, Browning was unable to contain the efforts of Congressman Albert Gore to build a statewide base for his senatorial ambitions. Many of Browning's friends made commitments to Gore, thus demonstrating the governor's inability to maintain discipline among his own following. This bickering among the forces of Browning and Kefauver and jockeying for positions by other political aspirants resulted in a lack of unity in the Democratic party in Tennessee. Although disunity was not an unusual situation, it did suggest that Governor Browning was not in firm control of the party nor was he able to determine the course and policies that it should take.[36]

One reason why Governor Browning failed to establish a more aggressive statewide organization was his concept of democracy and the requirements of leadership. The exercise of authoritarian power was repugnant to him, and he was sincere in his commitment to freedom of choice. In the tradition of an earlier Tennessean, Andrew Jackson, Gordon Browning had a sense of identity with the common people. Like the Jacksonians of the nineteenth century, he had a deep and abiding faith in the ability of the common man to determine right from wrong. This explains his frequent candor in discussing an issue, for he expected the people to see "right" as he saw it once a problem was explained to them. The people could, however, be exasperating. He once remarked that a governor's job was difficult:

And your enemies do not bother you as much as your friends. Your friends are always trying to get the state to smile in their direction. They want jobs. They want roads. They want pardons for their relatives and friends.

Do I handle them tactfully? . . . No I don't. I just let them pound me. Then I tell them I'll pray over it and do the best I can. As a matter of fact, my friends have all been rather good to me when I needed them and I am not actually complaining.[37]

Browning also had a strong sense of integrity and a naive faith that his political associates possessed the same degree of honesty. A close friend observed that the quality of "stubborn loyalty to those he loved" became one of his greatest "weaknesses."[38] Some of those closest to him conceded that he was simply unable to believe that any of his "friends" would take advantage of his loyalty to them. He was also taken advantage of because he was, perhaps, overly sympathetic to the less fortunate and had a compassion for those in trouble. He was easily moved by the clemency pleas of mothers, wives, and sweethearts for those in prison. In fact, his foes frequently accused him of granting excessive pardons and paroles and of releasing dangerous criminals to society. The executive secretary of the Pardon and Parole Board under Browning declared, however, that his record of pardons was not excessive and compared favorably with those of other recent governors. At any rate, in later years Browning expressed satisfaction that some of the criminals he released from prison had testified to his faith in them by leading fruitful lives.[39]

Browning's greatest failure as governor, in the long run, was not mishandling politics but his inability to comprehend the nature of, and to respond appropriately to, the rapid social and economic changes that were sweeping over postwar Tennessee. Sympathetic to rural Tennessee, he responded negatively to the increasing demands by the cities for a greater share of the state's material and human resources. And in the tradition of rural southerners, he viewed labor organizations with disdain and was repelled by the increasing activities of unions in Tennessee. His inability to adjust to the increasing power of labor was reflected in his response to a dispute in 1950. In March of that year, the workers at the American Enka Corporation's plant near Morristown went on strike when their demands for a wage increase and other benefits were not met. The walkout remained peaceful until late May when some workers, including nonunion members, began returning to work. Violence allegedly erupted, and Hamblen County Sheriff Robert Medlin, charging that "professional agitators" were present, called on the governor for assistance. Browning quickly, and perhaps hastily, sent in the highway patrol and alerted the National Guard. There was more violence two days later and Browning, without consulting Commissioner of Labor Lee Case, called out the Guard. Pickets were arrested and the press reported that some were roughly handled, but the governor denied any desire on his part to crush the strike and blamed the union for the violence.[40] Case believed that Browning listened to the wrong advice, overreacted, and made a mistake in sending the soldiers. The governor incurred the enmity of organized labor for his use of troops, and union leaders became his bitterest enemies from that point on.[41]

Gordon Browning was also mystified by the increasing restiveness and militancy of blacks. The governor was a racial moderate in the sense that he had never practiced "race baiting," though it should be noted that few politicians had successfully used that tactic in Tennessee. Browning had increased services to Tennessee's black population and a few jobs were provided in state agencies. But he did not challenge the traditional racial mores of the South, he accepted the wisdom of the doctrine of separate but equal facilities and he assumed that blacks were generally content with their status. Browning therefore did not fully understand the implications of the blacks' drive for equality. All of the social and economic changes that were taking place—increasing urbanization, activities of labor, and black militancy—seemed to challenge his agrarian values. Understandably he resisted.

Despite Browning's inability to understand the changes taking place, the accomplishments of his term were significant, and no controversial issue, except the strike at Morristown, developed to disturb the serenity of the political scene. Browning remained generally popular, and there was never any doubt that he would be a candidate in 1950 to succeed himself. Reelection to a second term was almost a certainty, for Tennessee voters had traditionally given governors an additional two years.[42] A popular and colorful candidate might have given him a good race, but such a candidate was not forthcoming in 1950 and few serious aspirants were willing to risk certain defeat unless they were simply making a trial run to gain future name recognition. Browning's only opposition for the Democratic nomination in 1950 was State Senator Clifford Allen of Nashville. Allen's reason for challenging the governor is not clear but he probably hoped to establish himself as the leading contender for 1952. Allen was a lawyer specializing in tax matters and the owner of several businesses that included a chain of restaurants.

After several terms in the Tennessee Senate, he had gained a reputation as something of an outspoken maverick and had developed a good following in the black community in Nashville and from organized labor. His platform included pledges to repeal the anti–closed shop law, to establish homestead exemption in property taxation, and to provide free textbooks for public school pupils. Allen was not regarded as a serious challenger, and in contrast to 1948, the campaign turned out to be a drab affair. No full-page advertisements by Crump appeared in the papers, as the Memphis boss, apparently having no enthusiasm for Allen, did not become involved in the primary. Browning captured most of the newspaper support, even from some of his old foes like the Memphis *Commercial Appeal*. The editor of that paper felt that there had been some doubts about Browning in 1948 but on the whole his record was good and he should be returned to the governor's office in preference to Clifford Allen.[43]

Without substantial opposition, Browning waited until 1 July 1950 to open his bid for renomination. He followed a policy of not mentioning his opponent' name at first, but Allen became somewhat abusive in his attacks on the governor, and Browning finally lashed out at his challenger late in the campaign. He charged Allen with being "the cheapest charlatan that ever disgraced politics in Tennessee."[44] The results in the quiet primary gave Browning a majority of 57,000 out of 477,000 votes cast. Allen won only the third and fourth congressional districts while Browning carried those remaining, including Shelby County. Memphis gave the incumbent an 11,000-vote majority out of almost 52,000 cast.[45] Senator Allen did surprisingly well, and the total vote cast was comparable to that in the governor's race in 1948. Why the challenger polled such a large vote is not easily explained. Organized labor gave Allen a good vote and his total in rural areas suggests that his homestead exemption and free textbook proposals may have had an appeal. Browning was obviously overconfident and did not put forth a strenuous effort. In addition, the incumbent did not have a personality like Kefauver on the ticket to help attract votes. The results of the primary left Browning's forces dismayed, depressed, and concerned about the future.

For the first time in the history of the Republican party in Tennessee, the GOP failed to have a candidate for the governor's race in the general election in November 1950. Browning did, however, have opposition in Dr. John R. Neal, candidate for the "Good Government and Clean Elections" ticket. Neal, a University of Tennessee law school professor and perennial candidate for a state office, did not carry a single congressional district and received only 51,757 votes to Browning's 133,680 in a very light turnout.[46]

When the Seventy-seventh General Assembly met in January 1951, Governor Browning did not submit an extensive legislative program. He declared that he was content to expand and build upon the programs enacted during the previous session. In his second inaugural, he suggested that the time was not right for broad new programs and gave as the reasons the crisis of the Korean War and the cold war conflict with the Soviet Union.[47] The ensuing legislature was generally quiet, except for a battle over congressional redistricting and a proposal to raise Memphis State College to a full four-year branch of the University of Tennessee. The latter measure was defeated despite the Governor's support.

The most significant action taken by the General Assembly was to submit again to the electorate the question of calling a convention to amend the constitution. The subjects to be considered were similar to those in the call proposed by the previous General Assembly, with one major exception: the assembly avoided the controversial proposal to permit the legislature to classify property for taxation and thus eliminated one issue that might have defeated the call in the referendum. The assembly also set the referendum for the election in August 1952 to ensure a larger turnout.[48] The call for a limited convention received a favorable vote in that election, delegates were elected in the general election in November 1952, and the convention met in April 1953. A number of proposed amendments generally following the proposals by the legislature were subsequently submitted to the voters. The amendments with the most political significance included greater home rule for municipalities and extension of the term of governor from two to four years. The electorate approved the constitutional changes in a special election in November 1953. The two amendments that Browning had considered important, a provision to permit the legislature to enact an income tax and a revision of property assessment procedures for taxing purposes, were not incorporated in the constitution.

When the Seventy-seventh General Assembly closed in March 1951 the *Tennessean* declared that, although the Assembly was inexperienced, it was independent, energetic, and very productive. It did not obstruct the governor's program, as most administration bills passed with only minor changes.[49] At that moment, Governor Browning was still the chief political figure in the state because he controlled party machinery, no controversial issue had appeared to anger the electorate, and no attractive challenger had surfaced. Even so, his control of the party was less than complete, for those who had opposed him in the past were still strong and there was evidence of independence in some of the factions within his alliance. The defeat of an ally, Tom Cummings, in the mayoralty election in Nashville in May 1951, coming soon after the close race Allen gave Browning in 1950, indicated that his alliance system was not as unified as it might have been.

Despite these problems, the years in the governor's office were good and happy ones for Gordon Browning. He worked hard at being governor and was one of the most active in the state's history. He was deeply involved in the work of the Southern Governors' Conference and was chairman of that organization's freight rates committee. His fame as an entertaining speaker spread far and wide, and he was often called upon to give an address at places distant from Tennessee. Despite a rigorous schedule, there was time for play. Nothing relaxed Browning more than being with his cronies, and he went about his passion for hunting and fishing with the same flamboyance that he ran the administrative branch of government in Tennessee. As one writer described it:

> The Browning day in office was fast and frantic, but the governor watched for a chance to slip out with the zeal of a schoolboy.
> He would call old friends and without much notice take off—hunting for geese on Hudson Bay with attorney John Hooker, Sr.; fishing in Florida's St. John River with Sam Neal of Carthage; long bull sessions with Nashville Mayor Tom Cummings and the late Silliman Evans, Sr., publisher of THE NASHVILLE TENNESSEAN; trips to Chicago to "eat and talk" with Attorney Jack Norman.[50]

Browning was a confirmed outdoorsman and seldom turned down an opportunity to go hunting or fishing. He especially liked fox hunting, perhaps because of the excitement of the chase. He would accompany contractor friends J. H. Hadly of Humboldt, J. B. Michael of Memphis, and Bob Guinn of Savannah to a duck hunting lodge near Stuttgart, Arkansas, and invariably the kill was brought back to the freezer in the governor's mansion. Browning enjoyed good food and his appetite was a source of amazement to his associates. Guinn observed that he had seen Browning consume two whole ducks at one meal in addition to side dishes.[51] Hugh "Swat" Scarborough, former sheriff of Carroll County, declared that he never saw a man eat as much as Browning: "Eat? What you talking about! . . . I've seen him put away, one after the other, big plates of barbecued possum, sheep, goat, coon and pork—all the time shaking hands and smiling and eating. I can eat. But Gordon Browning—he could really eat!"[52] An active man with an abundance of nervous

energy, Browning could burn up the calories from overeating; nevertheless, his weight reached a robust 225 pounds during his second term.

The governor also had time for levity. When the University of Tennessee was scheduled to meet the University of Texas in a postseason
football game, Browning, as a joke, placed a wager on the game with
the governor of Texas, Allan Shivers: the Tennessee River for the Brazos
River. Browning also won some notoriety for singing. It all began at a
party on New Year's Eve 1950, the night before the football game between Tennessee and Texas. "On a banter in a contest" with Governor
Shivers, Browning sang the "Tennessee Waltz." Written by "Pee Wee"
King and Redd Stewart as a theme for King's country music band, the
"Golden West Cowboys," the song became a popular hit after it was
recorded by singer Patti Page. Not long after the party with Shivers,
Browning was invited to appear on Nashville's famous radio program,
the "Grand Ole Opry" to render the song. Browning later declared face-
tiously: "I sang the 'Tennessee Waltz' on the Grand Old Opry stage and
I was such a big hit they wanted me to come back. But I told them
nothing doing. Not after the way they ran Roy Acuff against me in
1948."[53] But he returned more than once to the Opry stage, and although, as one commentator noted, he sang "with far more enthusiasm
than talent," his fame spread.[54] Everywhere he went he was asked to
sing the "Tennessee Waltz." He sang on a nationally aired radio program,
Don McNeill's "Breakfast Club"; on one of the early television shows,
"We The People"; and he entertained the Democratic National Convention in 1952 at 1:30 A.M. Browning also made a record of the song
with the proceeds designated to go to charity. He received a great deal
of "fan mail" which generally applauded his vocal efforts. He declared
that he was "having lots of fun" and he wrote to one constituent that he
was "undertaking to develop a new avocation [singing]" in the event he
was ever in need of a job.[55] Gordon Browning found joy in living and
humor in everything.

The Democratic primary in the summer of 1952 loomed as a vital
campaign that would determine who controlled the party in Tennessee
for the foreseeable future. Two offices would come before the electorate:
the governorship and the United States Senate seat occupied by
Kenneth McKellar. Long before the close of the legislative session in
1951 speculation was rife concerning candidates and factional alignments for both races. Politics had seldom been muddier as individuals
and factions jockeyed for positions. Despite the opposition of his wife,
Gordon Browning had not abandoned his ambition to become a United

States senator. The election of 1952 appeared to be his best opportunity yet because the electorate would determine a seat occupied by a West Tennessean, and McKellar, if indeed he chose to run, could be beaten. The senator would be eighty-three in 1952, his mental alertness was declining, his health was poor, and he was often unable to perform his duties. Some of McKellar's close friends, including Ed Crump, urged him to bow out gracefully and retire.[56] Very likely some who held positions at the senator's pleasure wanted him to run while others, anticipating his defeat, began looking for a "place to land." In the speculation concerning McKellar, the dialogue followed a logical sequence. First, the senator might decide to retire, but if he chose to run for another term, he might not live until the election. If he lived and did run, he could be defeated, but if elected he would certainly not live out the full term. McKellar ended speculation on one point very early. Unable to give up the office he had held for so long, the aging senator announced in June 1951 that he would be a candidate to retain his seat.

Rumors abounded throughout the year 1951 concerning Gordon Browning's course. During the session of the General Assembly, Leslie T. Hart, political writer for the *Banner,* repeated a story that the governor would soon resign and take a post in General Dwight Eisenhower's North Atlantic Treaty Organization staff. Speaker of the Senate Walter Haynes would then become governor and would in turn appoint Browning to the Senate should a vacancy occur.[57] The Governor experienced a mild boom for the Democratic presidential nomination in 1952. Leslie Hart noted the factors that made him an available candidate: he was well known as an advocate of states' rights; he was a "big cog" in the Southern Governor's Conference and several southern governors would support him for the nomination; he was well received when he addressed a meeting of more than a thousand industrial leaders in Philadelphia. Senator James H. Duff had introduced him as possibly the next Democratic candidate for president. Hart also suggested that Browning was a good prospect for the vice-presidential nomination if President Harry Truman sought reelection. His qualifications included a close friendship with the president, and his reputation as a states' right advocate would appeal to the South. Hart concluded that "Browning's national speech making marathon would indicate he has at least one eye on the proverbial greener pasture."[58] The *Banner* was in no way endorsing Browning for either the presidential or vice-presidential nomination but perhaps hoped to encourage the governor to seek one of those offices to remove him from the political scene in Tennessee. Those suggestions may have flattered Browning, but it is doubtful that he entertained the possibility of either nomination. He did keep everyone guessing as to his intentions and the uncertainty of his future course caused considerable maneuvering among his own forces. Several trial balloons were lofted by those who aspired to be governor, including Commissioner Charles Weyland, Senator Walter Haynes, Secretary of State Jim Cummings, and attorney Robert L. Taylor of Memphis. Browning did nothing to suppress that activity.

Certainly if Governor Browning still aspired to the Senate, 1952 was the time to make an attempt, for he was already sixty-two and time was playing out. It appears, however, that Congressman Albert Gore's candidacy for McKellar's seat had preempted the governor. Because he had not established a cohesive organization or firm control of the party, Browning had been unable to prevent some of his supporters from making commitments to Gore. Browning partisan Lucius Burch advised the governor that he would support Gore for the senate. Ed Meeman wrote that the *Press-Scimitar* was prepared to endorse the congressman's candidacy for the Senate, expressing also its willingness to back Browning for reelection.[59] The rift in the long-time friendship between Gore and Browning was complete by 1951. Although Gore had advised Browning before 1948 of his intention of running for the Senate, the governor always believed that they had an agreement that he would be the first to run. Gore admitted the break years later and observed that it was the result of "a conflict in our ambitions."[60] Rumors of the split were numerous during the meeting of the General Assembly in 1951, and Leslie Hart reported that Browning and Gore were near the parting of the ways because of the congressman's apparent intention to run for the Senate against McKellar. The governor gave substance to the report when he stated that he had not made up his mind about the senatorial race, asserting, "I certainly have no obligation to anyone that would keep me out of the race if I decide to make it."[61]

Factional realignments began to take shape and one was especially curious. Browning and Senator McKellar had always been on opposite sides but they had some pockets of common support. Sometime after 1950 some individuals in McKellar's organization began to cultivate Browning in earnest. Many of the senator's friends, especially those who had lived off his control of federal patronage, were aware that his ship was sinking; it was only a matter of whether he would retire, be defeated, or die. A story circulating among Senator Kefauver's staff suggested that Lipe Henslee, collector of Internal Revenue in Nashville and long-time McKellar loyalist, was openly courting Browning and publisher Silliman Evans. According to the story, Henslee was the secret mastermind behind the efforts of young gubernatorial hopeful Frank Clement. Once he had lulled Browning and Evans into an alliance with McKellar and thus neutralized them, Henslee would then coalesce Clement's campaign efforts with the senatorial candidate, Gore or McKellar, whichever would be to Clement's advantage.[62] However, neither Browning nor Evans could be easily duped by such a ploy. Actually the governor had little choice but to coalesce with the senator's organization. The morale of the Browning forces was at a low point because of the surprise vote for Allen in the 1950 primary and because of Gore's success in winning support for his candidacy. An alliance with McKellar's forces had certain advantages: should the senator retire or perhaps die prior to the primary in 1952, Browning would be in position to command the allegiance of McKellar's friends; and should the senator run for reelection and win, the governor could well be in a position to succeed McKellar should he not survive the term. Sometime in 1951 Browning made the decision that he would be a candidate for the Senate only if McKellar retired; a three-way race was rejected as too great a risk. He also tentatively decided not to seek reelection for governor.[63] But McKellar did not step down, and an old campaigner like Browning would not retire voluntarily. He decided to try to become only the third governor since before the Civil War to win a third consecutive two-year term. John Sevier and William Carroll were the only Tennessee governors to serve more than six years. Since the Civil war only governors Austin Peay and Prentice Cooper had been honored with a third consecutive term.

NOTES

1. *House Journal of the Seventy-Sixth General Assembly of The State of Tennessee, 1949* (Nashville, 1949), pp. 211–218.
2. Joe Hatcher, "Politics," *Nashville Tennessean*, 19 December 1948.
3. James Lee Case, interview with the author, Nashville, 19 July 1977.
4. Quoted in George Barker, "Three Times and You're Out," *Nashville Tennessean Magazine* (7 October 1962), p. 13.
5. Lucius Burch to Charles Neese, 16 February 1949, 4ᶜ, Box 7, The Estes Kefauver Collection, University of Tennessee Library.
6. Jack Norman, Sr., interview with the author, Nashville, 20 March 1978;

Mrs. Bill Bowers, interview with the author, Milan, 24 June 1976; Mrs. W. S. Field, interview with the author, Milan, 24 June 1976, confirmed that F. L. was a restraining influence.

7. Gordon Browning, "Gordon Browning: An Oral Memoir," ed. Joseph H. Riggs (Memphis Public Library, 1966), p. 16.

8. Barker, "Three Times and You're Out," p. 18.

9. James A. Barksdale, interview with the author, McKenzie, 12 August 1976.

10. W. R. Jarrell, interview with the author, Springfield, 21 June 1966.

11. Jack Norman, interview; James H. Cummings, interview with the author, Woodbury, 8 June 1976.

12. Leslie T. Hart, interview with the author, Nashville, 29 June 1977.

13. *Tennessean*, 7 January 1949; *Public Acts of the State of Tennessee, Passed by the Seventy-Sixth General Assembly, 1949* (Nashville, 1949), pp. 98–101.

14. *Tennessean*, 20 January, 12 February 1949; *Public Acts, 76th GA*, pp. 91–98; James E. Thorogood, *A Financial History of Tennessee Since 1870* (Sewanee: University of the South Press, 1949), p. 187.

15. E. W. Eggleston to Browning, memorandum, 29 June 1950, Gordon Browning Papers, Tennessee State Library and Archives.

16. *Public Acts, 76th GA*, pp. 26, 19–25, 206, 215, 352–356, 526–544, 722–724, 729–730, 491–506, 884–885.

17. Hatcher, "Politics," 13 July 1950.

18. Ibid., 31 March 1949; *Tennessean*, 29 March 1949; James H. Cummings, interview.

19. *Public Acts, 76th GA*, pp. 177–186; *Tennessean*, 15 November 1949.

20. Browning to William D. Baird, 5 March 1949, Browning Papers.

21. Herbert Bingham, interview with the author, Nashville, 29 June 1977; see also Lee S. Greene, David H. Grubbs, and Victor C. Hobday, *Government in Tennessee*, 3rd ed. (Knoxville: University of Tennessee Press, 1975), p. 223.

22. Matthew Lynch, interview with the author, Nashville, 7 July 1977; *Trades and Labor News*, 14 April 1949.

23. William Goodman, *Inherited Domain: Political Parties in Tennessee* (Knoxville: Bureau of Public Information, 1954), p. 37.

24. Browning to John B. McKinney, 22 July 1949, Browning Papers.

25. Browning to Dr. John E. Rowsey, 2 August 1949, Ibid.

26. Browning to W. G. Anderson, 1 August 1949, Ibid.

27. Browning to Tom Robinson, 14 April 1951, Ibid.

28. Abe L. Roberts to Browning, 28 January 1949, Ibid.

29. Meeman to Browning, 15 March, 2, 17 November 1949, 13 July 1950, Ibid.

30. Browning to Lucius E. Burch, Jr., 27 June 1949, Ibid.

31. Browning to Grover C. Gibbs, 10 October 1949, Browning to Anthony Aspero, 1 April 1950, Ibid.

32. Browning to John B. McKinney, 20 September 1949, Ibid.

33. Goodman, *Inherited Domain*, p. 37. Allen Hampton Kitchens, "Political Upheaval in Tennessee: Boss Crump and the Senatorial Election of 1948," *The West Tennessee Historical Society Papers* 16 (1962): 125–126, argues that Crump was well on the way to regaining statewide political control when death overtook him in 1954.

34. William D. Miller, *Mr. Crump of Memphis* (Baton Rouge: Louisiana State University Press, 1964), p. 341.

35. Browning to Estes Kefauver, 24 May 1952, Browning to Frank Bryant, 5 February 1952, Browning Papers.

36. G. Edward Friar to Kefauver, 3 June 1949, 4ᶜ Box 7, Kefauver Collection; Kefauver to Meeman, 26 May 1952, Box 11, No. 27, Edward J. Meeman Papers, Memphis State University Library; Martha Ragland, "Governor Gordon Browning" (authors copy of unpublished essay, 30 December 1976); Martha Ragland, interview with the author, Nashville, 7 July 1977.

37. Quoted in Leslie T. Hart, "Capitol Hill," *Nashville Banner*, 13 April 1951.

38. Barker, "Three Times and You're Out," p. 18.

39. Ibid.; Gordon Browning, interview with the author, Huntingdon, 28 December 1965; Priestly Miller, interview with the author, Nashville, 30 September 1966, declared that Governor Cooper pardoned few because he opposed pardons in general; McCord pardoned only 357; but Governor McAlister pardoned or commuted 1,266 felons. From January 1949 to the summer of 1952, Browning pardoned or commuted a total of 338 felons. Miller argued that his record appeared high because of the publicity gained by two or three criminals who were pardoned and later committed heinous crimes.

40. *Knoxville News-Sentinel*, 25 May–12 June 1950.

41. James Lee Case, interview; Matthew Lynch, interview; Dan Powell, interview with the author, Memphis, 10 August 1976; *Trades and Labor News*, 1 June 1950.

42. Tennessee ranked number one among the southern states for incumbents winning reelection, Cortez A. M. Ewing, *Primary Elections in the South* (Norman: University of Oklahoma Press, 1953), p. 67.

43. *Commercial Appeal*, 28 July 1950.

44. *Tennessean*, 2 August 1950.

45. *Tennessee Blue Book, 1951–1952* (Nashville, 1951), pp. 290–291.

46. Ibid., pp. 308–309.

47. *House Journal of the Seventy-seventh General Assembly of the State of Tennessee, 1951* (Nashville, 1951), pp. 166–174.

48. *Public Acts of the State of Tennessee, Passed by the Seventy-seventh General Assembly* (Nashville, 1951), pp. 525–533.

49. *Tennessean*, 18 March 1951.

50. Barker, "Three Times and You're Out," p. 18. Norman recalled that

Browning liked Chicago and the two may possibly have made as many as 30 trips to the Windy City; Jack Norman, interview.

51. Bob Guinn, interview with the author, Savannah, 23 June 1977.

52. Quoted in George Barker, "Of War, Peace, and Politics," *Nashville Tennessean Magazine* (23 September 1962), p. 11. Hugh Scarborough (interview with the author, McKenzie, 12 August 1976) declared that Browning's favorite dishes were barbecued coon and rabbit.

53. Quoted in Barker, "Of War, Peace, and Politics," p. 11.

54. Ibid.

55. Browning to W. T. Parrott, 31 December 1951, Browning to Wilks T. Thrasher, 12 December 1951, Browning Papers.

56. Miller, *Mr. Crump*, pp. 344–345; W. R. Davidson, interview with the author, Tullahoma, 1 September 1977.

57. Hart, "Capitol Hill," 18 February 1951.

58. Ibid, 2 April, 16 June 1951.

59. Lucius Burch to Browning, 7 February 1951, copy, Box 4, No. 1, Meeman Papers; Meeman to Browning, 12 February 1951, Browning Papers.

60. Albert Gore, interview with the author, Nashville, 15 May 1977.

61. Hart, "Capitol Hill," 8, 22 February 1951.

62. Charles G. Neese to Kefauver, n.d., 4[b] Box 6, Kefauver Collection.

63. Whit LaFon to Frank Clement, 14 May 1951, Correspondence: General, 457–4–8, Frank Clement Papers, Tennessee State Library and Archives.

9

The Fall

GORDON BROWNING announced on 1 March 1952 that he would be a candidate to succeed himself as governor, saying "as usual I shall stand squarely on my own two feet, with no entanglements in other races, if they respect me in like manner."[1] The governor had three opponents for the Democratic gubernatorial nomination: Clifford Pierce of Memphis, State Senator Clifford Allen of Nashville, and attorney Frank G. Clement of Dickson. The campaign for Pierce simply did not get off the ground and he played no significant role in the outcome. Allen had polled a suprisingly large vote in the 1950 gubernatorial primary, and he had hoped that it would provide him with sufficient momentum to become the front-runner. Instead, Allen's fortunes declined as Clement quickly became Browning's chief rival.

Only thirty-two years old, Clement had no previous experience as a legislator or administrator. After obtaining an education at Vanderbilt University, he became a special agent for the Federal Bureau of Investigation and later served in the army late in World War II. Following the war, he was made a general counsel for the Tennessee Railroad and Public Service Commission. Clement had known from his high school days that he possessed a good speaking voice and he deliberately cultivated the talent. He was also deeply religious and impressed his listeners with his sincerity. He quoted Biblical scriptures so easily and frequently that his political rallies sometimes took on the appearance of a religious revival. Shortly after World War II, Clement began making contacts, obtaining commitments, giving speeches across the state, and in general establishing the nucleus of a gubernatorial campaign organization. His early boosters obtained his selection as the outstanding young man of the year by the state Junior Chamber of Commerce and his election as president of the state's Young Democrats for added exposure. There were those across the state who liked to think that they were the first to recognize Clement's potential and masterminded his rise from obscurity. However, the young Dickson attorney was intelligent and needed little in the way of guidance. He shrewdly and carefully selected some of the most astute political minds in the state as advisors.

Clement's greatest handicap, although not an insurmountable one, was lack of name recognition. Relative obscurity is probably the reason why he announced his candidacy a full year before the primary. However, he may have initially regarded the campaign as a trial run for a future contest; clearly a loss would not have been disastrous for a young man with a future. Clement based his campaign on an indictment charging Browning and his associates with political profiteering, waste and extravagance in government, general corruption, and favoritism in awarding state contracts. His theme was neither rare nor ingenious, but a set of circumstances conspired to make his charges seem valid and, by the spring of 1952, it was apparent that the unknown attorney from Dickson was a serious contender and not to be taken lightly.[2]

Browning had liabilities that were readily apparent in the beginning. Organized labor was bitter about the governor's use of the National Guard during the strike at Morristown in 1950, and he could not count on support from union membership. Labor support was divided between Allen and Clement. Allen had a core of support among Nashville's blue-collar workers but, although some labor leaders regarded Clement as too inexperienced, the Political Action Committee of the CIO endorsed him. Clement also gained significantly with an informal endorsement by the membership of the Tennessee Municipal League. The TML adopted a pledge not to support any candidate who failed to incorporate in his platform a promise to return to muncipalities one cent of the state's gasoline tax. Allen rejected the pledge and, although both Clement and Browning signed it, the governor's having failed to press such a measure during the legislative sessions in 1949 and 1951 made his sincerity suspect; Clement's public statement of support was more convincing. Finally, the third term, an admittedly hard to measure issue, conspired against Browning. Undoubtedly a few Tennesseans were opposed as a matter of principle to a governor serving more than two consecutive terms. Despite the liabilities, the governor had obvious advantages: he was the incumbent, controlled the party's machinery, and commanded the allegiance of the state's vast bureaucracy. Browning received the endorsement of most of the black leaders across the state with the exception of the membership of the CIO and Clifford Allen's local black support in Nashville. Some black leaders were concerned about the slow pace of economic improvements for their race and had doubts about Browning's sincerity, but the governor had fulfilled his promises to place blacks in state jobs, to raise teacher's salaries, and to improve recreational facilities. Furthermore, he was largely responsible for elevating the state's only black institution, Tennessee State College in Nashville, to university status.[3]

Conforming once again to the tradition of Democratic factionalism in Tennessee, no coalition was formed between any of the gubernatorial candidates and either of the senatorial hopefuls, Albert Gore and Senator Kenneth McKellar. Demonstrating the complex nature of factionalism in the Tennessee Democratic party, there were no clear cut alignments. Browning of course made no public endorsement of either senatorial candidate, but some of his closest friends, like Jim Cummings, I. D. Beasley, and Priestly Miller, worked very hard for McKellar. Other Browning loyalists such as Ed Meeman were openly committed to Gore. And both the Allen and Clement camps also divided their support between the senatorial hopefuls. McKellar refused to endorse a gubernatorial candidate because, as he wrote, he had some support in the organizations of all four candidates. The senior senator made only one speech during the campaign, a disastrous appearance at Cookeville. The rambling and frequently incoherent effort clearly revealed that his health and physical stamina had declined and McKellar retired from the scene and let his organization continue the campaign. Gore, even more than McKellar, remained aloof from the governor's race. The senatorial challenger waged a spirited, constructive, and efficient campaign in which he did not abuse the senator in any way; Gore even praised McKellar, declaring that the senator had done much for Tennessee, but he always referred to him "in the past tense."[4]

The political boss of Memphis, Ed Crump, still not without influence in his own district, endorsed Clement because he "looked 'like a winner.' " He also announced for McKellar, although, as Crump's biographer points out, he tried to persuade the senator to retire. But the Memphis boss was not active in the campaign because he too was getting old and, unlike McKellar, was gradually retiring from the political arena.[5] Despite Crump's lack of activity, Gordon Browning continued to make the Memphis boss an issue. He wrote that he was "entering a campaign, which will be about the most strenuous of my life" and that "my opponent is for all intents and purposes E. H. Crump of Memphis."[6] In his opening campaign speech in Huntingdon, Browning pledged that the rule of Crump would not return to the state of Tennessee. The governor's leading press supporter, the *Tennessean*, continued to harp on the theme that "Crumpism" versus freedom was the most important issue in the campaign and charged that Clement was a creature of the Memphis boss and Crump's hatchet man, Willie Gerber.[7] The fact was, however, that the subject of Crump was barren because it no longer interested the voters. Browning faced a real challenge from his youthful opponent, and he kept bossism alive for want of a better theme; but Clement also lacked a clear-cut issue initially. However, two factors entered the race and gave the Dickson attorney significant issues: the governor authorized the lease-purchase of the Memorial Apartments in Nashville as an office building for the state, and he made an all-out commitment to assist Senator Estes Kefauver in his efforts to win the Democratic presidential nomination in 1952.

The first issue stemmed from the fact that Governor Browning had put the state of Tennessee into the real estate business in a big way. The rapidly mushrooming bureaucracy in government required increased office space. During the meeting of the General Assembly in 1951, Browning persuaded the legislature to authorize bonds for the construction of a large modern office building, which, when completed, was named in honor of Cordell Hull. The governor also induced the legislature to authorize the purchase of the old twelve-story Cotton States Building on Sixth Avenue in Nashville, one block from the Capitol Building, for $744,518. The method of obtaining a third office building for the state, the Memorial Apartments on Seventh Avenue, became a political issue.

Although it was a state office, the Department of Employment Security had the responsibility of implementing federal programs and was funded by the federal government. Like other agencies of the state, the department had gradually expanded its services and staff and was strapped for office space. It is probable that E. A. Adams, the official charged with procuring and maintaining facilities for Employment Security, discovered in his search for housing that the owners of the Memorial Apartments were desirous of selling. Indeed the owners had offered on at least one occasion, and possibly others, to sell to the state. The property, however, was encumbered by a mortgage and the state was unable to pursue the matter until it was cleared of indebtedness. At that point a private company was formed for the specific purpose of buying the Memorial Apartments, clearing the indebtedness, and then selling or leasing the building to the state. The originator of this idea is still unknown, nor is it known whether the idea came from within the administration of Governor Browning. But Rube McKinney, chief fund raiser for the Browning organization, appeared on the scene and probably was the one responsible for securing investors. Whether Browning was aware of the scheme in the beginning is not clear, but the details were probably worked out before it was brought to him for approval. At any rate, on 18 July 1951 Cumberland Properties, Incorporated, was chartered with Nashville tax consultant J. Marshall Ewing and attorney Andrew Ewing listed as incorporators. The stockholders were R. S. "Pup" Doggett of the Southern States Paving Company of Nashville, Karl Martin of the Machinery and Supply Company of Knoxville, and John and Stirton Oman of Oman Construction Company of Nashville. Browning may not have been acquainted with the Oman brothers, as he later claimed, for neither had been politically active and they had bought into Cumberland Properties purely as an investment. But the governor most certainly was acquainted with Martin and Doggett, for both were heavy campaign contributors. Immediately after being chartered, Cumberland Properties purchased the Memorial Apartments for a reported $625,000 and Marshall Ewing began negotiating with Governor Browning. According to the agreement, Cumberland Properties would lease the building to the state under a lease-purchase agreement, providing the Department of Employment Security with much-needed space for its small army of officials and clerks. The rental would be $115,000 per year and would be paid out of operating funds provided by the federal government. All of the rent would go toward paying the purchase price, for a total of approximately $1,725,000 over fifteen years. Title to the building would be transferred to the state at that time. The governor routinely forwarded the proposal to Attorney General Roy Beeler for a ruling. Beeler replied that the governor did not have the authority to bind the state to such an agreement and he gave three reasons: Employment Security's revenue depended upon the uncertainty of appropriations by Congress; current funds could not be spent beyond the biennium; and money could not be drawn except by due appropriation. In the meantime Browning had received an opinion from the counsel for Employment Security that the lease-purchase could be made under a legislative act of 1943 that authorized the acquisition of property using funds in the state's treasury not otherwise appropriated. That act's intention, however, was concerned with small acquisitions such as garages and patrol stations. Nevertheless, Browning accepted the opinion of Employment Security's counsel in preference to Beeler's ruling and signed an executive order on 3 August 1951 authorizing the lease-purchase. The lease was signed on 10 September 1951, with the provision that the state must take up the option by 31 December 1952. The parties involved in the negotiations unnecessarily created an impression of conspiracy by keeping the transaction under wraps until it was completed. But political reporters got wind of the deal near the end of August and Fred Travis of the *Chattanooga Times* broke the story.[8]

The governor's press opponents immediately sensed an issue. His most severe critic, the *Nashville Banner,* charged that the owners of Cumberland Properties were Browning's "friends" and they would make an enormous profit of 180 percent in fifteen years. The paper declared that the deal should be aired, the names of the stockholders revealed, and the taxpayers be given a closer look at the "dummy" corporation.[9] The newspaper exaggerated. The investment would have produced a return of a little less than 7 percent, compounded annually, before taxes and insurance. It was not, in fact, a good deal for the stockholders. Joe Hatcher, political writer for the *Tennessean,* in defense of the governor, agreed that the names of the stockholders should be made public but argued that the fact that they were not general knowledge did not justify insinuations of a corrupt bargain.[10] Another note of suspicion was injected into the picture when the *Times* reported in early September that Attorney General Beeler had informed the governor that he lacked authority to bind the state to a contract of the nature of the lease-purchase. The paper reported correctly that the Employment Security Office had bypassed the attorney general's office and submitted the plan to its own general counsel for his ruling.[11] The governor's press opponents maintained a thorough campaign against the lease-purchase. Leslie T. Hart, political writer for the *Banner,* frequently asked whether Browning had received the Attorney General's ruling that he had no authority to bind the state to the lease. If so, he should have informed the people. The

Banner contended without reservation that it was an illegal deal carried out in a clandestine atmosphere. In addition, the paper charged that certain individuals in the administration had participated in other questionable deals, including excessive purchases of road machinery and building materials. [12]

Stung by such charges, Browning denied any wrongdoing in the purchase of the Memorial Apartments. He declared that the deal had not been prearranged for the benefit of his friends, that he did not know any of the stockholders, and that he did not receive any benefit from the purchase. He insisted that the federal government asked him to make the transaction, that the state would receive the building at no cost, and that it did not require legislative approval because it did not need appropriations. Moreover, he claimed that the attorneys for the owners of Cumberland Properties later offered the state $150,000 not to take up the option. Browning was so outraged by the charge of corruption that he went to great lengths to defend the transaction. The many letters he received protesting the lease-purchase seemed to require a denial of wrongdoing. He contended that some newspapers gave false information and misrepresented the transaction. To one individual he wrote: "There is nothing wrong with our purchase which was one of the finest the State ever made. The State gets a million and a half dollars worth of property for nothing. Employment Security pays about one-half as much as they would have to pay for rent for 15 years and pays for the property and will have it from now on."

To the charge that he completed the deal in order to benefit his friends, he declared:

> When I deal with a corporation I never know the owners of it. When I bought the Cotton States Building I had no idea whose property it was and did not feel called upon to try to investigate so long as I was dealing with a reputable agent. I would be glad for every name to be published who owns the Cumberland Properties, Inc., but I do not know who they are and I will not be brow beaten into giving up such a fine transaction because somebody is unscrupulous enough to try to attribute wrongdoing to the legitimate and fair and open transaction of the State's business. [13]

Browning was especially sensitive to the suggestion that he had received a cut from the deal. To Colonel Enoch Brown, an official of the Memphis *Commercial Appeal* and a comrade in France in the 114th Field Artillery Regiment during World War I, he wrote that the paper slandered him by requesting that he answer such a charge. He accused the *Commercial's* political writer, Maurice Cunningham, of giving false information and withholding facts about the purchase. He declared that Cunningham had made derogatory statements about his friends and had hinted that the two Oman brothers, part owners of Cumberland Properties, were his friends. He insisted that Cunningham knew "that I did not know either of the Omans if I met them on the street and that neither of them had ever been a personal or political friend of mine. He further knew that when he said that the State is paying for the remodeling cost that it was a lie and that we were not paying any of it." Browning concluded that the withholding of facts confirmed his charge "that Maurice Cunningham is a low character and unworthy to represent a decent paper." He declared that in all fairness, the true record should be published in reply to the charge of wrongdoing. [14]

Clifford Allen was the first gubernatorial candidate to seize the issue. He wrote to Attorney General Beeler requesting that he reveal his opinion on the Memorial Apartments lease-purchase. Beeler responded that his relationship with the governor was that of "attorney and client" and "the release of any of these opinions" should be made by the public official to whom the opinion was rendered. Although the attorney general maintained discreet silence on the subject for nearly a year, Browning claimed that Beeler was an opponent and the opinion was the result of political animosity. However, if there were differences between the attorney general and Browning, they were not pronounced because no evidence exists of serious friction in the relationship of the two officials. [15]

Frank Clement cited the Memorial Apartments lease-purchase as evidence to support his charge of widespread corruption in Browning's administration. The challenger presented to the electorate a long list of allegations which included the claim that convicts were used to do personal work for members of the administration; that individuals were placed on the state's payroll in order to produce votes; that there was no competitive bidding on many state purchases and the Governor's friends had profited by those purchases; that there was excessive purchase of road machinery; that the state owned too many automobiles, some of which were for the personal use of state employees; and finally, that there were instances of voting frauds committed by the governor's allies. To this list he added the charge that Browning had a dangerous pardon and parole policy. He charged that the governor had pardoned or commuted 1,181 felons during his tenure in office and many of those released were returned to prison for committing additional crimes. Clement promised that, if elected, he would conduct an exhaustive investigation of Browning's administration. "By their fruits ye shall know them," he declared. "People know Gordon Weaver Browning by the fruits of graft his administration has produced and they want no more of it."[16] Clement conducted a vigorous and hard-hitting campaign, but he devoted more time to attacking the incumbent administration than to constructing a positive platform and legislative program. The challenger was assisted in his attack by the *Banner*, which frequently referred to Clement as a man of honesty, integrity, and decency, and denounced the governor because he presumably lacked those qualities. Abusive editorial cartoons became a regular feature in the paper.

In response to Clement's ferocious attack, many of Browning's campaign speeches were devoted almost exclusively to categorial denial of charges. In the untenable position of being on the defensive, he noted in anguish that he had lived for sixty years without being found corrupt, but that now a youthful upstart was challenging his integrity. In regard to the Memorial Apartments transaction, Browning declared, "anyone who is honest and intelligent will not say this purchase is corrupt. If an honest person says it is corrupt, he is not intelligent. And if an intelligent person says it is corrupt, he is not honest." Browning insisted that he was proud of the deal: "If I could make a trade like that for you, I'd do it everyday."[17] He chided the challenger for his lack of a positive platform and insisted that most of Clement's proposals were already in effect: "He wants bidding on State purchases; we already have that. He wants civil service and training for the State Highway Patrol; we already have that. This candidate has come out for so many things already in effect, I would not be surprised if he came out for the Ten Commandments and the Sermon on the Mount before he gets through campaigning."

Browning also charged, "Mr. Clement proposes an agriculture program which he knows very little about. In fact, he probably doesn't know a pea vine from a morning glory."[18] In addition, the governor claimed that his opponent would turn the state over to the interstate truckers and radical labor leaders. He declared that Clement had promised to raise trucking weights on state highways in return for support, a charge that may have had some substance. One of Frank Clement's chief fund raisers was Robert M. Crichton, a trucking executive. Conceding the radical element in organized labor to his opponent, Browning said, "I tried to get along with them for four years. . . . They got mad at me because I have the courage of my convictions [to end violence in a labor dispute]." Browning also demonstrated that he could still vent his fury on an opponent. Referring to Clement's FBI service, he declared that his opponent "couldn't track an elephant in six feet of snow." He intimated that the challenger, a reserve army officer, had successfully avoided combat in both World War II and the Korean War: "Clement has been in two of the biggest fights the world has ever seen and hasn't found either of them yet." Finally, he insisted that he would welcome an investigation of his administration by Clement. Despite frequent assaults upon the challenger, the governor seldom departed for long from what he regarded as the central issue in the campaign: "the efforts of the E. H. Crump political machine to regain control of the political machinery of the State."[19]

Despite the furor raised by Browning's opposition, the Memorial Apartments lease-purchase and other charges of corruption did not become significant issues until late in the campaign. One observer contended that the charges of wrongdoing were "answered carefully and, apparently, with some success." But then Browning made a trip to the Democratic National Convention in Chicago late in July 1952 that led to disaster.[20]

In that year Senator Estes Kefauver became a serious contender for the Democratic presidential nomination. A number of factors contributed to making him a viable challenger. The popularity of the incumbent, Harry Truman, had declined sharply because of prolonged war in Korea, taxes, inflation, and the belief that his administration contained both "corruptionists" and Communists. Kefauver, on the other hand, had earned publicity by conducting nationally televised Senate hearings on organized crime and had thereby gained an image as a champion of justice and decency. The senator committed himself to the presidential race and demonstrated his popular appeal when he entered the New Hampshire primary in March 1952, the first of the preferential races, and upset President Truman. The Kefauver bandwagon then began to roll, and he amassed victories in primaries in Wisconsin, Nebraska, Illinois, Massachusetts, Pennsylvania, New Jersey, Maryland, Oregon, South Dakota, and California. The senator had, however, incurred the hostility of party leaders. He had offended President Truman, embarrassed the Democratic party by implicating several prominent leaders during the crime hearings, and had bypassed the professionals by appealing directly to the people. Nevertheless, he was popular at the grass roots, and after building a commanding lead in committed delegates to the convention it appeared that Senator Kefauver had a good chance of winning the nomination.[21]

Gordon Browning and Estes Kefauver had been allied in common cause before, and it came as no surprise when the governor boarded the senator's presidential bandwagon. His principle motive was clear: he needed the votes of Kefauver's Tennessee supporters to fight off the stiff challenge from young Frank Clement, and should the senator win the presidency, Browning would be able to appoint an interim successor. There were potentially even greater rewards. One loyalist suggested that he would be a good candidate for attorney general in Kefauver's cabinet. Browning replied that he expected to remain governor for two more years, but, he added significantly, "no doubt if Kefauver is nominated and elected I could have what I want."[22] Probably no one in Tennessee or elsewhere put forth more effort in Kefauver's cause than Browning. Prior to the preferential primary circuit, the governor, his cabinet, and the constitutional officer of the state made a sizeable contribution to the senator's campaign chest. Kefauver was most appreciative and wrote: "I can't tell you how much I appreciate this kindness and generous expression of your interest and friendship. Our funds have been troubling us, Gordon, and you can imagine what this means to us, coming just when it did."[23] Despite the difficult race confronting him, Browning eagerly volunteered his services and campaigned for the senator in the Florida, Kansas, and Nebraska primaries. Kefauver was profuse in his expression of gratitude for the governor's efforts. Browning responded that he was "tickled to death at the prospects" of Kefauver's nomination. "What I have done in the matter has been a privilege," he wrote.[24]

Kefauver's bid for the presidential nomination generated some turbulence in Tennessee. The followers of both had always viewed each other with suspicion and the governor's people were especially concerned about the more liberal Kefauver. One loyalist to both Browning and Kefauver acknowledged that some of the governor's friends were lukewarm toward the senator and "would knife him if it was to their interest to do so."[25] Reflecting the feeling of some in Kefauver's Tennessee organization, one ally wrote: "The Governor himself, as you know, has stated emphatically that he is for you. But, as we in the second District so well know, what the Governor says and what his organization ultimately does, are often in no way similar."[26] But Kefauver needed the Browning-controlled party machinery to ensure a totally committed delegation to the Democratic convention from Tennessee. He therefore, made an effort to keep his supporters in line for Browning; he reminded dissidents that Browning was working hard for his cause. And on one occasion, he was able to inform the governor, "I put the QT to some of my boys whom I found supporting Frank Clement. Let me know if there are any others, and I will get after them."[27] As a result, Browning's organization was soon caught up in the drive for Kefauver; in fact, his forces became so enthusiastic that they almost pushed aside some of the senator's fanatics in their efforts to help Kefauver's campaign. And Browning was able to assure the senator that Tennesseee Democrats would be committed to his nomination: "When our Convention meets here," he wrote, "there will not be a ripple on the surface and the only thing we will permit them to do is take positive action on your case."[28] And as Browning predicted, there was no ripple of dissension as the combined forces of the two leaders dominated the Democratic state convention of 1952. Therefore, the Tennessee delegation selected to go to the national convention in Chicago in July was a combination of Browning and Kefauver supporters, and the governor was elected chairman of the group.

Despite a big lead in committed delegates and the enthusiasm of his supporters, Kefauver's bandwagon ran into a roadblock at Chicago in the form of the hostility of party leaders. President Truman controlled party machinery and parliamentary maneuvers and committee decisions were often unfavorable to the senator. Then Kefauver made a mistake by committing himself to a party loyalty oath. A resolution to put into effect a loyalty pledge was passed by the convention because some southern delegatons threatened to repeat the 1948 Dixiecrat revolt and not support the national ticket if the party adopted a civil rights plank in the platform. Although Senator Kefauver endorsed the pledge, Tennessee's delegation appeared to be ready to cast a vote in favor of seating the Virginia delegation which refused to sign the pledge. Kefauver made a personal appeal to the delegation to cast its unit vote against Virginia. Browning was in a difficult position; he did not want to embarrass the senator but he still voted with the minority in the caucus when the delegation determined that Tennessee would cast its unit vote against seating Virginia. Thus Tennessee, at Kefauver's request, became the only southern state to vote against the Old Dominion. The senator ultimately lost his bid for the nomination to Governor Adlai Stevenson of Illinois in part because of the pledge, but the greater factor was the opposition of the party's professionals.[29]

The action of the Tennessee delegation at Chicago produced repercussions at home. Few issues could have angered the electorate more than the negative vote on seating a neighboring southern state. The great outburst of protest was caused in part, perhaps, by the fact that

thousands had witnessed the convention on television and had seen the
vote cast. And Governor Browning, despite his vote in the caucus, was
regarded as an accomplice to the act because he was present at the
convention as chairman of the delegation. There was a deluge of letters to editors protesting the stand at the convention and insisting that
Browning did not deserve the vote of a single Tennessean because of
what had been done. The opposition immediately took up the issue by
charging that Browning had deserted the South and disgraced and humiliated Tennessee by acting as a stooge of the left wingers. A hoax was
perpetrated when someone released a statement allegedly issued by
liberal Senator Hubert Humphrey of Minnesota defending Browning.
The *Banner* cited this bogus statement as proof that the governor had
joined the radicals. Clement made no public criticism—he did not have
to. His supporters displayed banners that read: "Frank Clement loves
the South! We Love Frank Clement!" Browning had become a "scalawag."[30]

The governor was not without his apologists, but most of them were
already committed to him. Joe Hatcher stated that neither Tennessee
nor Browning betrayed the South; instead, the South had been betrayed
by the "Republicrats." The *Kingsport Times-News* and the *Johnson City
Press-Chronicle* expressed regret at the vote against Virginia, but held
that Browning deserved reelection on his record of accomplishments
in East Tennessee. The *Clarksville Leaf-Chronicle* asked a thoughtful
question: who betrayed whom? The paper believed that the pledge was
justified and forty-six states accepted it, why did Virginia fail to adopt
it? The *Chattanooga Times,* one of Kefauver's most vocal supporters,
commented that Virginia was really to blame and that Browning was a
true Tennessean. If he had not fought so courageously for Kefauver, he
would not have deserved the vote of any Tennessean. The *Times* declared that the real issue in the gubernatorial contest was still "Crumpism." The *Knoxville News-Sentinel* also defended Browning's action at
the convention and agreed with the *Times* that the issue was still
freedom versus dictatorship. The paper stated that it had supported
Browning since he entered office because "no cane-toting gauleiter from
Shelby had stalked the Hermitage Hotel lobby while the Legislature
was on, dictating every move."[31]

Lucuis E. Burch, Jr., of Memphis, and Tennessee's delegate on the
Credentials Committee of the Democratic National Convention, tried
to calm the storm raised against Browning. He made a public statement
pointing out that Browning, as chairman of the delegation, was bound
by the rule to carry out the wishes of the majority. After the convention,

a tired and disappointed Kefauver returned to Tennessee for a rest. Prevailed upon publicly to defend his ally's actions, he appeared on television to accept full responsibility for the delegation's stand. He stressed that Browning was simply following his wishes and demonstrated that he was a "courageous friend" who "stood by me." He asked the voters to forgive their governor.[32] The Dyersburg *State Gazette* probably expressed the feeling of many when it suggested that the governor could not be blamed for being loyal to the senator, but that there was a deeper loyalty to the state and the party. Therefore, Browning must assume full responsibility for what was done at the convention.[33] Kefauver's appearance did little good, for no matter how hard he tried, Browning could not explain why the Tennessee delegation had cast a vote against seating Virginia, and some who were opposed to the seating of Virginia were disturbed by the governor's attempt to explain the action. Browning must have been sincere when he commented that he "shouldn't have gone (to Chicago) in the first place," for a big city made him uncomfortable. However, he insisted, "I am not ashamed of the action of the Tennessee delegation in Chicago."[34]

The charges of unethical and illegal deals in the administration seemed to carry more weight after the debacle at Chicago. Clement became even more emphatic in his claim that the lease-purchase of the Memorial Apartments was corrupt. Browning, on the defensive once again, insisted that he would not defend the deal, but he would brag about it because it was "the best real estate deal the state has ever made."[35] Clement continued to ask the governor to reveal Attorney General Beeler's opinion on the lease-purchase. The challenger waited until the last week of the campaign to announce that he had written to Beeler requesting that he make public his ruling on the transaction. Browning had just acknowledged that the attorney general's opinion was negative but Clement's move was good showmanship. Released from the client-attorney relationship by Browning's admission, Beeler revealed to the challenger that he did indeed advise the governor that he was "wholly without authority" to make the purchase.[36] A few days after Beeler released his letter, Browning again admitted that the attorney general had rendered an opinion against the lease-purchase. Stating that, while he respected Beeler's opinion, he disagreed with him; Browning declared: "The newspapers have published an opinion from the Attorney General of the state in which he told me I did not have any right to obligate the state to pay for that building. I did not propose to obligate the state. Employment Security obligated itself. I did it with some of the best counsel in Tennessee backing me."[37]

Browning's defense of the Memorial Apartments transaction was no more convincing than his explanation of the events at Chicago. The Democratic electorate in Tennessee repudiated the governor decisively in the primary on 7 August. Clement polled 302,491 votes to the incumbent's 245,166. The defeat was general; Browning carried only two congressional districts, the first and second, by narrow margins. The governor usually polled a large vote in his home community, but he even lost Carroll County by almost 1,000 votes. He did receive something like 31,000 in Shelby County, but Clement received more than 50,000 there. Clifford Allen polled only 75,000 votes statewide, far less than he had received in 1950. Although the Clement forces had been concerned about Allen and had tried on at least one occasion to get him to withdraw from the race, the vote for the Nashville attorney was not a significant factor in the final outcome of the primary.[38] As expected, Congressman Albert Gore retired Senator McKellar 335,000 votes to 245,000. The aging senator won only the first and ninth congressional districts, and his slender majority of only 3,000 votes in Shelby County was indicative of his waning strength.

How much effect the Memorial Apartments transaction had on the outcome of the gubernatorial election was not clear. Politically, it was not a wise deal but Browning's opposition proved no dishonesty. The governor's loyalists continued to insist that it was favorable to the state, although it might have been unconsititutional and it would have been better if Browning had rejected it. Browning had no regrets about the purchase, saying that his opponents would have raised another bugbear if that deal had not been made.[40] Most observers believed that the events at the Democratic convention were primarily responsible for Browning's defeat in the primary. And Browning himself also believed that it was the major factor in his loss.[41] Why did he insist on going to the convention in the first place? Jack Norman, chairman of the state Democratic Executive Committee, and vice-chairman of the delegation, declared that he had seen the issue of civil rights and the party loyalty pledge developing and realized that nothing but bitterness would come from the convention. He had advised Browning to stay at home, saying that he could easily excuse himself because of the campaign. But the governor felt obligated to Kefauver and insisted on going.[42] Browning was also a stubborn man once he took a stand, as in the Memorial Apartments lease-purchase, and would not retreat, es-

pecially when it involved loyalty to a friend and ally. He was also motivated, in part, by the need for the votes of Kefauver's organization.
In the final analysis, however, W. R. Jarrell was probably correct when
he suggested that if Kauver had won the Democratic presidential nomination, no one would have criticized Browning.[43]

Factors other than the backlash of the convention contributed to the
governor's defeat. Perhaps many people wanted a change; 1952 was a
"throw the rascals out" year across the nation and, according to Joe
Hatcher, the prospect of a third term displeased some voters.[44] The contrast in the styles of Browning and Clement was also significant. An old-
fashioned stump orator using colorful invectives did not appeal to the
more sophisticated among Tennessee's electorate as much as Clement's
more polished manner. In addition, by 1952, an increasing number of
Tennesseans were making a habit of watching television. Politicians
were quick to see the new medium's potential for reaching large audiences, and the primary of that year was the first in which TV was used
extensively. Browning's extemporaneous style, more suited to an open-
air platform on the court square, did not project a good image on the
new medium. He appeared stiff and uncertain before the camera; as
one observer noted, "Browning looked as comfortable in the TV glare
as a man trying to scratch his nose in an iron lung."[45] Organized labor
and the Tennessee Municipal League both worked hard to defeat the
governor. Herbert Bingham, executive director of the TML, believed
that his organization brought about Browning's defeat.[46] He over-
estimated the power of the TML alone but scarcely its intent. In reality,
a number of immediate issues and factors combined to defeat Browning;
but in a very real sense the times brought about his downfall. His philosophy was a blend of southern states' rights conservatism and Tennessee populism, and his sympathies were with the countryside; he had
tended to ignore the needs of the more industrialized society of the
1950s. A new generation of leadership which would be more responsive
to those needs was required.

On the surface, Gordon Browning took his defeat at the hands of
Frank Clement cheerfully and perhaps a bit stoically. In response to a
wire of condolence from Senator Kefauver, he wrote, "this result came
as a distinct surprise to me." He admitted, however, "the load is bur-
densome and my wife is so overjoyed I feel ashamed to even want to
stay." In fact, "Ida is so happy over gettting out of the surroundings that
I am almost glad I lost for her sake."[47] Browning was deeply hurt, however, and found it difficult to accept forced retirement. The charges of

dishonesty in his administration made his repudiation by the electorate even more unpleasant. He remarked later that Clement was the only man he found "it hard to forgive." "So far as I know," he said, "Governor Frank Clement is the only person to impute dishonesty and crookedness to me in public office."[48] Unable to accept retirement, he began planning a political comeback soon after his defeat.

Browning was also concerned about his ally, Senator Kefauver. Aware that the senator was despondent over his loss at the convention, Browning urged his friend to bounce back: "Do not grieve over spilled milk—just get another cow," he wrote. Conscious that the senator's popularity in the state had declined, he declared that he was confident that his "friends" would support Kefauver's bid for renomination and reelection in 1954.[49] He also sought to keep his organization alive and loyal to Kefauver. Shortly after the primary in 1952, Browning wrote to an ally in Memphis to suggest that all of his friends should join forces with the friends of Senator Kefauver to crush Clement and the revived Crump machine at the next primary. Pointing out that Kefauver might need help since his popularity was at a low ebb after the vote against seating the Virginia delegation at the convention, he stressed that if all worked together, the restored Crump machine could be destroyed.[50]

Browning apparently believed that Clement was the figurehead of a revived Shelby machine. He did not perceive that the voters were no longer interested in the Crump issue and that the Memphis boss was no longer influential in statewide politics. Clement undoubtedly attracted to his organization individuals that had once been allied with the Crump-McKellar axis, but the new political force was a different generation. And the factions that Browning represented were as demoralized and disorganized as they had been after his defeat in 1938. An attempted comeback by Browning would be difficult for he could hardly expect enthusiastic support from either of the senators or their supporters.

Conforming to tradition, Democratic factionalism in Tennessee remained a complex system of highly personalized organizations. Although the new state leaders, Clement, Kefauver, and Gore, received support in common from some local leaders and groups, each organization was an independent entity. Kefauver had to be especially careful in his relations with Clement, who now controlled state patronage and party machinery. Friction had developed between the two organizations during the 1952 campaign when Clement irritated Kefauver loyalists by not endorsing the senator's bid for the presidential nomination, and

Kefauver incurred Clement's hostility by becoming openly involved in Browning's campaign. Thus, the two leaders emerged from the primary as enemies.[51] Governor Clement demonstrated his hostility by retaliating against Kefauver's friends in state positions, and the senator's forces quickly came to view the young governor as a potential if not a probable challenger for the senatorial nomination in 1954. Because of Clement's enmity and his own ebbing popularity, Kefauver wisely maintained a low profile and avoided controversial issues while he quietly tried to mend his political fences in Tennessee.[52]

Tennessee's newest senator, Albert Gore, with an organization based on individual friendships, was even more independent than either Clement or Kefauver. Although he steered clear of public commitments with other leaders, in his quiet way he cooperated with the senior senator.[53] And neither Gore nor Kefauver were willing to hitch their fortunes to the chances of a moribund politican such as Browning. The opposition of Browning and his friends during the senatorial primary of 1952 was sufficient reason for Gore to avoid any alliance. And as one of the senior senator's partisans wrote, "It is clear and definite that Kefauver cannot align himself with the old Browning outfit. They are out of business and there is not much prospect for a revival."[54]

The issues in the campaign of 1952 were not dead, for much to Browning's displeasure, the lease-purchase of the Memorial Apartments continued to be a live subject. On 31 December 1952, on his instructions, the state exercised its option on the building. He intended to carry out the transaction despite the charges of wrongdoing brought out in the campaign. As he prepared to vacate the governor's office in January 1952, Browning submitted his final report to the new General Assembly. He summed up the progress of his administration and cited the accomplishments of his leadership: improved schools, better pay for teachers, much needed construction on college campuses, institutional improvements, and better roads. He declared that much more was needed and suggested that the assembly should exert every effort to continue improvements. Finally, Browning pointed out that he was leaving the office of chief executive with the state in sound financial condition. His report, much longer than usual, reflected his desire to convey to the legislators and the people the impression that his administration was one of progress.[55]

A week later, on the day of Clement's inaugural, Gordon Browning gave his farewell address to the people of Tennessee. He remarked that it was difficult to give a farewell address after what had transpired but that he was grateful for the support and the confidence of his many friends. He called attention, briefly, to the accomplishments of his service to the state with particular emphasis on the debt retirement program inaugurated in 1937. He revealed that he had planned a long and much needed vacation, but rumors that the assembly would make an investigation of his administration caused a change in his plans. He declared that an investigation insinuated dishonesty, so he would remain in Nashville to be ready to offer the truth and defend any action of his tenure as chief executive. He insisted that every possible feature of the Memorial Apartments purchase had been made public. He concluded that the members of the General Assembly might better spend the time in performance of their duties than in throwing "poisoned arrows and darts."[56] True to his promise, Browning remained in Nashville for the time being and set up a law office with attorney Jack Norman, but he eventually returned to Huntingdon to live.

In compliance with his campaign pledge to examine the Memorial Apartments lease-purchase carefully, Governor Clement's forces introduced a resolution in the General Assembly to create a special committee to investigate the transaction along with the Purchasing Department and the Highway Department. The resolution, in effect, called for a sweeping probe of Browning's administration, and was quickly passed. Considering the accusations of the previous year and a half, a complete airing of the charges of misconduct was necessary to set the record straight. Investigation of charges of corruption and fraud is a legitimate function of the General Assembly and Clement had obligated himself to a probe which had to be carried out. On the other hand, an investigation of Browning's administration by Clement's administration could not have been impartial, and the probe smacked of an attempt to embarrass the former governor.

The probe began early in February 1953 and after a week of hearings columnist Joe Hatcher reported that Clement's forces were disappointed at the committee's inability to find fraudulent or even illegal operations in the previous administration.[57] The investigation also appeared to be one-sided, since neither Browning nor any of the owners or officials of Cumberland Properties were called before the committee. Attorney General Beeler testified that he had not filed suit to void the transaction for the apartment building because the owners were willing to have the property returned to them; prospects of an even greater return than was possible under the fifteen-year lease agreement was given as the reason.[58] The probe ended the last week in February when the committee submitted a seventy-three-page report to Governor Clement. The report stated that, to the committee's knowledge, the participants in the Memorial Apartments lease-purchase were not guilty of criminal acts, but the manner in which the state acquired the structure was questionable. The report further said that the total cost was exorbitant and "alleged" personal friends of the former governor had profited. Moreover, the purchase had been consummated before the formation of Cumberland Properties and the stockholders obviously wanted to keep their identities secret. The committee insisted that the transaction needed legislative approval in order to make it binding. Finally, the committee recommended to Governor Clement that he file suit to have the lease voided. On other aspects of the investigation, the committee reported that undoubtedly the Department of Highways and Public Works was mismanaged and misused. "It had been the focal point of corruption, graft, and had unquestionably been susceptible to outside influences dictating purchases and policies of the department with the view of securing campaign funds," the report stated. It cited as evidence the state's purchase of more materials for the Highway Department than were necessary and its abuse of the practice of competitive bidding in the purchase of heavy road machinery. Finally, the report said that the Department of Conservation was subject to the same pressures and irregularities, and cited the Purchasing Department with being guilty of condoning or encouraging all of those activities.[59]

In reality, the investigation proved little in the way of wrongdoing. The only charge that may have had substance was that administration officials bought excessive amounts of materials from friends of the governor. The evidence was not sufficient to bring criminal action against any member of Browning's administration for any reason. The résumé of the committe's report which appeared in the *Senate Journal* did not mention the Memorial Apartments lease-purchase. It merely stated that the Department of Accounts was negligent in preventing the purchase of materials, supplies, and equipment through a favored few with the result of waste, extravagance, and corruption.[60] In April 1953 the Clement administration asked the Chancery Court of Davidson County to set aside the Memorial Apartments lease-purchase on the grounds that Cumberland Properties had fraudulently influenced the state. The disposition of the case was not forthcoming, but the court held that the state had to continue paying rent because it was still using the building.[61] More than a year elapsed before the case was finally settled.

Because he wanted vindication above anything else, Gordon

Browning determined to try for the governor's office once again. He had been able in the past to recover from defeat but the odds this time were against a revival. Not only had he been decisively defeated in 1952 but time was also running out, for he was already sixty-four years old. His family pleaded with him to retire gracefully, and many of his friends tried to talk him out of running again. Their efforts, however, were to no avail. Joe Hatcher recalled, "we tried to talk him out of it, tried every way in the world," but he was a hurt man who insisted on running because of what the Clement forces had said about him.[62] Hatcher therefore spoke with authority when he wrote in January 1954 that Browning acted very much like a candidate and that he would probably try again for the governor's office in the August Democratic primary.[63] The former governor confirmed the prediction two weeks later when he announced that he would seek the four-year term established by the recently ratified constitutional amendment. Soon afterwards, Governor Clement, declining to contest Kefauver for the Senate, declared for reelection.

The campaign that followed was almost a carbon copy of the campaign of 1952. Browning opened his drive in Trenton on 4 June with a furious attack on Clement's administration, charging the governor's forces with fraud, deception, and mismanagement. He did not ignore Ed Crump in the campaign but the Memphis boss was not as prominent in Browning's attacks as before. Instead, he insisted that the governor's father Robert Clement or "Pa-pa" as Browning termed him, was the real power behind the throne. He declared that Clement's father had a sinister influence in state affairs, and the charge was reinforced by a parody on the song "Clementine," "Happy Pappy Clementine," and played by a country music band. Clement successfully destroyed the issue by calmly admitting that he did indeed look to his father for his advice because he subscribed to the scriptural admonition, "Honor thy father."[64]

Browning also insisted that Clement was an ally of the old dictatorship in Memphis. That charge failed to elicit much response from the electorate, for the Memphis machine was no longer a force in state politics. Moreover, Crump was not enamored of the governor and made no attempt to dictate state policy. He was, in fact, in failing health and would be dead within three months after the primary. He endorsed Clement in 1954, not because he liked him, but because he considered him the lesser of two evils, remarking that the incumbent had made mistakes but had tried to be a good governor.[65]

The public endorsement disappointed some of the administration's opponents for they hoped that Crump would repudiate Clement because of a truck weight scandal. In February 1953 the Seventy-eighth General Assembly, with the governor's support, passed a bill raising trucking load limits from 42,000 pounds to over 55,000. Foes charged that trucking interests had contributed to Clement's campaign in 1952, and Crump had accused the governor of pushing a measure designed to benefit special interests. The weight issue was emphasized by Browning after it was revealed that Robert M. Crichton, a trucking industry leader who had been one of Clement's chief fund raisers in the 1952 campaign, gave the governor-elect $5,000 in currency on inaugural day in 1953 to buy a Cadillac. Although Crichton admitted the gift, the governor denied it; in so doing he revealed that he had broken with Crichton and his close friend and advisor, Secretary of State G. Edward Friar.[66] Browning tried to take advantage of the truck weight and gift scandal but he became excessively strident in his charges of corruption and the issue probably backfired. The electorate apparently felt that the increase in truck weights and the gift were petty compared to the Memorial Apartments transaction and Gordon Browning was unable to generate enthusiasm for his candidacy.

Frank Clement had important advantages: he was the incumbent with control of patronage and party machinery, and Tennesseans customarily rewarded governors with a second term. Clement emphasized morality in his campaign oratory in an attempt to maintain his image "as the essence of decency, morality, and honesty." He reinforced the portrait by wearing a white linen suit and often repeating the expression "Precious Lord, Take My Hand and Lead Me On."[67] Clement counterattacked with the themes that had produced votes in 1952: the Memorial Apartments transaction and sellout at Chicago. The Memorial lease-purchase remained an issue largely because the case was still in litigation. Browning charged that the governor's forces were trying to delay the decision until after the primary because they could not find enough evidence to sustain the accusation of wrongdoing. The charge may have had substance because the case had been delayed from time to time. However, the investigation into state affairs under Browning was still fresh in the minds of the people and many simply believed that his administration had committed numerous illegal deals.

The most volatile issue to develop in the summer of 1954 was public school desegregation. What came to be called the Second Reconstruction had been gaining momentum since the end of World War II. The American black emerged from the idealism and fervor of war years in a more militant mood and began to challenge aggressively the long-standing racial discrimination in the South. A number of minor victories had already been won and the issue of civil rights had disrupted the Democratic party. Even so, the Supreme Court's decision in the case of *Brown* v. *Board of Education, Topeka*, in May 1954, exploded with a surprising suddenness. The court unanimously declared that in public education, the "separate but equal" doctrine enunciated in the case of *Plessy* v. *Ferguson* (1896) was no longer valid; in short, segregated schools were inherently unequal and must therefore be desegregated. The decision caused a wave of anger to sweep across the South and denunciations were emotional and bitter. In Tennessee, however, the decision was generally received with some moderation and the state's press urged compliance with the "law of the land."[68]

Tennessee's geographical and economic diversity and its more diverse population had resulted in its having a more pluralistic society than the deep South. As a result, the state's electorate had seldom responded positively to candidates spouting racist rhetoric. Conforming to this tradition, in part because he also had ambitions for political office beyond Tennessee, Governor Clement took a moderate, noncommittal stance of "wait and see."[69] Browning expressed his convictions when he issued a statement denouncing the Brown decision shortly after it was announced. He declared that he stood for segregation because he considered it the best way to prevent friction between the races. He stated emphatically that no mixing of the races in the schools of the state would be allowed if he were elected governor. Despite that statement, Browning remained popular among blacks. The editor of a black newspaper in Memphis, the *Tri-State Defender*, acknowledged that Browning's denouncement of the *Brown* decision was unfortunate but the paper would support him because of what he had done for blacks.[70] If the circumstances of the campaign had been more favorable to Browning, he would not have made desegregation a big issue, but he started from far behind and he had failed to generate enthusiasm for his cause. Therefore, late in the campaign, he revived the issue, lashing out at the Supreme Court and others he characterized as agitators stirring up conflict, and again declaring that race mixing would not take place in Tennessee schools if he returned to the governor's office. He took a calculated risk in his stance because of Tennessee's large black voting population. Browning may have picked up a few white votes in counties heavily populated with blacks but his stand for white supremacy and segregation may have cost him the major portion of the black vote. The

Tri-State Defender finally abandoned Browning and endorsed Clement near the close of the campaign.[71]

Desegregation became an important issue in the senatorial primary where Estes Kefauver was making a bid to succeed himself. After the debacle at the Chicago convention in 1952 the senator quietly mended his fences. His forces were concerned about the Clement threat and were relieved when he opted to try to succeed himself rather than make the race for the Senate. The challenge to Kefauver came from Pat Sutton of Lawrenceburg, the congressman who represented the seventh district. Sutton conducted an innovative campaign; he traveled by helicopter, a novelty in 1954, and appeared in television marathons. He also waged an especially vicious campaign charging that Kafauver was part of a communist conspiracy in the United States and was in league with the radicals who were trying to force the *Brown* decision on the South. Kefauver was greatly concerned about Sutton's exaggerated anti-communist pitch.[72]

As usual, the gubernatorial and senatorial primaries were kept separate although Browning, in desperation, tried to link the two contests. He charged that Clement had offered him a deal: he would endorse Browning for the Senate against Kefauver if he would stay out of the gubernatorial contest.[73] The allegation had little influence on Kefauver's supporters, some of whom were working for Clement. One Browning loyalist wrote to the senator, "Browning placed himself on the altar of sacrifice in your behalf [at Chicago]. . . . I understand that you have your race to think of; the same was true with G. Browning when he stood with you in Chicago."[74] Kefauver, however, wisely kept his distance from Browning's feeble campaign.

Browning's lack of popular support was demonstrated by the fact that only one major daily newspaper, the *Nashville Tennessean*, remained loyal to him. Even Ed Meeman's Memphis *Press-Scimitar*, long a Browning partisan, announced that it would endorse neither of the candidates. The *Chattanooga Times* commented that Browning should be given credit for the sound condition of Tennessee's finances but that Clement should be returned because he gave the state good government.[75]

The results of the Democratic primary in August 1954 surprised no one. Governor Clement received over 481,000 votes to Browning's humiliating 185,000. The former governor failed to win a single congressional district, although he did at least obtain the majority in his own Carroll County. The electorate thus spoke in a resounding manner and retired Gordon Browning permanently. In the Senate contest, Kefauver easily defeated Sutton 440,000 to 186,000.[76]

The controversial issue, the Memorial Apartments lease-purchase, was finally disposed of shortly after the primary in 1954. On 26 August Chancellor William J. Wade of the Davidson County Chancery ended three years of stormy charges and litigation when he ruled that the state did not have legal authority to enter the lease-purchase agreement and held that Browning needed legislative approval in order to make the transaction binding. Chancellor Wade also cleared Browning, members of his administration, and owners of Cumberland Properties of any fraud. In addition, the chancellor ruled that the state was not entitled to recover the $240,000 spent in converting the building from apartments to offices. The Clement administration appealed the decision concerning recovery of the money, but in November 1954 the chancery court dismissed all action and litigation ended. After the court's decision in August, Governor Clement declared that the "people have won a great legal and moral victory."[77] But it was Gordon Browning who won a moral victory in that he was freed legally from any taint of dishonesty. In 1956 Cumberland Properties was dissolved, and the title to the Memorial Apartments went to two insurance companies which had guaranteed the loans to purchase the building. In 1957 National Life Insurance Company of Nashville bought the structure for a reported $450,000.[78]

NOTES

1. *Nashville Tennessean*, 2 March 1952.

2. Leslie T. Hart, interview with the author, Nashville 29 June 1977; Leslie T. Hart, taped interview with Stephen D. Boyd, Nashville, 18 August 1971, Tennessee State Library and Archives; Robert Clement, Sr., taped interview with Lee Greene, 25 March 1975, TSLA; Joe Carr, taped interview with Lee Greene, 16 September 1975, TSLA; Stepen D. Boyd, "The Campaign Speaking of Frank Clement in the 1954 Democratic Primary: Field Study and Rhetorical Analysis" (unpublished Ph.D. dissertation, University of Illinois, 1972), pp. 15–16, 28–30, 56–58.

3. *Trades and Labor News*, 10 July 1952; Matthew Lynch, interview with the author, Nashville, 7 July 1977; Dan Powell, interview with the author, Memphis 10 August 1976; Herbert Bingham, interview with the author, Nashville, 29 June 1977; see also Lee S. Greene, David H. Grubbs, and Victor C. Hobday, *Government in Tennessee*, 3rd ed. (Knoxville: University of Tennessee Press, 1975), p. 223; *Tri-State Defender*, 19 April, 5 July, 16 August 1952.

4. J. Carlton Loser to McKellar, 25 January 1952, McKellar to J. Carlton Loser, 1, 2 February 1952, Political Correspondence, Box 64, The Kenneth Douglas McKellar Papers, Memphis-Shelby County Public Library and Information Center; Whit LaFon to Clement, 14 May 1951, Correspondence: General, 457–4–8, Frank Clement Papers, Tennessee State Library and Archives; W. R. Davidson, interview wih the author, Tullahoma, 1 September 1977; Albert Gore, *Let the Glory Out: My South and Its Politics* (New York: The Viking Press, 1972), p. 78; Albert Gore, interview with the author, Nashville, 15 May, 1977. Gore's slogan was "Vote For Albert Gore—He's Only 44."

5. William D. Miller, *Mr. Crump of Memphis* (Baton Rouge: Louisiana State University Press, 1964), pp. 344–345.

6. Browning to G. Hurst Paul, 16 May 1952, Gordon Browning Papers, Tennessee State Library and Archives.

7. *Tennessean*, 25 May, 22 June, 1952.

8. Leslie T. Hart, interview with the author; Milton Rice, interview with the author, Nashville 19 July 1977; *State of Tenn. v. R. S. Doggett, et al.* (Memorial Hotel Litigation), Davidson Chancery, Part II, No. 73212, Att. Gen. office file, 2015, Tennessee State Library and Archives; *Chattanooga Times*, 29 August 1951.

9. *Nashville Banner*, 4 September 1951

10. Joe Hatcher, "Politics," *Tennessean*, 9 September 1951.

11. *Chattanooga Times*, 6 September 1951.

12. Leslie T. Hart, "Capitol Hill," *Banner*, 11 July 1952; *Banner*, 5 August 1952.

13. Browning to George Allmendinger, 29 February 1952, Browning Papers.

14. Browning to Enoch Brown, 3 April 1952, Ibid. Browning advanced $240,000 from his emergency fund to cover the cost of remodeling but he claimed that the money would ultimately be repaid when the state gained title to the building.

15. *State of Tenn. v. R. S. Doggett.* Beeler later explained why he did not attempt to block the lease-purchase. He believed in the separation of powers. and, according to that concept, the judicial department was equal and not superior to the executive branch of government. The governor's violation of the law was minor and subject to legislative review; the lease-purchase could be investigated by proper legislative authority and the legal department then given proper directions to void the transaction. He admitted, however, that he would have moved quickly if the lease-purchase had been a serious offense; Gordon Browning, "Gordon Browning: An Oral Memoir," ed. Joseph H. Riggs (Memphis Public Library, 1966), p. 66.

16. Quoted in *Banner*, 11, 12, 13, 14, 20 June 1952. Browning had been christened Gordon Weaver but had never used his middle name.

17. Quoted in Ibid., 18, 28 July 1952.

18. Quoted in Ibid., 12 June, 4 July 1952.

19. Quoted in Ibid., 11, 12, 28 June 1952.

20. William Goodman, *Inherited Domain: Political Parties in Tennessee* (Knoxville: Bureau of Public Information, University of Tennessee, 1954), p. 77.

21. Joseph Bruce Gorman, *Kefauver: A Political Biography* (New York: Oxford University Press, 1971), p. 103–105; Philip A. Grant, Jr., "Kefauver and the New Hampshire Presidential Primary," *Tennessee Historical Quarterly* 31 (Winter 1972): 372–381.

22. Browning to Pugh Moore, 26 June 1952, Browning Papers.

23. Kefauver to Browning, 5 March 1952, Browning Papers. The contribution was $1,500 of which five hundred was Browning's personal check.

24. Kefauver to Browning, 5 April, 10, 20, 28 May 1952, Browning to Kefauver, 19 May 1952, Ibid.

25. Lucius Burch to Dick Wallace, 31 March 1952, 4ᶜ Box 7, The Estes Kefauver Collection, University of Tennessee Library.

26. Gene Joyce to Kefauver, 16 March 1952, Ibid.

27. Kefauver to Robert Kelso, 17 March 1952, Ibid; Kefauver to Browning, 17 March 1952, Browning Papers.

28. Browning to Kefauver, 19 May 1952, Browning Papers.

29. Goodman, *Inherited Domain*, pp. 68–75; see also Paul T. David, Malcolm Moos, and Ralph M. Goodman, eds., *Presidential Nominating Politics in 1952*, vol. 3, *The South* (Baltimore: Johns Hopkins University Press, 1954), pp. 176–181. The Democratic presidential nominee, Adali Stevenson, failed to carry Tennessee, and some of Kefauver's supporters bolted to the Republican candidate, Dwight D. Eisenhower. The *Chattanooga Times*, for example, a Kefauver backer, endorsed Eisenhower.

30. *Commercial Appeal* 3 August 1952; *Press-Scimitar*, 28 July 1952; *Banner*, 28 July, 2, 3 August 1952.

31. Hatcher, "Politics," 28 July 1952; *Kingsport Times-News*, 27 July 1952; *Johnson City Press-Chronicle*, 5 August 1952; *Clarksville Leaf-Chronicle*, 1, 4 August 1952; *Chattanooga Times*, 28 July 1952; *Knoxville News-Sentinel*, 30 July 1952.

32. *Press-Scimitar*, 26 July, 1 August 1952; see also Gorman, *Kefauver*, pp. 35–63.

33. Dyersburg *State Gazette*, 25, 28 July, 1 August 1952.

34. Quoted in *Banner*, 31 July 1952.

35. Quoted in *Press-Scimitar*, 31 July 1952.

36. *Banner*, 30 July, 4 August 1952; *State of Tenn. v. R. S. Doggett*.

37. Quoted in *Banner*, 6 August 1952.

38. Sam Coward to Frank Clement, 28 June 1951, Correspondence: Political 457–4–8, Clement Papers.

39. *Tennessee Blue Book, 1954* (Nashville, 1954), pp. 314–315, 318–319.

40. W. R. Jarrell, interview with the author, Springfield, 21 June 1966; Jim Cummings, interview with the author, Woodbury, 28 June 1976; Milton Rice,

interview; Bob Guinn, interview with the author, Savannah, 23 June 1977; Gordon Browning, interview with the author, Huntingdon, 28 December 1965.

41. Browning, interview, 28 December 1965.

42. Jack Norman, interview with the author, Nashville, 20 March 1978; see also George Barker, "Three Times and You're Out," *Nashville Tennessean Magazine* (7 October 1962), p. 18.

43. Jarrell, interview.

44. Hatcher, "Politics," 3 August 1952.

45. Gore, interview; Barker, "Three Times and You're Out," p. 19.

46. Herbert Bingham, interview.

47. Browning to Kefauver, 11 August 1952, Browning to Kefauver, 12 August 1952, Browning Papers.

48. Quoted in Barker, "Three Times and You're Out," p. 19.

49. Browning to Kefauver, 12 August 1952, Browning Papers.

50. Browning to Gilmer Richardson, 15 September 1952, Ibid.

51. Charles Neese to Frank Clement, 16 June 1952, 4ᶜ Box 7, Kefauver Collection; Dan Powell, interview.

52. James I. Bell to Kefauver, 11 May 1953, Kefauver to Bryan Hicks, 5 August 1953, George R. Dempster to Kefauver, 19 June 1953, W. M. Barr to Edmund Orgill, 3 December 1953, copy, 5ᶠ Box 1, Kefauver Collection; Gorman, *Kefauver*, pp. 160–174.

53. Mary Elizabeth Gore to Kefauver, n. d., Robert E. Lafferty to Kefauver, 4 March 1953, 5ᶠ Box 2, Ibid.

54. C. W. Owens to Kefauver, 19 May 1953, Ibid.

55. *House Journal of the Seventy-eighth General Assembly of the State of Tennessee, 1953* (Nashville, 1953), pp. 52–91.

56. Ibid., pp. 156–163.

57. Hatcher, "Politics," 8, 13 February 1953.

58. Ibid., 24 February 1953.

59. *Banner*, 24 February 1953, gave the full text of the report.

60. *Senate Journal of the Seventy-eighth General Assembly of the State of Tennessee, 1953* (Nashville, 1953), pp. 1292–1298.

61. *Tennessean*, 16 April 1953. An assistant in the attorney general's office at the time of the Memorial Apartments issue suggested that the administration may have had second thoughts about the valuable and badly needed property. But because he had made it a campaign issue, Governor Clement felt compelled to take legal action to void the transaction; Milton Rice, interview.

62. Mrs. Bill Bowers, interview with the author, Milan, 24 June 1976; Jarrell, interview; Joe Hatcher, interview with the author, Nashville, 21 June 1966.

63. Hatcher, "Politics," 5 January 1954.

64. Boyd, "The Campaign Speaking of Frank Clement," pp. 83–87; Robert Clement conceded that, although Frank Clement had a "mind of his own," he was influential in his son's administration; Robert S. Clement, taped interview

with Stephen D. Boyd, Dickson, 11 August 1971, Tennessee State Library and Archives.

65. Miller, *Mr. Crump*, p. 349.

66. *Tennessean*, 28 February 1953; *Press-Scimitar*, 21 July 1954; Boyd, "The Campaign Speaking of Frank Clement," pp. 73–79.

67. Boyd, "The Campaign Speaking of Frank Clement," pp. 101–103, 132–133.

68. Hugh Davis Graham, *Crisis in Print: Desegregation and the Press in Tennessee* (Nashville: Vanderbilt University Press, 1967), pp. 29–61.

69. Ibid., pp. 62–63; Boyd, "The Campaign Speaking of Frank Clement," pp. 87–91.

70. *Tennessean*, 1 June 1954; *Tri-State Defender*, 10, 17 July 1954.

71. *Tri-State Defender*, 7 August 1954.

72. Gorman, *Kefauver*, pp. 174–191.

73. *Tennessean*, 1 August 1954.

74. Ruby Todd to Kefauver, n. d., 5ᶠ Box 1, Kefauver Collection.

75. *Press-Scimitar*, 2 August 1954; *Times*, 1 August 1954.

76. *Tennessee Blue Book, 1956* (Nashville, 1956), pp. 375–376.

77. *Tennessean*, 27 August, 20 November 1954.

78. Ibid., 19 June 1957.

Epilogue

IN THE PAST, Gordon Browning had proven his ability to come back from overwhelming defeat to win again, but age perhaps more than anything else would prevent his return to political office after 1954. He was bitter for the moment at the circumstances that forced his retirement from public service. "The people," he observed, "expect full bodily sacrifice on the public altar. . . . But I love people and I have enjoyed serving them." He soon became reconciled to retirement: "A man in politics has to accept defeat when it comes."[1] There was one consolation in defeat; Miss Ida was happy. "Poor girl, she had to wait a long time . . . she never had a home of her own—Washington apartments, two different governor's mansions in Nashville, living with her folks or her sister in between times and when I was overseas."[2] In 1953 the Brownings built, on a choice lot on the edge of Huntingdon, a red brick house with white columns across the front and paneled throughout with wood from Tennessee trees. Miss Ida had the life-style she preferred: a home, a yard for flowers, a garden club, her church, and the close-knit society of a small town. It was also consoling to bask in the warmth of the admiration and respect of his fellow townspeople who still affectionately greeted him as "Cap."

Upon returning to Huntingdon, Browning entered law practice with the firm of Maddox and Lassiter in a shabby office on the second floor of an old building on Huntingdon's court square. Shortly thereafter he purchased a substantial block of stock in Tennessee Valley Life Insurance Company of Jackson, Tennessee, and accepted the chairmanship of the board of directors. For a decade he daily drove the thirty-five miles to his office in Jackson. When asked why he did not move to Jackson to be near his office, he replied that he "married a Huntingdon girl. She just won't go. And I'm too old to start living alone—or to organize another woman."[3]

Despite his age, and in spite of the onset of Parkinson's disease, Gordon Browning remained active and on the go with seemingly unflagging energy. The disabling disease, which causes tremors and loss of mobility of the face, developed gradually probably appearing as early as 1954. When the drug L-dopa was brought out as a possible remedy for Parkinson's disease, Browning had no hesitation about being a guinea pig, and participated in the drug's experimental use, with some apparent benefit. Browning remained mobile, assisted by the state patrolman assigned to him, and sometimes would be off to a picnic, barbecue, or fish fry. He seldom missed Democratic party rallies or conventions of veterans' organizations such as the American Legion and Veterans of Foreign Wars, and he was regular in his attendance at meetings of the Tennessee Historical Commission of which he was a member. Tennessee's former governors and their wives began meeting periodically, very possibly at Browning's suggestion, to socialize and reminisce.[4] The highlight of each year was the annual reunion in Memphis on 11 November of the veterans of Battery A. It was a happy and emotional experience, and the former captain was a regular in attendance, even after he was confined to a wheelchair.

Browning had always been a political man, and his interest in politics did not diminish. He declared, "There will never be a time in my life when political interest will be lost by me. There is no way to get rid of me!"[5] However, despite his many friends and admirers, he had no organization and his influence over the state was minimal. In the Democratic gubernatorial primary in 1958 he actively campaigned for Andrew "Tip" Taylor of Jackson in a three-way race which involved, in addition to Taylor, Buford Ellington (the Clement administration's candidate), and the mayor of Memphis, Edmund Orgill. By the 1960s, Browning's political activities had declined to the point where he merely announced his endorsement of candidates and did not actively participate in campaigns. He had become simply an elder statesman of the Democratic party.

In retrospect, Gordon Browning could take pride in the fact that his administrations were dynamic and characterized by solid accomplishments. His greatest achievement by far was solving financial problems, especially in reorganizing the state's debt and placing it on a sound retirement program. Browning's economic philosophy was the result of early conditioning, modified by time, experience, and political expediency. The result was a bundle of conflicting ideologies. On the one hand, he advocated a more responsive government to meet the needs of his rural constituents. On the other hand, he was a states' right conservative who resisted change. He believed in fiscal integrity: balance the budget and reduce the debt. His gubernatorial administations demonstrated that he followed his philosophy with some degree of consistency. Yet he opposed President Franklin D. Roosevelt's economy measure in 1933 because it called for a reduction of veteran's benefits. He rationalized that the immediate needs of individuals transcended the needs of a balanced budget. Browning was not afraid to spend, but he preferred to raise taxes rather than to finance projects with bonds. He observed, however, that because General Assemblies were always reluctant to increase taxes, it was easier to get legislators to raise funds by authorizing the sale of bonds.[6] He recognized that the demands of a growing society required greater expeditures, and he had the courage to propose the adoption of a state income tax, a proposal that was generally unpopular and failed to be incorporated in the constitutional revisions of 1953.

Gordon Browning demonstrated both a pragmatism necessary to successful political existence and an awareness that the alliance systems were not permanent but ever shifting. He was not, for example, inclined to condemn allegedly corrupt practices in Shelby Country when he was the beneficiary of those activities. He once stated that it was not a good policy to destroy an opponent because an opponent at any given time might be a needed friend sometime in the future: "There's not a bit of need in killing anyone off, especially in politics, because you never know who's going to be your best friend the next time. It's absolutely foolish to shut the door on them just because they are against you."[7] The hard core of his voting strength was among veterans, and he gathered about him a coterie of his former World War I comrades. In Congress he became one of the leading spokesmen for veterans' benefits and he was sincerely interested in helping former servicemen, especially the disabled and the widows and orphans of those killed in service. In that respect, he demonstrated the human tendency to use benevolent motives for personal benefit.

Although Browning was not above a measure of demagoguery if it meant the difference between victory and defeat in a political campaign, he could hardly be likened to the typical southern demagogue. He did not rise to power on the crest of a popular reform movement, as did Tom Watson or Leonidas L. Polk, nor did he participate in race baiting as did Eugene Talmadge or Theodore Bilbo. He was, however, a strong racial segregationist and an advocate of southern conservatism tempered by political expediency. He was a typical southern politician in that he advocated the mythical doctrine of states' rights, and the retention of the prevailing relationship between the races.

Browning realized that much of what was said in the heat of campaign oratory was magnified beyond the fact. He could, therefore, hold no animosity toward old foes like Prentice Cooper and Jim McCord, and he agreed to the appointment of another past opponent, Burgin Dossett, to the presidency of East Tennessee State College.[8] He also revealed a capacity to forgive his political enemies when he and Senator McKellar buried the hatchet soon after the senator left office in 1953. He recalled, "I'm awfully glad that I had the courage and the appreciation to make up with him" because, as he said, McKellar had become a helpless old man without friends or attention.[9] Browning could also reclaim old friends such as World War I comrades Abe Waldauer and Walter Chandler. He maintained a deep respect and admiration for Chandler despite his association with the Crump machine.[10] Close friends and relatives disputed whether Browning and Waldauer truly regained the spirit of comradeship that held them together before October 1937, but at least a portion was recaptured in the warm reunions of Battery A.[11] Browning did not bury the hatchet with Crump. But there was evidence of some admiration for his chief political enemy in his estimate of the Memphis boss:

> He was a man of medium ability, but with an uncanny power of organization to keep people and eliminate opposition to him. He was unusually strong in this regard. In his four years in Congress, I never had a closer friend in the world than Crump. When I left Congress and started running for Governor I thought anybody was a fool that suggested you couldn't get along with Ed Crump. But I got my awakening. . . . The only man that ever passed away with any grievance against me that I know of was Mr. Crump. I don't remember the things he did to me; I just don't have time. I've always

lived under the conviction that the Master, when He was on earth, had the biggest heart in the universe and there wasn't room in it to harbor the memory of a wrong. He never did. I'm not that good but I'd like to shoot at it. And I don't think I have any particular enemies.[12]

The implication was clear: had Crump lived, Browning might well have been agreeable to a reconcilation, but the leader of the Memphis machine died before that could be accomplished.

Gordon Browning was a fighter par excellence. His motto was attack and in so doing, he tended to exaggerate charges directed against his opponents. Paradoxically, his opponets ended his political career with exaggerated charges against him of corruption and unethical deals. His freewheeling and flamboyant manner tended to lend credence to those charges and the more sophisticated electorate was repelled. There was substance to the charge that some of Browning's "friends" participated in unethical practices but there was no evidence to link Gordon Browning to anything dishonest. The only thing he could have been charged with was responsibility for activities within his official family and perhaps for protecting his friends when charges were made against them. In that respect, he was not unlike other political leaders who hesitated to expose their own administrations to public censure. An observer wrote that one of Browning's greatest problems was a "stubborn loyalty" and trust of his friends:

> Good men, such as Browning, are too often naive as to the intentions of their contemporaries. . . . Good men indulge too deep in the presumption that others are as good—and that their intentions are as correct. Evil men will attach themselves to such a man to share his mantle of dignity. And when, finally, their evil deeds become known, the good man must share their guilt before an undiscerning public which is often cruel in its wrath.[13]

Dishonesty was indeed present in Browning's administration, but, as Jim Cummings observed, there would always be corruption in every administration at all levels of government from Washington all the way down to the court house at Woodbury in Cannon County.[14] But there was no evidence to suggest that it was more widespread in Browning's tenure than in any administration before or since. Nevertheless, his opponents in 1952 and a portion of the news media created an image of wholesale wrongdoing which caused Browning to leave office under a cloud. That image tends to obscure his very real achievements and deny to him his rightful place as one of the outstanding governors of Tennessee and one of the spokesmen and directors of the course of the Tennessee Democracy.

Gordon Browning and his rival in the struggle for control of the Democratic party, Ed Crump, were representatives of two different socioeconomic groups. Crump, the modern heir of the old paternalistic planter aristocracy, was symbolic of progressivism in Tennessee and the trend toward urbanization. Browning represented the rural block—the "wool hat" element. He was the son of the agrarian tradition, having learned his politics in a populist environment, and his policies as governor reflected the remnants of populism he retained. He was imbued, like the populists of the nineteenth century, with a belief in democracy and the theory that the cure for the ills of society was more democracy. The populists of the 1890s had seen urban party bosses manipulating nominating conventions and elections, and the people denied a fair count of their votes. Browning saw those same evils in the regime established by Ed Crump. As a remedy he sought to democratize elections and restore control of government to the people. His efforts in 1937 to install a unit system for primaries reflected the agrarian fear of dominance by the big cities. The election reforms in 1949 and some of the consitutional amendments of 1953 were the direct result of his desire for clean elections. Other policies revealed his populist background: he advocated a progressive income tax because he believed it to be the most equitable form of taxation; his rural roads program was designed to aid the farmer; the refinancing of the state debt was, in part, an effort to prevent Tennessee money going into the hands of eastern bankers; and his fight against the trucking lobby in 1949 reflected his opposition to preferential treatment for corporate interests. Browning's populism was also in evidence in his work in the Southern Governors' Conference. He was chairman of the freight rates committee which pressed for equalization of rates in the South. He actively participated in cases before the Interstate Commerce Commission and saw the work he began on freight rate equalization in 1937 reach fruition before he left office in 1953. [15]

Browning played an important part in the transition of political leadership from the old states' right conservatism to a new breed of public servant more responsive to the needs of modern society. After the downfall of the Lea-Horton-Caldwell regime in the 1930s, Browning became the figurehead for the forces opposed to the Crump-McKellar axis. Both Crump and McKellar had originally been reformers, but in the 1940s, after having reconciled the Bourbon tradition with progressivism, they became the conservative defenders of the status quo. In short, by 1948 both Crump and McKellar had lost touch with the times, and the more sophisticated electorate was ready for a change in leadership. And

Browning, because he was the most widely known anti-Crump leader, was swept back into office along with the new generation in a unique coalition of the conservative rural block and more liberal urban interests. But he was out of place with the new breed, for he, like Crump, was of the old generation. He was returned to the governor's office because he was a popular figure who represented the general desire to end bossism in Tennessee. It was inevitable, however, that Browning would be overthrown by the very forces that had helped him to return to office in 1948. His defeat in 1952 signaled the defeat of the rural block by the more urbanized and sophisticated electorate.

Browning left office as change was accelerating in Tennessee. In the quarter of a century following his retirement, the twin forces of the Second Reconstruction and the bulldozer revolution brought about a remarkable transformation in the Volunteer State. The Second Reconstruction brought the state's blacks more into the mainstream of life, and the bulldozer revolution transformed Tennessee in a predominantly urban and industrial state with a burgeoning middle class. Of poltical significance was the Supreme Court's "one man, one vote" ruling in 1962 in the case of *Baker* v. *Carr* which ended the rural "rotten boroughs" and the political domination of the countryside over the cities. But neither the Second Reconstruction nor the bulldozer revolution forced a dramatic shift in the political inclinations in Tennessee. Despite the apparent liberalism of leaders like Estes Kefauver and Albert Gore, the gubernatorial leadership in the years after Browning remained essentially conservative. Postwar Tennessee governors have in fact demonstrated a continuation of Bourbon conservatism in the South.[16] In short, Browning's sucessors like the Bourbons of the late nineteenth century who reconciled tradition with innovation, adjusted and made concessions to the Second Reconstruction and the bulldozer revolution. "Built into their synthesis," George Brown Tindall concluded, "was the persistent tradition of community in the South."[17]

The nature and character of Gordon Browning were clearly illustrated in his declining years. Despite a variety of physical infirmities, he demonstrated a will to live and a determination to enjoy life to the fullest. In his last five years, in addition to battling Parkinson's disease, he broke both hips which required lengthy hospital stays on each occasion. He also suffered from cerebral arteriosclerosis and other problems with vital organs. Yet he remained cheerful and alert most of the time and he still liked to talk and reminisce. His appetite also remained good and he continued to enjoy his favorite delicacy, barbecued coon. In 1975 he celebrated his eighty-sixth birthday in the hospital but the next day he insisted on attending a postseason football game named in his honor the Browning Bowl. But sheer determination alone could not long delay the inevitable. He reached the end of his strength and death came peacefully on 23 May 1976. The Memphis *Press-Scimitar* observed, "Browning was perhaps the last of the old political warhorses of Tennessee politics in the days when thundering oratory and fighting speeches were necessary to win."[18] He was indeed a remarkable man and the central figure in one of the most exciting eras in Tennessee's political history.

NOTES

1. Quoted in George Barker, "Three Times and You're Out,"*Nashville Tennessean Magazine* (7 October 1962), p. 19.

2. Quoted in Ibid., p. 13.

3. Quoted in Ibid.

4. Mrs. Prentice Cooper, interview with the author, Shelbyille, 7 October 1976. The former governors included Cooper, McCord, and after 1958, Clement.

5. Quoted in Barker, "Three Times and You're Out," p. 19.

6. Gordon Browning, interview with the author, Huntingdon, 23 June 1966.

7. Gordon Browning, "Gordon Browning: An Oral Memoir," ed. Joseph H. Riggs (Memphis Public Library, 1966), p. 10.

8. Ibid., pp. 105–106, 124.

9. Ibid., pp. 90–91.

10. Ibid., p. 96.

11. Mrs. Abe Waldauer, interview with the author, Memphis, 10 August 1976; Mrs. W. S. Field, interview with the author, Milan, 24 June 1976; Mrs. Bill Bowers, interview with the author, Milan, 24 June 1976; Mrs. Julian Duvault, interview with the author, McKenzie, 12 August 1976.

12. Browning, "Oral Memoir," p. 84.

13. Quoted in Barker, "Three Times and You're Out," p. 18.

14. Jim Cummings, interview with the author, Woodbury, 8 June 1976.

15. Gordon Browning, interview with the author, Huntingdon, 28 December 1965. The Browning papers in the Tennessee State Library and Archives contain a large volume of correspondence concerning freight rate equalization.

16. Numan Bartley and Hugh Davis Graham, *Southern Politics and the Second Reconstruction* (Baltimore: Johns Hopkins University Press, 1975), p. 23.

17. George Brown Tindall, *The Persistent Tradition in New South Politics* (Baton Rouge: Louisiana State University Press, 1975), p. xii.

18. *Press-Scimitar*, 24 May 1976.

BIBLIOGRAPHICAL ESSAY

INDEX

Bibliographical Essay

Many sources, including a large number of monographs and articles in both scholarly journals and popular periodicals, were examined in preparing this narrative and virtually all made a contribution. But because the overall value of most was at best minimal it would be superfluous to list here every source used or for that matter all sources cited in the text. It would also, perhaps, be ostentatious to include every biographical directory or popular magazine article that added only slightly to the final product. With the exception of identifying individuals interviewed, only the principal and pertinent sources which contributed significantly to the narrative are included in this essay.

ORAL INTERVIEWS

A number of observers and participants in the events recorded in this narrative were available for oral interviews and the information elicited was valuable. Some factual information that is not in the written record was obtained as well as the opinions, emotions, and animosities of those observers and participants. Just as important, their recollections added what journalists call "color." Nevertheless, interviewing has certain limitations: the passage of time and the process of aging tends to dim memories, and, although the emotionalism of past political battles had subsided, none of those interviewed were entirely unbiased. All revealed the human tendency to recall the actions and events of the past as they preferred to remember them; this was especially true of those directly involved in events. At times interviewees gave factual data contrary to documentary evidence, not in a deliberate attempt to deceive, but simply because they believed the information to be true. It was therefore necessary to use special care in interpreting the material obtained orally.

Forty-eight interviews were conducted with forty-four individuals. A few of the participants in past political battles refused to submit to questions—Abe Waldauer, for example—but most of those contacted were at least willing, if not eager, to tell their side of the story. Although a recording device was used on occasion, notes were taken in every case

243

because some individuals objected to the use of a tape recorder. A few interviews were brief, twenty minutes or so, while others lasted up to an hour and a half; three were conducted by telephone. Three people gave information they regarded as confidential and requested that the source not be divulged. Those requests have been honored but the information was either not critical to the narrative or was obtained from another source.

The central figure in this narrative, Governor Gordon Browning, was interviewed on three occasions for a total of a little over four hours. He was a source of a great deal of information although much of what he said was a repetition of his unpublished "Gordon Browning: An Oral Memoir," edited by Joseph H. Riggs (Memphis Public Library, 1964). Moreover, most of the quotations attributed to Browning in three articles by George Barker, "Of War, Peace and Politics," *Nashville Tennessean Magazine* (23 September 1962), pp. 14–15, 18–19; "Victory, Defeat, and Victory," *Tennessean Magazine* (30 September 1962), pp. 8–9, 20–21; and "Three Times and You're Out," *Tennessean Magazine* (7 October 1962), pp. 12–13, 18–19 were uttered again almost verbatim during the interviews. Browning's sister, Mrs. W. S. Field (Halford), his niece, Mrs. Bill Bowers, and his sister-in-law, Miss Mary Leach, gave informative interviews on family matters; a family friend, Mrs. Julian Duvault added some useful information on Browning's personality and character, as did a longtime Carroll County politician, Hugh Scarborough. Two of Browning's World War I comrades, J. Chester Shields and Charles Gallina, contributed stories about the escapades of Battery A and of the spirit of comradeship among the veterans in later years. Mrs. Abe Waldauer gave her observations about the relationship between her husband and Browning.

More valuable in interpreting Tennessee politics were interviews with Browning's associates and political allies: Senator Albert Gore, commissioner of labor during the first administration; George Cate, commissioner of the Department of Welfare and Institutions in the first administration; James Lee Case, commissioner of labor in the second administration; W. R. Jarrell, state purchasing agent in the second term; the Reverend Priestly Miller, chairman of the Pardon and Parole Board in the second administration who graciously gave two interviews; Jack Norman, Sr., Nashville attorney and a close personal friend; Joe Hatcher, political writer for the *Nashville Tennessean;* Clark Porteous, political writer for the Memphis *Press-Scimitar;* Pugh Moore, at one time a reporter for the *Press-Scimitar;* Federal Judge Robert L. Taylor of Knoxville, Browning's state campaign manager in 1948; attorney Robert L. Taylor of Memphis who served as Shelby County campaign manager in 1948; attorney William Farris, a Memphis ally; Bob Guinn, Savannah contractor and campaign contributor, two interviews; and longtime member of the General Assembly, Jim Cummings of Wood-bury, who gave one of the most candid interviews. Two important allies of Senator Estes Kefauver gave useful information: Federal Judge Charles Neese of Greenville and Martha Ragland of Nashville.

Interviews reflecting the opposition included: Leslie T. Hart, political writer for the Nashville *Banner* in the 1940s and 1950s; Brainard Cheney, *Banner* writer in the 1930s; Mrs. Prentice Cooper, wife of Governor Cooper; Chancellor Frick Stewart, son of Senator Tom Stewart; W. R. Davidson, an administrative assistant to Senator Kenneth McKellar; Herbert Bingham, Executive Secretary of the Tennessee Municipal League; and labor leaders Dan Powell of Memphis and Matthew Lynch of Nashville. One of the most valuable interviews because it resulted in leads to other sources was with Milton Rice, who was on the Attorney General's staff at the time of the Memorial Apartments transaction. Other interviews were with Miss Elizabeth Haynes and J. L. Haynes, sister and brother of legislator Walter M. Haynes; two former members of the General Assembly, Joe Bean of Winchester and Basil McMahon of Manchester; William C. Bateman, Memphis attorney; and finally, Burgess and Ethel Hamm of Ramer for the story of a visit by Governor Browning to their home and a subsequent fox hunt with Burgess' father.

Oral interviews conducted by others were useful and included: Burgin Dossett, interviewed by Frank Williams, Jr.; interviews with Joe Carr, Robert Clement, Sr., and Joe Henry by Lee S. Greene, on tape in the Tennessee State Library and Archives; and interviews with Robert Clement, Sr., Leslie T. Hart, Joe Hatcher, and Anna Belle Clement O'Brien, by Stephen D. Boyd, also on tape in the Tennessee State Library and Archives.

MANUSCRIPTS

The most pertinent information came from manuscript collections. The Papers of Governor Gordon Browning, 1937–1939, and 1949–1953 in the Tennessee State Library and Archives was a major source, which, incidentally, was examined prior to cataloging for orderly research. Much of the collection pertains to routine day-to-day matters and correspondence. Because Browning had an inclination to oral communication, his public papers are somewhat disappointing in that they do not reveal a great deal about the political battles of his terms in the governor's office. For reasons not entirely clear access to a small uncatalogued collection of his papers on deposit in the McKenzie Memorial Library was denied.

One of the most valuable collections relative to Tennessee politics is the voluminous Senator Kenneth Douglas McKellar Papers on deposit in the Memphis-Shelby County Public Library and Information Center. Especially important are McKellar's correspondence catalogued as "Crump-McKellar Correspondence 1911–1955" and "Political Correspondence 1911–1952." Equally valuable in interpreting politics in the Volunteer State is the large Estes Kefauver Collection in the James D. Hoskins Library at the University of Tennessee. The Watkins Overton Papers in the Mississippi Valley Collection at Memphis State University reveal much about the years of Crump's ascendancy in Memphis as do the Edward Meeman Papers, also in the Mississippi Valley Collection. Other manuscript collections that have useful but limited value are the Papers of Governor Jim McCord, the Papers of Governor Frank Clement, the Roy H. Beeler MS newspaper clipping scrapbooks, 1932–1953, and the Tom Henderson Papers in the Tennessee State Library and Archives; the Edmund Orgill Papers in the Mississippi Valley Collection; and the Southern Politics Collection in the Joint University Library at Vanderbilt University. Finally, the papers of C. L. Majors, a private collection, provides some insight into the political activities of veterans of World War I.

PUBLIC DOCUMENTS

The most important source for Gordon Browning's years in Congress is the *Congressional Record*, volumes 65–77 (Washington, 1923-1933). Valuable for Browning's participation in congressional hearings on the proposed Tennessee Valley Authority are the *Hearings Before the Committee On Military Affairs on Muscle Shoals, April 11 to April 15, 1933* (Washington: Government Printing Office, 1933). Another publication, *Report of the Special Committee to Investigate Senatorial Campaign Expenditures and the Use of Governmental Funds in 1938*, Senate Report 1, Part 1 (Washington: Government Printing Office, 1939), reveals a good deal about the bitter Democratic primary in Tennessee in 1938. The most important source for governmental reports, legislative debate, and legislation for Browning's years as governor are the various issues of *Tennessee House Journal,* 1937, 1938, 1949–1953, *Tennessee Senate Journal,* 1937, 1938, 1949–1953, and the *Public Acts of the State of Tennessee,* 1937, 1938, 1949–1953. The *Tennessee Handbook and Official Directory,* 1921–1923, and its successor, the *Tennessee Blue Book,* 1929–1956, are important for election results as well as biographical data on numerous public servants. The case of *Gates et al.* v. *Long et al.,* 113 S. W. 2d 388, is the Tennessee Supreme Court's ruling on the unit bill of 1937 and a file on deposit in the Tennessee State Library and Archives labeled "*State of Tennessee* v. *R. S. Doggett, et al.* (Memorial Hotel Litigation), Davidson Chancery, Part II, No. 73212, Attorney General Office File, 2015," reveals a great deal about the Memorial Hotel issue.

<h2 style="text-align:center">NEWSPAPERS</h2>

Newspapers were an invaluable source for this narrative as a record of events as well as for editorial comment. In a very real sense Tennessee's press mirrored factional struggles and played an important role in political battles by creating images and by emphasizing issues. The two most extensively perused newspapers were the *Nashville Tennessean* and the *Nashville Banner,* in part because as state capital papers, they gave better statewide coverage of news and because they reflected conflicting political philosophies. Since its editor was so vocally anti-Crump, the Memphis *Press-Scimitar* was examined extensively and for balance, the more sedate Memphis *Commercial Appeal.* Other major daily papers, examined selectively, were the *Chattanooga Times*,' the *Chattanooga Free-Press* and its successor, the *Chattanooga News-Free Press,* and the *Knoxville News-Sentinel.* Small city papers examined selectively included the Dyersburg *State Gazette,* the *Jackson Sun,* the *Clarksville Leaf-Chronicle,* the *Columbia Daily Herald,* the *Johnson City Press-Chronicle,* and the *Kingsport Times-News.* The *Tri-State Defender,* a black newspaper published in Memphis in the 1940s and 1950s reflected the opinion of a portion of the black community, while the attitude of organized labor was revealed in the *Labor Advocate,* published in Nashville in the 1930s and the *Trades and Labor News,* published in the same city in the 1940s and 1950s.

<h2 style="text-align:center">SECONDARY SOURCES</h2>

No state, of course, exists in a vacuum, and Tennessee politics in the years between 1934 and 1954 cannot be understood out of context from both regional and national history. The number of works dealing with the national evolution from the nineteenth century through populism and progressivism to the middle of the twentieth century is endless but several interpretive works are especially useful: Richard Hofstadter, *The Age of Reform: From Bryan to F. D. R.* (New York: Vintage Books, 1955); Robert H. Wiebe, *The Search for Order, 1877-1920,* in David Donald, ed., *The Making of America* (New York: Hill and Wang, 1967); William E. Leuchtenburg, *The Perils of Prosperity, 1914–1932* (Chicago: The University of Chicago Press, 1958); Richard Hofstadter, "The Myth of the Happy Yeoman," *American Heritage* 7 (April 1956): 43–53; and J. Joseph Huthmacher, "Urban Liberalism and the Age of Reform," *Mississippi Valley Historical Review* 49 (September 1962), pp. 231–241. Three works on the South are helpful: C. Van Woodward, *Origins of the New South, 1877–1913,* Vol. 9., *A History of the South* (Baton Rouge: Louisiana State University Press, 1951); George Brown Tindall, *The Emergence of the New South, 1913–1945,* Vol. 10, *A History of the South* (Baton Rouge: Louisiana State University Press, 1967); and George Brown Tindall, *The Persistent Tradition in New South Politics* (Baton Rouge: Louisiana State University Press, 1975). Also useful are Arthur S. Link, "The Progressive Movement in the South, 1870–1914," *The North Carolina Historical Review* 23 (1946): 172–195, and Blaine A. Brownell, *The Urban Ethos in the South, 1920–1930* (Baton Rouge: Louisiana State University Press, 1975).

Several studies on politics in the South are valuable in interpreting Tennessee. They include: V. O. Key, Jr., *Southern Politics in State and Nation* (New York: Alfred A. Knopf, 1949); Alexander Heard, "Interviewing Southern Politicians," *The American Political Science Review* 64 (December 1950): 866–896; Alexander Heard, *A Two Party South?* (Chapel Hill: University of North Carolina Press, 1952); Dewey Grantham, Jr., *The Democratic South* (Athens: The University of Georgia Press 1963); Cortez A. M. Ewing, *Primary Elections in the South: A Study in Uniparty Politics* (Norman: University of Oklahoma Press, 1953); Numan V. Bartley, *The Rise of Massive Resistance: Race and Politics in the South During the 1950s* (Baton Rouge: Louisiana State University Press, 1969); William C. Havard, ed., *The Changing Politics of the South* (Baton Rouge: Louisiana State University Press, 1972); and Numan V. Bartley and Hugh Davis Graham, *Southern Politics and the Second Reconstruction* (Baltimore: The Johns Hopkins University Press, 1975). Social and economic development in the South in the 1940s is analyzed in two articles: Howard W. Odum, "Social Change in the South," *The Journal of Politics* 10 (May 1948): 242–258, and B. U.

Ratchford, "Recent Economic Developments in the South," *The Journal of Politics* 10 (May 1948): 259–281. Both articles were reprinted in Taylor Cole and John H. Hallowell, eds., *The Southern Political Scene, 1938–1948* (Gainesville: The University of Florida Press, 1948).

The only general histories of Tennessee which survey the era covered in this narrative are Stanley J. Folmsbee, Robert E. Corlew, and Enoch L. Mitchell, *History of Tennessee*, 3 vols. (New York: Lewis Historical Publishing Co., Inc., 1960) and the abridged version, Stanley J. Folmsbee, Robert E. Corlew, and Enoch L. Mitchell, *Tennessee: A Short History* (Knoxville: The University of Tennessee Press, 1969). Both are superficial in coverage, largely because of the dearth of scholarly studies on Tennessee in the twentieth century on which to base a survey.

Because political patterns in modern Tennessee evolved from those of earlier generations, two monographic studies on the late nineteenth century are valuable in interpreting the twentieth century: Daniel M. Robison, *Bob Taylor and the Agrarian Revolt in Tennessee* (Chapel Hill: University of North Carolina Press, 1935) and Roger L. Hart, *Redeemers, Bourbons, and Populists: Tennessee, 1870–1896* (Baton Rouge: Louisiana State University Press, 1975). J. A. Sharp, "The Farmer's Alliance and the People's Party in Tennessee," *East Tennessee Historical Society's Publication* 10 (1939): 91–113, is a useful study. Two important works treating the early part of the twentieth century are William D. Miller, *Memphis During the Progressive Era, 1900–1917* (Memphis: Memphis State University Press, 1957) and Paul E. Isaac, *Prohibition and Politics: Turbulent Decades in Tennessee, 1885–1920* (Knoxville: University of Tennessee Press, 1965).

Scholarly studies on Tennessee politics in the 1920s are limited to three articles, a dissertation, and one monograph. Gary W. Reichard in two articles, "The Aberration of 1920: An Analysis of Harding's Victory in Tennessee," *The Journal of Southern History* 36 (February 1970): 33–49 and "The Defeat of Governor Roberts," *Tennessee Historical Quarterly* 30 (Spring 1971): 94–109, analyzes the election of 1920. The governorship of Austin Peay is discussed in Joseph T. McPherson, "Democratic Progressivism in Tennessee: The Administration of Governor Austin Peay, 1923–1927," *East Tennessee Historical Society's Publications* 60 (1968: 50–61. A well researched monograph by David Dale Lee, *Tennessee in Turmoil: Politics in the Volunteer State, 1920–1932* (Memphis State University Press, 1979) emphasizes the struggle between rural and urban Tennessee. The other monographic study that relates to Tennessee politics in the 1920s is John Berry McFerrin's *Caldwell and Company: A Southern Financial Empire* (Nashville: Vanderbilt University Press, 1969). McFerrin's work, originally published in 1939, is marked by a strong antipathy toward Rogers Caldwell, Luke Lea, and Governor Henry Horton; it was, perhaps, written too close in time to the subject for objectivity and sources were limited in the main to public documents, memoranda, court cases, and newspapers. It is, however, a valuable contribution to the literature on Tennessee and the only source in publication to attempt to describe the enigmatic Colonel Luke Lea. A little of Lea is revealed in T. H. Alexander, "They Tried to Kidnap the Kaiser,"*The Saturday Evening Post*, 25 October 1937, pp. 5–7, 84–89; Luke Lea, "The Attempt to Capture the Kaiser,"ed. William R. Alderson, *Tennessee Historical Quarterly* 20 (September 1961): 222–261; and Cromwell Tidwell, "Luke Lea and the American Legion," *Tennessee Historical Quarterly* 28 (Spring 1969): 70-83. The political collapse of the Lea-Caldwell-Horton regime and the transition of power in Tennessee in 1932 is documented in two articles by David Dale Lee, "The Attempt to Impeach Governor Horton," *Tennessee Historical Quarterly* 34 (Summer 1975): 188–201 and "The Triumph of Boss Crump: The Tennessee Gubernatorial Election of 1932,"*Tennessee Historical Quarterly* 25 (Winter 1976): 393–413. John Dean Minton's "The New Deal in Tennessee, 1932–1938"(unpublished Ph.D. dissertation, Vanderbuilt University, 1959), provides some insight into Tennessee in the 1930s.

Boss Ed Crump attracted writers, especially during his lifetime. A great deal of anti-Crump literature appeared in popular periodicals during his ascendancy but most of it clearly lacked any pretense at objectivity. The most hostile treatment of Crump is Jennings Perry's exaggerated *Democracy Begins at Home: The Tennessee Fight Against the Poll Tax* (New York: J. B. Lippincott, 1944), cited here only because the little volume became an issue in the running battle between the Memphis boss and the publisher Silliman Evans. More thoughtful criticism of Crump may be found in Gerald M. Capers, "Memphis, Satrapy of a Benevolent Despot" in *Our Fair City*, ed. Robert S. Allen (New York: Vanguard Press, 1947), and in Shields McIlwaine, *Memphis Down in Dixie* (New York: E. P. Dutton, 1948). William D. Miller's *Mr. Crump of Memphis* (Baton Rouge: Louisiana State University Press, 1964), is a readable biography and the best source on Crump. Miller had access to Crump's papers and, while he is critical at times, the biography is generally sympathetic. His "The Browning-Crump battle: The Crump

Side," *East Tennessee Historical Society's Publications* 37 (1965): 77–88 is a more detailed account of the political struggle in 1937–1938. In contrast to Crump, scholarly work on Senator Kenneth McKellar is limited. Robert Dean Pope, "Senatorial Baron: The Long Political Career of Kenneth D. McKellar" (unpublished Ph. D. dissertation, Yale University, 1976), is the most complete study to date.

Three studies discussing the events in the crucial Democratic primary in 1948 are useful: Allen Hampton Kitchens, "Political Upheaval in Tennessee: Boss Crump and the Senatorial Election of 1948," *West Tennessee Historical Society Papers* 16 (1962): 104–126; Robert G. Everett, "The 1948 Senatorial Primary in Tennessee: A History and an Anlaysis" (unpublished M. A. thesis, Memphis State University, 1962); and Marshall F. Priest, Jr., "Politics in Tennessee: The 1948 Democratic Gubernatorial Primary" (unpublished M. A. thesis, Memphis State University, 1963). The biography of Senator Estes Kefauver by Joseph Bruce Gorman, *Kefauver: A Political Biography* (New York: Oxford University Press, 1971) is disappointing because it deals largely with the senator on the national scene and adds little to an understanding of the part he played in Tennessee politics. Although limited to one campaign, Stephen D. Boyd, "The Campaign Speaking of Frank Clement in the 1954 Democratic Primary: Field Study and Rhetorical Analysis" (unpublished Ph. D. dissertation, University of Illinois, 1972), describes Governor Clement's speaking ability and campaign style.

Three works on Tennessee government and politics are valuable. Lee S. Greene, David H. Grubbs, and Victor C. Hobday, *Government in Tennessee*, 3rd ed. (Knoxville: University of Tennessee Press, 1975) is especially helpful in understanding the state's constitution and governmental processes. Although differing only slightly from the interpretations in the chapter on Tennessee in V. O. Key, Jr., *Southern Politics in State and Nation*, William Goodman, *Inherited Domain: Political Parties* (Knoxville: Bureau of Public Information, University of Tennessee, 1954) is a useful study. Just as valuable is Lee S. Greene and Jack E. Holmes, "Tennessee: A Politics of Peaceful Change," in *The Changing Politics of the South*, ed. William C. Havard (Baton Rouge: Louisiana State University, 1972).

Finally, there are a number of works on a variety of subjects of varying value that provide insight into Tennessee's political struggles: James E. Thorogood, *A Financial History of Tennessee Since 1870* (Sewanee: University of the South Press, 1949); Thomas Harrison Baker, *The Memphis Commercial Appeal: The History of a Southern Newspaper* (Baton

Rouge: Louisiana State University Press, 1971); Hugh Davis Graham, *Crisis in Print: Desegregation and the Press in Tennessee* (Nashville: Vanderbilt University Press, 1967); Edward J. Meeman, *The Editorial We: A Posthumous Authobiography,* ed. Edwin Howard (Memphis: Memphis State University Printing Service, 1976); Mingo Scott, Jr., *The Negro in Tennessee Politics and Governmental Affairs, 1865-1965* (Nashville: Rich Printing Co., 1964); Ralph J. Bunche, *The Political Status of the Negro in the Age of FDR,* ed. Dewey Grantham (Chicago: University of Chicago Press, 1973); David M. Tucker, *Lieutenant Lee of Beale Street* (Nashville: Vanderbilt University Press, 1971); David M. Tucker, *Black Pastors and Leaders: The Memphis Clergy, 1819–1972* (Memphis: Memphis State University Press, 1975); Lester C. Lamon, *Black Tennesseans, 1900–1930* (Knoxville: University of Tennessee Press, 1977); Preston J. Hubbard, *Origins of the TVA: The Muscle Shoals Controversy, 1920–1932* (Nashville: Vanderbilt University Press, 1961); Wilmon Henry Droze, *High Dams and Slack Waters: TVA Rebuilds a River* (Baton Rouge: Louisiana State University Press, 1965); and Thomas K. McCraw, *TVA And the Power Fight, 1933–1939)* (New York: J. B. Lippincott, 1971).

Index